W9-CTZ-762

REDEEMING

AMERICAN POLITICAL

THOUGHT

Judith N. Shklar

Redeeming American Political Thought

*Edited by Stanley Hoffmann and
Dennis F. Thompson*

Foreword by Dennis F. Thompson

THE UNIVERSITY OF CHICAGO PRESS / CHICAGO AND LONDON

JUDITH N. SHKLAR (1928–1992) was Cowles Professor of Government at Harvard University from 1956 to 1992. She was the author of nine books, including *Ordinary Vices* and *The Faces of Injustice*.

STANLEY HOFFMANN is the Paul and Catherine Buttenwieser University Professor at Harvard University.

DENNIS F. THOMPSON is Alfred North Whitehead Professor of Political Philosophy in the government department at Harvard.

The University of Chicago Press, Chicago 60637
The University of Chicago Press, Ltd., London
© 1998 by The University of Chicago
All rights reserved. Published 1998
Printed in the United States of America
07 06 05 04 03 02 01 00 99 98   1 2 3 4 5

ISBN: 0-226-75347-6 (cloth)
ISBN: 0-226-75348-4 (paper)

Library of Congress Cataloging-in-Publication Data

Shklar, Judith N.
    Redeeming American political thought / Judith N. Shklar ; edited by
Stanley Hoffmann and Dennis F. Thompson ; foreword by Dennis F.
Thompson.
        p.   cm.
    Includes bibliographical references and index.
    ISBN 0-226-75347-6 (cloth : alk. paper). — ISBN 0-226-75348-4
(pbk. : alk. paper)
    1. Political science—United States—History. I. Hoffmann,
Stanley.   II. Thompson, Dennis F. (Dennis Frank), 1940–   .
III. Title.
JA84.U5S525   1998
320'.092'273—dc21   97-25
                                                                       CIP

⊗ The paper used in this publication meets the minimum requirements of the American National Standard for Information Sciences—Permanence of Paper for Printed Library Materials, ANSI Z39.48-1984.

CONTENTS

FOREWORD
Dennis F. Thompson

Judith Shklar taught American political theory for many years, but began to write about it in a sustained way only late in her life, resisting many invitations to produce a book on it. Asked why, she once said simply, "the subject is too hard." A surprising comment from a scholar who wrote major books on Hegel and Rousseau, taught advanced courses on Greek political philosophy, produced sophisticated commentary on Renaissance painting and European history and literature, learned large parts of constitutional and international law, and kept up with developments in contemporary biology and medicine.

What Shklar found hard about American political theory could scarcely have been any intrinsic conceptual difficulty posed by individual theorists. She had higher regard for the theoretical achievements of American thinkers than did most of her colleagues in political theory, but she certainly did not think that the Americans posed intellectual challenges greater than those of the venerable European theorists she had mastered. The difficulty lay not in the theorists themselves but in the interpretations that commentators had laid upon them. A search for the unifying theme, a single key that could unlock the significance of American thought, had come to characterize the study of the subject. The themes that had done the most to promote misunderstanding, she believed, were liberal consensus and American exceptionalism.

In the essays collected here, Shklar sets out to redeem American political theory from these monolithic interpretations, and thereby to recover its intrinsic intellectual importance and its significance for the contemporary study of politics. Shklar's strategy of redemption is indirect. Instead of trying to remove one by one the encumbrances with which other interpreters have burdened American theory, she transcends them all at once by broadening our understanding of its mission and widening the circle of those who have carried it out.

Shklar acknowledged that her aim was ambitious, and she would not have claimed that this volume fulfills it. At the time of her unexpected death in 1992, she had not yet prepared most of these essays for publication. (Only four had been previously published in English; one had appeared in her own French but had not been translated.) Although the essays range widely, they do not capture all the aspects of American thought she considered important. The consequential role of law in American thought is more explicitly discussed in *Legalism,* and the critical influence of slavery is more fully treated in her *American Citizenship.* These books, along with *The Faces of Injustice,* are essential reading for anyone seeking a more complete view of her conception of American political culture. But even standing alone, these essays succeed brilliantly in showing that American political theory is much richer and more substantial than either its critics or its friends have generally suggested.

Far too many commentators describe an America that marches "single file down a single straight liberal highway."[1] Whether they celebrate or criticize this consensus, they turn American theory into "compulsive repetition of the same theme."[2] (She had in mind chiefly but not exclusively her Harvard colleague Louis Hartz, whose *Liberal Tradition in America* set the intellectual agenda of the field for many years.) Those interpreters who find conflict instead of consensus come closer to the truth, but they also tell too simple a story—"a single fall from grace . . . when [American thought] abandoned a premodern republicanism in favor of an amoral, atomized individualism."[3] Liberal consensus remains the foil. The true story has neither a simple plot nor a standard cast of characters.

The "fundamental social condition" of Americans, Shklar maintains, is the tension between relatively expansive political equality and distinctly persistent social inequality.[4] This tension "set a permanent pattern for political discourse" and still significantly guides public argument. Political equality, by which she means primarily the right to vote and the conditions necessary to exercising it with dignity, has been a long time in coming, and she is under no illusion that it has been fully realized in practice. But as an ideal "inherent" in the logic of American representative democracy it must prevail.[5]

Social equality is quite another matter. Even as an ideal, it finds less support in American thought. Indeed, its counterideals—meritocracy, libertarianism, self-reliance—have enjoyed much greater influence. So have even its more objectionable opponents—racism, sexism, nativism, and Social Darwinism. Shklar is concerned, as she thinks all thoughtful citizens should be, about this incongruity between social inequality and political equality, and its threat to the future of democracy. These essays display her fascination with the variety of (mostly unsuccessful) ways that American thinkers have tried to come to terms with it. Unlike the overarching interpretations that other commentators try to impose on the American experience, Shklar's account focuses not only on conflict instead of consensus but also on the multiple sources of conflict itself.

To readers who know Shklar's views mainly from a quick reading of her most cited article, "Liberalism of Fear," the egalitarian temper of many of these essays may be surprising. After all, in that essay she asserts that "liberalism has only one overriding aim: to secure the political conditions that are necessary for the exercise of personal freedom."[6] This sounds very much like what is usually called negative liberty, which by itself does not require or indeed allow the state to act energetically to promote positive liberty, let alone social or political equality.

Yet as discerning readers of that article have recognized, Shklar is laying the groundwork there for a much more robust liberalism, one in which personal liberty depends on securing equal citizenship.[7] The right to participate in politics and the opportunity to earn a living are not only necessary conditions for personal freedom but also expressions of equal respect. As Shklar makes clear in her analysis of negative and positive liberty translated for this volume, the distinction between the two kinds of liberty has much less relevance in America than in Europe.[8] So many of the rights that Americans assert in the name of negative liberty inevitably (and justifiably) compel the state to act in support of positive liberty. Because liberal governments should protect citizens from cruelty whatever the source, liberal legislation will have to deal with illness, hunger, unemployment, poverty, and other conditions that threaten the effective use of liberty.

Shklar's concern with equality is sometimes seen as continuing the project begun by Tocqueville in *Democracy in America*. Both bring their Old World experience to their observations of the New World; both emphasize the potential conflicts to which equality gives rise; and both treat America not as an aberration in the history of government but as the harbinger of its future. It is true that like Tocqueville, Shklar first viewed America through European eyes. She was born in Riga, Latvia, and with her family fled to Sweden to avoid the Nazis, finally settling in Canada, where she went to school and college. She believed that she might not have taken up the study of American thought at all had she not decided to accept an unexpected offer to teach in this country.[9]

But not only was the Europe from which she came far different from Tocqueville's, so also was her own relationship with America. She became an American citizen, and lived an American life in the fullest sense. She knew more about the nation's history, politics, and culture than most of her fellow citizens (including her Harvard colleagues), and she spoke and wrote with as much personal engagement with its successes and failures as any of them. In her writings, the praise she bestows on those American thinkers who succeed, and the scorn she heaps on those who fail, are not the reflections of a detached observer visiting from abroad.

Shklar reminds us that Tocqueville came to America to report back to his own people.[10] Because he wrote for a French audience, his warnings about the threat that equality poses to liberty have less force in America than has usually been assumed. America seemed so egalitarian only in comparison with his own country. By "equality of conditions," he meant the absence of castes with hereditary political and social ranks as in the ancien régime. It is therefore a mistake to invoke him, as later American social critics did, to condemn the "conformism of mass-men" or the "egalitarian radicalism" of political dissenters.[11] Shklar views this kind of criticism as just another manifestation of the American jeremiad—that persistent rhetoric of reproach that beginning with the Puritans in the seventeenth century sees nothing but the falling away from earlier standards. Throughout these essays, Shklar never misses an opportunity to expose the errors of this way of interpreting democracy in America, but she does not blame *Democracy in America* for them.

Yet Shklar could have faulted Tocqueville, more explicitly than she did, for defining the problem the way he did. Her view of equality in America is in a fundamental respect the opposite of his. For him, the problem is social equality, because it threatens political liberty. For her, the problem is social *in*equality, because it endangers political equality. In his account, social equality will lead inevitably to political equality: "To conceive of men remaining forever unequal upon a single point, yet equal on all others, is impossible: they must come in the end to be equal upon all." [12] Perhaps not forever, Shklar would concede, but for a very long time, for the whole of American history so far and for the foreseeable future. Furthermore, the pressure for equality comes, to the extent that it comes at all, from political rather than social conditions and ideals.

The American thinkers who appear in these essays are nothing if not resourceful in their responses to the tensions of equality. That is in no small measure because Shklar is so resourceful herself in casting familiar thinkers in new roles. Hamilton, not Madison, emerges as the theorist who pioneered the political science that has the most democratic potential.[13] Madison receives his due as the father of the political analysis of interest groups, but Hamilton is credited with explaining (even while disapproving of) the nature of the power that the electorate exercises in the American system. Voting may be a ritual, but it is a consequential one, and one consequence is that the representatives desperately want to find out how their constituents will vote. That gives the political science that Hamilton began an important job in a democracy. As political scientists go about their professional business, they serve the function, whether they know it or not, of providing some of the information that representatives want, and more generally of enhancing the sense of the ultimate importance of the ritual.

In her affectionate account of the correspondence between Jefferson and John Adams, Shklar's heart may have been with the Virginian but her head favored the New Englander.[14] Jefferson's system of education had egalitarian political aims: it was to foster a "natural aristocracy" of talent to replace the artificial "pseudo-aristocracy" of wealth and privilege. In this way social inequality could work to the political benefit of everyone. Adams did not think much of this solution, for the simple reason that there was no way to distinguish natural from artificial aristocrats, and moreover both kinds were equally dangerous for democratic politics. Adams knew what he was talking about because, as the most perceptive theorist of the American idea of aristocracy, he had developed the concept of what is now called elitism in a way that made much more sense in the New World than did the earlier European versions. In Adams's rendering, the elite is not merely a category of class: it comprises any of "the successful few who would take more than 'their fair share of political influence,' who could command more than their own vote."[15] Shklar did not of course suppose that Adams had resolved the conflict between social inequality and political equality, but she believed that he had clarified one of the most common forms it takes in America.

Shklar's Emerson struggles with a similar conflict. Shklar regards him as *the* American philosopher,[16] and paints a sympathetic and vivid portrait of his democratic faith.[17] She also approves of his good taste: his one and only hero is Montaigne, one of *her* few idols. But she is quick to point out the contradiction between his admiration for the great men and his faith in the "unexpressed greatness of the common farmer and laborer."[18] His solution—that great men should serve only as our representatives and help us to learn to do without them—is ingenious, Shklar believes, but "there are many reasons to believe that this is not the whole story."[19]

For more of the story, Shklar turns to literature, which she considers an essential but neglected source for understanding American political theory. Here it is Hawthorne from whom we have the most to learn.[20] With his year-long experience as a (hesitant) member of the Brook Farm community and his fine skills as a novelist, he was well positioned to present a powerful case against the utopianism of radical democracy (though not a wholly negative one, Shklar is careful to point out). At the other extreme are the Inspector and the Collector in "The Custom House," characters who represent "mindless traditionalism."[21] Having disposed of the extreme forms of egalitarianism and traditionalism, Hawthorne is free to concentrate on exploring the kind of character that a balanced democratic order requires. This is exemplified by the third man in the custom house, "the perfect Yankee," the "ideal young American" who also appears in most of Hawthorne's other novels. Neither an aristocrat nor a plebeian, he is competent, open, practical, and above all a man of integrity.[22] Hawthorne's character studies, Shklar fully realizes, do not overcome the theoretical tensions in democratic equality. But she argues that they make an important contribution to the theory of virtue that American liberalism is often mistakenly said to lack.[23] Hawthorne (along with Emerson) supplies the moral psychology of democracy—"America seen from within"—that Tocqueville and his social science successors neglect.[24]

Ever critical and never completely satisfied with any of the solutions her theorists offer, Shklar nonetheless finds insights in the writings of all of them. Even Southern political theory has something to teach us, and indeed "in a way the South won the war of ideas." For a long time after the Civil War, political theory adopted the sociological fatalism that had marked so much Southern thought.[25] The belief that the social world is fully determined underlies the recurring cynicism about political reform that persists in the North as well as the South, as reform movements rise and fall.

Only one writer of those considered here—Henry Adams—comes close to exhausting Shklar's interpretative patience, nearly defeating her effort to find something of value in every thinker. Her essay on *The Education of Henry Adams,* which originally appeared in a collection revisiting some twentieth-century classic works, concludes that the only reason Adams's autobiography is not a failure is that its author confesses that his life is a failure.[26] His confession redeemed his life, and has taught his readers much, including the lesson that if you claim to support the cause of reform you must be willing to do something to bring it about.[27] Elections may often be dishonest, and politicians corrupt, as the heroine of Adams's novel *Democracy* believed, but that does not mean that democracy is just like every other form of government, and certainly does not excuse anyone, especially an Adams, from doing his share of the public service.[28]

The other set of interpretive encumbrances that Shklar seeks to overcome grows out of the idea of American exceptionalism. She believes that the claim that American theory is distinctive, though obviously correct in some sense, has been badly misconstrued. It has led to the mistaken belief that American theory is "a peculiarly local phenomenon, 'a poor thing but our own.'"[29] This is doubly wrong.

American theory is in the first place not a poor thing at all, but part of "an intellectual adventure of the first order."[30] As a distinguished student of European theory, Shklar is able to affirm, with more than ordinary scholarly authority, that American thought is intrinsically important and intellectually serious. In the second place, it is not so distinctive as is often assumed. Shklar argues that "apart from the early establishment of representative democracy and the persistence of slavery, which do give it a special character, American political thought is just an integral part of modern history as a whole."[31] In any case, the dispute about American exceptionalism, as her essays implicitly remind us, is also such an integral part of the ongoing debate about so many other issues in American history that it cannot serve as the key to understanding American theory.

A distinction that Shklar does not herself draw can help clarify her position on exceptionalism. Ideas may be exceptional in two different ways: in their *origin* (when they arise in response to new problems in distinctive social contexts), and in their *relevance* (when they are appropriately applied only to problems in that same specific context). Shklar certainly believes that American theory is in some respects exceptional in the first sense, but just as certainly that it is not in the second sense.

In their origin, some leading ideas in American theory must be seen as responses to the nation's peculiar experience with representative government and slavery. Shklar agrees with Burke, for example, that Americans wrote more passionately about freedom in part because they saw up close what slavery was like.[32] More generally, the "wholly unique pattern of political controversy" about equality already discussed would not have emerged in a society that was either more aristocratic or more egalitarian than America.[33]

Furthermore, the idea of innovation itself is "inherently a part of an American democratic ideology."[34] The founders who thought they were creating a new constitution were right. Shklar agrees with Franklin, who in his frustration with appeals to ancient constitutions in the Convention, suggested that the delegates try prayer instead, which for Franklin was "an expression of despair."[35] Much the same could be said of most of the positive uses of European theory and experience. Locke is of course relevant, but is best understood as simply a respectable addition to the Puritan conception of religious government.[36] Montesquieu, with his doctrine of separation of powers and his appreciation of commerce, is more helpful, but even he is too mired in the world of ancient republics.[37]

It may seem surprising that Shklar, herself so historically oriented, should so warm to this rejection of the past. But her enthusiasm does not imply any rejection of history. One cannot understand how novel American theory was, and in what its novelty consists, without knowing in some detail the theory that preceded it in other times and places. Furthermore, most of those thinkers who wanted to reject the European past did not reject history altogether. They hoped that American historians would write a new, democratic sort of history.[38] If the spirit of innovation did not authorize early American theorists to ignore history then, it certainly should not license its contemporary interpreters to neglect it now.

As for the present and future, Shklar believes that American ideas speak to citizens of all democracies. In their relevance, the ideas are not exceptional. On this question, Shklar is more inclined to follow Paine than the Puritans. Her inclination leads her to another act of redemption, this time to save American theory from those who claim (in the strictest sense) to be redeemers themselves. The Puritans saw America as a "redeemer nation," chosen to carry out a divine mission that God could not entrust to other nations or other peoples.[39] But the Puritans were not the only or even the most important voice on this question. Paine argued, more cogently, that the "cause of America is in a great measure the cause of all mankind."[40] His influential pamphlet, *Common Sense*—the very title of which implies a shared and universal understanding—helped "turn a local squabble into a struggle for the salvation of the world."[41] If this was redemption, it was an entirely secular kind, and far more inclusionary than any the Puritans had imagined.

Even representative government, America's most impressive contribution to the gallery of political institutions, is now "far from peculiarly American."[42] If this institution set America apart during much of the nineteenth century, the ideas that "cluster around it have now become generally significant." Shklar allies herself with those "democrats [who] thought that America was the nation of the future, and its great task was to remove the intellectual and institutional impediments to that aspiration."[43] She is under no illusion that this progressive democratic spirit is the only or even the dominant force in American theory. Many currents, driven not only by realities but also by ideals, run counter to this force today, just as they always have in American history. Our best prospect, she thinks, is the process of democracy itself: "If we can learn to do better, it will be because democracy is itself dynamic."[44]

These essays are replete with intimations of how that process might proceed, and what we may learn as we engage in it. The themes emphasized in this Foreword are only a sample of the subjects that the essays illuminate. Among the many others enriched by Shklar's trenchant analysis are the place of religion in politics, the uses of history in political discourse, the nature of political friendship, the effect of skepticism in politics, the psychology of leadership, the origins of contemporary social science, the character of civic virtue, and the problem of immigration. The immigrant experience, hers and America's, led her to consider the plight of exiles—those who, sometimes by choice, more often under duress, emigrate without immigrating. She believed that by analyzing their moral status, she could expose some deficiencies in the American idea of citizenship, and more generally in political theories of obligation and loyalty. This was the aim of the major project on which she was working at the time of her death.[45]

Except in the suggestive survey in the last few pages of the first essay in this collection, Shklar does not carry the story of American theory beyond 1860. That is in a sense perfectly appropriate. She believes that the basic patterns of American thought were set in its early years, and that the moral and political beliefs they reflect tend to persist. "The ideas born in the first fifty years of [America's] independent political life remain relatively unaltered and are as vigorous as ever."[46] But readers may be excused for wishing that she could have continued her story and developed its implications for the controversies of our time. It is a wish that would have been fulfilled had she lived. In her later work her attention turned increasingly toward current problems, as she carried out a responsibility that she considered an essential part of the vocation of a political theorist. Yet her commentary on the contemporary would have remained, as it always had been, deeply informed by her insight into the complexities of the history of American political theory. Those who wish better to understand that history, for whatever worthy intellectual or political purpose, will find these essays indispensable.

Notes

1. *American Citizenship: The Quest for Inclusion* (Cambridge, MA: Harvard University Press, 1991), p. 13.
2. "Redeeming American Political Theory," in this volume, p. 92.
3. Ibid.
4. "Democratic Customs," in this volume, p. 188.
5. *American Citizenship*, p. 38.
6. "Liberalism of Fear," in *Liberalism and the Moral Life*, ed. Nancy Rosenblum (Cambridge, MA: Harvard University Press, 1989), p. 21.
7. This more robust liberalism comes to fruition in *American Citizenship*.
8. "Positive Liberty, Negative Liberty in the United States," in this volume.
9. "A Life of Learning," in *Liberalism without Illusions: Essays on Liberal Theory and the Political Vision of Judith N. Shklar*, ed. Bernard Yack (Chicago: University of Chicago Press, 1996), p. 277.
10. "An Education for America," in this volume, pp. 68–69.

11. Ibid., p. 66.

12. Alexis de Tocqueville, *Democracy in America,* ed. Phillips Bradley (New York: Random House, 1990), 1: 53.

13. "Alexander Hamilton and the Language of Political Science," in this volume.

14. "A Friendship," in this volume.

15. "The American Idea of Aristocracy," in this volume, p. 157.

16. "Redeeming American Political Theory," p. 101.

17. "Emerson and the Inhibitions of Democracy," in this volume.

18. Ibid., p. 53, quoting *Emerson in His Journals,* ed. Joel Porte (Cambridge, MA: Harvard University Press, 1982), p. 408.

19. "Emerson and the Inhibitions of Democracy," pp. 56, 58.

20. "Hawthorne in Utopia," in this volume.

21. "An Education for America," pp. 73–74.

22. Ibid.

23. "Democracy and the Past," in this volume, p. 183.

24. "An Education for America," p. 71.

25. "Redeeming American Political Theory," p. 103.

26. "*The Education of Henry Adams,* by Henry Adams," in this volume, p. 90.

27. Ibid., p. 86.

28. "Democratic Customs," pp. 187–88.

29. "A Life of Learning," p. 277. Also see "The American Idea of Aristocracy," p. 146.

30. "Redeeming American Political Theory," p. 108.

31. "A Life of Learning," p. 277.

32. *American Citizenship,* p. 40.

33. "Democratic Customs," p. 197.

34. "Democracy and the Past," p. 186.

35. "A New Constitution for a New Nation," in this volume, p. 164.

36. "The Boundaries of Democracy," in this volume, p. 131–32.

37. "A New Constitution for a New Nation," pp. 165–66.

38. "Democracy and the Past," pp. 184, 186.

39. "The Boundaries of Democracy," pp. 131, 134.

40. Thomas Paine, *Common Sense,* ed. Isaac Kramnick (London: Penguin, 1976), p. 63, quoted by Shklar, "The Boundaries of Democracy," p. 135.

41. "The Boundaries of Democracy," p. 134.

42. "The American Idea of Aristocracy," p. 146.

43. "Democracy and the Past," p. 186.

44. "Redeeming American Political Theory," p. 108.

45. "Obligation, Loyalty, Exile," *Political Theory* (May 1993): 181–97.

46. "The American Idea of Aristocracy," p. 157.

PART ONE

American Thinkers

CHAPTER ONE

Alexander Hamilton and
the Language of Political Science

In a striking article about medieval scholars, Georges Duby has written "[In] political relations, we can observe changes that are sometimes very rapid . . . however, the history of systems of values does not display sudden changes."[1] That sentence instantly brought the history of America to my mind. As we all know, universities are held together by an intricate series of rituals, and this, one might suppose, is not unrelated to the continuity of their values. There are other rituals which have survived in a comparable way, and so have, with some interruptions, the intellectual dispositions that are associated with them. Consider for example elections in the United States. They were part of its political life well before the Revolution, to be sure, but it is only with the ratification of the Constitution that the present rhythm of representative democracy began. For two hundred years now Americans have voted for a president every four years and every two in congressional elections. For all citizens the "simple act of voting" is a ritual profoundly reinforced by the deepest "democratic myth"—that even the federal government acts with the "consent of the governed." Elections are what I should like to call "consequential rituals"; that is, they have very real political effects, not only on the ultimate choice of office holders, but also on their attitudes and conduct. They have also had an enormous impact upon the most typical forms of social theory, which is now political science and which has

This chapter was previously published as "Alexander Hamilton and the Language of Political Science," in *The Languages of Political Theory in Early Modern Europe,* ed. Anthony Pagden (Cambridge: Cambridge University Press, 1987), pp. 339–55. Reprinted with the permission of Cambridge University Press.

all along been a part of the culture of representative democracy. From the first, democracy has required a considerable amount of accurate information. Along with regular elections, Americans also have, as mandated by the Constitution, a national census that is published every ten years without fail (Act I, sect. 2). And beyond that there is the need, recognized inevitably by any group of freely elected representatives, to know as much as possible about their constituencies.

The demand for information about essentially the entire white male population, for the suffrage was very broad, even before all property and tax qualifications for voting disappeared in the 1840s, imposed a radical democratization on political inquiry. How to assess the behavior and attitudes of the anonymous many who compose the electorate was a wholly novel intellectual task. So new a democratization of inquiry and values demanded considerable theoretical effort in 1787, and again when it was taken up with new vigor in the 1930s. Among the earliest political thinkers, it has always seemed to me, Alexander Hamilton's voice was the most significant in setting the terms of what is now called political science. For then as now it is the tortuous and long road from the individual voter to the public policies of the federal government that has excited the greatest interest. It obsessed Hamilton and it is central to a very substantial part of contemporary survey research. The active, planning, central state of which Hamilton merely dreamed is, to be sure, the political actuality of this science which has its present origins in the 1930s. The sources of authority and its ultimate exercise are however in either case the focus of calculation. It is of course true that the mathematical refinement and therefore the accuracy of the framed hypotheses and of their disposition are far greater now than they were in the eighteenth century; nor is the population being counted and viewed the same. The real puzzle, however, is that—given that the culture, geography, economy, and technology of America have been transformed—the structure of political discourse has changed so little and that the most characteristic institutions of its representative democracy seem so immune to change. The claim that political science is a new enterprise and that it must first imitate and then catch up with the natural sciences is more an expression of a multiplicity of frustrations than a reflection of either the age or the inner structure of America's typical political science. In fact, the practices of political science are responses to the oldest and most enduring political values and as such prove, if anything, the resilience of at least one of America's earliest vocabularies.

There were two other early forms of social science. The most significant arose not from the experience of representative democracy, but from the contact of Europeans with native American Indians and imported black slaves. Though such encounters were to be widespread everywhere, they were more enduring and integral to American society than to any other group of Europeans. Hence the habit of "looking at" and describing these alien peoples along with the fauna and flora of the continent became a settled intellectual style. One need only glance at Jefferson's *Notes on the State of Virginia* to recognize the origins and character of American anthropology, so much of it concerned with the Indians. That is, however, another avenue of research. For political science Jefferson's friend and Hamilton's collaborator on the *Federalist,* Madison, is more significant. His great claim is that he began that part of political sociology that flourishes in a pluralistic society and which concerns itself with the formation and interactions of interest groups. The model of these was the multiplicity of Protestant sects which Madison knew in his native state and from which he extrapolated the likely behavior of those other groups that regional diversity and a free and growing economy nurtured. This is also a field now cultivated by survey research and it has obvious bearings on every aspect of politics. However, as general public opinion is not identical with specifically electoral opinion, the relationship between the two is itself a subject of scholarly dispute. What is significant here is that major part of political science for which ultimately electoral acts and their implications count most heavily, not the sociology of public attitudes generally. Indeed, as an aside, even radical American social scientists use elections as their focus of investigations of social change in American history. It is not surprising, because it is impossible to think of American politics apart from the processes of representative democracy with its peculiar terms: majority and minority rather than class; local and central, partly because elections are geographically determined, and also because of federalism; voters and candidates; choice and its limits; indifference and activity; habits and issues and parties. And these terms impose themselves whatever the ideological preferences of the observer-speaker may be. Hamilton, as it happened, was not a supporter of the system he helped others to understand, while most of today's political scientists tend to be ardently loyal to the constitutional order. It makes no difference; when you enter a ritual, you are going to speak its language. And that language tells us of a huge premium put upon prediction: for everyone cares about the outcome of elections and that itself stimulates science.

The intellectual structure of electoral survey research is not particularly complicated. It works to establish valid generalizations about voters by correlating increasingly detailed and accurate versions of expressed opinions. Mathematically sophisticated and now computerized, it remains basically within the realm of common sense. You test probable abstract statements by correlating the responses of individuals, the only directly observable indivisible unit: the voter. This is solid Baconian science and it is just what Hamilton wished to develop as well. A known reader of Hume's essays, and of Montesquieu, he was sure that "history" taught political psychology. According to his friend Chancellor Kent, he contemplated "a full investigation of the history and science of civil government . . . and to have the subject treated in reference to past experience upon Lord Bacon's inductive philosophy."[2] The questions that such a science would ask were not remote from those of voting studies. They were about the responsiveness of governments to the governed, the ability of systems to reconcile groups of people in conflict, and the governability specifically of the American people.[3] It is indeed not surprising that at fifty years of age survey research recognizes itself as a legitimate part of political historiography, intellectually and, as a contributor to the public good, ethically.

Unlike Hume, whom history taught that whatever lasted must be good, Hamilton, no less than his successors, was open to novelty and to the constructive efforts of the political will. "The science of politics . . . like most other sciences, has received great improvement. The efficacy of various principles is now well understood, which were either not known at all, or only imperfectly known to the ancients."[4] Among the things that the science of politics had discovered was the efficacy of representative democracy. Moreover, there was something that the very act of establishing a completely new form of government could prove: "whether societies of men are really capable or not of establishing good government from reflection and choice, or whether they are forever destined to depend for their political constitution on accident and force." If Americans chose to make the wrong decisions it would be not only a mistake for them, but a "general misfortune of mankind."[5] Electoral politics obviously implied a fair degree of voluntarism; voters made their destiny, especially when they voted for a constitution in the first place. That also introduced an element of unpredictability into politics. Discussing the future of military policies, Hamilton, for instance, admitted that "how the national legislature may reason . . . is a thing which neither [his adversaries] nor I can foresee."[6] And this again was an invitation to calculation and inferences from past to present. Voters changed, representatives had wills. Politics as voting was, in short, a subject for constant investigation, because it was uncertain and yet needed to be grasped.

The kind of information that was really needed was psychological. It was taken for granted that both social groups and individual political agents were moved by "ambition, avarice, and vindictiveness." Of these the first two were the most important, which made political behavior relatively predictable, at least when the most active political people were involved. Hamilton was not disposed to "view human nature" other than "as it is, without either flattering its virtues or exaggerating its vices."[7] That made him neither anxious, nor excessively optimistic. Indeed, "utopian" was a word of scorn in his vocabulary.[8] What really impressed him politically, however, was "[t]he alarming indifference discoverable in the exercise of so valuable a privilege" as voting.[9] All these observations referred back to known behavior in the several states. Moreover, this mix of ambition, avarice, and voter indifference was not random in his view. Like everything else it occurred in a setting that was also subject to reasonably accurate descriptions. The relevant circumstances were the natural wealth and "genius" of the citizens, the degree of information they possessed, the state of commerce, of acts of industry—and "many more too complex, remote or adventitious to admit of particular specification." This constituted "the wealth of nations" and it was measurable.[10] Apart from voting, politics were in fact highly depersonalized and, indeed, this was necessary for a predictive science of politics. It was also inherent in representative democracy, and for Hamilton that was a sign of the durability of the "great" republic. Majorities were aggregates, solid wholes. That in any case was given; there could be no alteration of majority rule. The "fundamental maxim of republican government . . . requires that the sense of the majority should prevail" and that "the deliberate sense of the community should govern the conduct of those to whom they intrust the management of their affairs."[11] Majority government as such was simply "there," and it was subject to objective investigation.

Like most political scientists Hamilton thought little of the intelligence or knowledge of the voters.[12] Nevertheless he did not blame them for defects in their conduct. It was always the fault of the candidates and of those who misled or failed to present issues properly to the voters. Among distinguished political scientists it was particularly

V. O. Key who came to emphasize that the quality of voters' choices depended on the choices that were put before them and articulated for them by candidates. The political science profession's long-standing *cri de coeur* for a "responsible" two-party system carries the same message. It was Hamilton's as well, especially when he argued, for example, for a single executive, whom voters could easily size up and hold fully responsible for his performance in office.[13] It must be said that recently voters have certainly exercised that real if rather negative power.

With all these considerations in mind Harrington had turned to the composition of the majority, given its primacy in the whole political scheme. How do electors behave? Like present-day researchers, Hamilton was no formalist; he looked to "social alignments." Today these are region, ethnicity, religion, and status. Since it was a white Protestant electorate, Hamilton looked at region and status, the South and North, as ever also the more agricultural and the more commercial areas, respectively. Status was, however, the chief object of interest. What he saw in New York, his own state, was as follows: "Mechanics and manufacturers will always be inclined, with a few exceptions, to give their votes to merchants in preference to persons of their own professions or trades." They regarded a merchant who traded in their products as their "patron and friend" and they thought their interests safer in his hands than in their own. What you have here is an account of deferential voting, but without the usual sneer that often accompanies such observations. The confidence that small landowners had in great planters, Hamilton went on to observe, was equally strong and again rooted in well-understood self-interest. For the psychology was here not one of class deference, but of calculated self-interest, brought out by capable candidates. "If we take fact as our guide," in short, we would know that rural voters elected moderate proprietors as a rule. Even more than these statistical constants, what mattered was the confidence that an individual candidate, rich or poor, could arouse in voters.[14]

That is indeed the argument today of those interested in accurate short-term predictions of voting behavior, which makes sense, given the very low ideological temperature of American voters and their declining tendency to identify with one of the two parties.[15] There would, therefore, be candidates who succeed without being members of any of the obvious economic groups: the "learned professions . . . who truly form no distinct interest in society" but who "according to their situation and talents" would be "objects of the confidence and choice" of their communities. By "learned professions" Hamilton meant lawyers. Voters certainly wanted candidates who understood "their feelings and interests," but to bring diverse groups together to frame policies the latter needed to do more. They needed to amalgamate in the legislatures and make governable their very heterogeneous electors. Mediation and brokerage in Hamilton's view were the chief tasks of the "neutral" representatives, those who belonged to the learned professions.

What of the candidates? Information was their greatest need if they were to function at all. "Extensive inquiry" would inform a potential or actual representative of "the dispositions and inclinations" of the voters. He must, therefore, whether he was learned or not, be a primary consumer of local political and general psychological knowledge, the kind that only scientifically sampled survey research can and did, in fact, yield.[16]

Hamilton, of course, had special reasons for emphasizing the possibility of representatives being equipped with "sufficient knowledge of local circumstances" and also of their ability to forge solid majorities out of disparate interests. For these were the necessary basis for policy planning, especially for centralized economic and fiscal policy grounded in political economy. Because members of the same class, such as different kinds of artisans, often had more conflicts with each other than with people who might be better off than themselves, but engaged in their own line of production, they voted not in keeping with their social status but with their vertical economic interest group. This was fortunate as it was likely to result in a representative assembly whose members could be reconciled for purposes of fiscal policy, not to mention the sort of economic planning Hamilton hoped for, and which the contemporary federal government pursues. Voters, in short, chose not necessarily their own mirror image as individuals or members of groups, but as their more diffuse sense of confidence in an individual dictated. That was, of course, not a quality that could be divorced from issue voting. Especially when the issues were as confounding as welfare, defense, race relations and, as ever, taxation.

There are few papers in the *Federalist* that can match the two on which I have just drawn. There is in them, as in many others, a larger purpose that must and does inspire the scientific temper in all its manifestations. That is the necessity to combat nonscientific or prescientific modes of thought. Americans are notoriously, though not, I believe, uniquely, addicted to one form of prescientific thinking: conspiratorial explanations of political events. In a brilliant essay Gordon Wood has argued that conspiratorial thinking in this period of American history was a response to a new intellectual climate created by science and naturalistic philosophy generally. There now had to be a causal, natural explanation for all events, social as well as physical. Given the rather frightening and complex events, the appeal to common sense and suspicion that conspiracy offers—not to mention its psychological gratifications, its certainties and simplicities, it was and is the most obvious answer for those who are remote from scientific modes of thought.[17] Among the Anti-Federalists there were indeed many such men who, fearful of the new constitution and terrified by the men who had drawn it up, saw deep plots behind the proposals. Monarchies, standing armies, and generally the connivance of "the wealthy and well-born" were seen as dooming republican freedom. "Where in the name of common sense," Hamilton exclaimed, "are our fears to end if we cannot trust our brothers, our neighbors, our fellow citizens?"[18] But he also argued from the analogy of the natural sciences to try to induce his readers to think through complexities, rather than to look for sinister agents.[19] Above all he wanted to persuade them to try "rational calculation of probabilities," to think carefully of the "permanent causes, moral as well as physical" rather than to abandon science in favor of wild speculation.[20] The other sources of irrationality in politics were obviously passion and self-interest. In Hamilton's view, these were "utopians, who disdain the admonitions of experimental instruction," who thought, he claimed, that one could have government without coercion.[21]

Clearly there are many far from "utopian" dreamers who also resist the instructions of scientific thought. Prescientific, unscientific, antiscientific thinking about politics generally and elections specifically flourishes, right and left, north and south. The newspapers and television often conduct unscientific surveys, and then treat them as solid public opinion though it is often vaguely defined; they regard guesswork, moralism, and ideology as definitive; they use polls to promote candidates and policies. All of these—and of course every form of conspiracy thinking—are rampant forms of semiscience in the United States. It is impossible to understand the passion for accuracy apart from these essentially nonscientific mind-sets which play at being scientific even though they are in truth antiscientific. The refinements of survey research have other sources and intellectual justifications, to be sure, but the spectacle of science abused and misapprehended must always figure as an important one. Exposing fallacies was one of Hamilton's self-set tasks and it remains one for political science.

The scientific study of voters—specifically, their psychology, responses to events, and the outcome of elections—has finally a bearing on what survey researchers frankly call the "democratic myth": that the voter decides. The voter does not care, is ignorant, and generally feels that what he does on election day does not matter. For him it is a civic ritual. Nevertheless, it is psychologically extremely important that representatives and officials think of themselves as dependent upon "grass roots." They want and need the security of this base which guarantees their place in the structure of representative democracy as a whole. To this quandary science has no answer.[22] It may not need to worry, because its findings are not new politically and indeed have always reflected these realities. Political science need not look back with regret to the formalism of the nineteenth century, which was always subject to challenges, even in its strongest period. There is, in fact, every reason to suppose (especially when one considers Hamilton, writing all that *before* legal and political institutions had become established) that an informal, demystifying, scientific, and individualizing political science is built into the rituals of electoral politics and is in fact a part of their structure. Those who seek votes will want to know all they can about the voters, and they will always have reason to fear their constituents. There is therefore a built-in impetus to scientific surveying and one that in the end sustains rather than unsettles the whole ritual because far from diminishing, they enhance the sense of its ultimate importance. For looked at historically, scientific historiography, which is what survey research knows itself to be by now, is itself an integral part of the complex dialectic of democratic political culture.

There is of course one objection of great weight to be made against my argument. Did not the active state of the ancien régime, especially under such statesmen as Colbert and later Turgot, also undertake the most extensive search for social information? And did not at least one of Turgot's younger disciples, the mathematician Condorcet, apply mathematics at once to parliamentary voting after the French Revolution?[23] Is there not a continuity that moves from bureaucratic to parliamentary social science? I do not, in fact, deny that bureaucratically devised policies are a part of the picture. That is why Hamilton, the first and most significant early American partisan of such policies, is so prophetic and why his language re-emerges in the age of the New Deal and after. The uniqueness of his political science as contrasted to the purely policy-oriented studies of bureaucratic governments is that the behavior of the electorate is primary. The science of understanding the voters is not subservient to policy. The voters count and active public policy only makes them more problematic. Within the context of representative democracy the science of politics remains, in fact, subordinate to the imperatives of "the consent of the governed," though it becomes vital only when it is confronted by national politics framed and executed *far* from the arena in which "the simple act of voting" occurs. For political science to be a science, as it now is, it must make the understanding of the individual, elementary phenomena its primary goal, and that occurs only within the cultural context of democracy. American political science may well be stimulated by the political demands of an active central state, but it looks first to its ultimate basis in the rituals and habits of two centuries of uninterrupted (even by a Civil War!) electoral activity.

Notes

1. Georges Duby, "The History of Systems of Values," in *The Chivalrous Society*, trans. Cynthia Postan (Berkeley: University of California Press, 1980), p. 216.

2. William Kent, *Memoirs and Letters of James Kent* (Boston: Little, Brown & Co., 1898), pp. 327–28.

3. Norman H. Nie, Sidney Verba, and Jolen R. Petrocik, *The Changing American Voter* (Cambridge: Harvard University Press, 1979), pp. 2–13.

4. *The Federalist*, ed. Clinton Rossiter (New York: New American Library, 1961), no. 9, p. 72.

5. Ibid., no. 1, p. 33.

6. Ibid., no. 29, p. 185.

7. Ibid., no. 76, p. 458.

8. Ibid., no. 6, p. 54.

9. Ibid., no. 61, p. 373.

10. Ibid., no. 21, pp. 142–43.

11. Ibid., no. 22, p. 146; no. 71, p. 432.

12. John C. Miller, *Alexander Hamilton and the Growth of the New Nation* (New York: Harper and Row, 1959), pp. 185–86.

13. V. O. Key, *The Responsible Electorate* (Cambridge: Harvard University Press, 1966); *Federalist*, no. 70, pp. 427–31.

14. *Federalist*, no. 35, pp. 214–17.

15. E.g., Stanley Kelley Jr., *Interpreting Elections* (Princeton: Princeton University Press, 1983).

16. *Federalist*, no. 35, pp. 214–17; no. 36, pp. 217–20.

17. Gordon S. Wood, "Conspiracy and the Paranoid Style: Causality and Deceit

in the Eighteenth Century," *William and Mary Quarterly,* 3d ser., 39 (1982): 401–41.

18. *Federalist,* no. 29, p. 186.

19. Ibid., no. 31, pp. 193–94.

20. Ibid., no. 60, p. 367.

21. Ibid., no. 28, p. 178.

22. These are the implications of both Angus Campbell, Philip E. Converse, Warren E. Miller, and Donald Stokes, *The American Voter* (New York: Wiley, 1960); and Nie et al., *The Changing American Voter.*

23. Keith Michael Baker, *Condorcet* (Chicago: University of Chicago Press, 1975).

CHAPTER TWO

A Friendship

Political philosophers since classical antiquity have given much thought to friendship and for very good reasons. The kinds of friendship people have may depend on the governments they live under. And it is not clear that friendship and politics mix all that well. First of all the tensions created by political ambition are likely to strain even the most intense personal loyalties. And then there are many occasions when our political and personal obligations come into conflict. What if one's friend turns out to have broken the law, possibly even to the point of treason; do you stick by him or turn him in to the FBI? This sort of dilemma is particularly acute if one has a very extreme sense of what friendship involves. "One soul in two bodies," as it has often been called, speaks of an identity, not just of feeling and opinions, but of personality. This is often how people think of friendship in oppressive or anarchic societies. Indeed, friendship often flourishes in despotic states as it does in no others. Friends form their private polity which protects them against the state and gives them an alternative moral universe. Here freedom and spontaneity reign, while oppression and hypocrisy are the universal rule in the larger society. In the one, people comfort each other and share whatever they may have; in the other, they exploit and abuse others. That is also why some of the finest essays on friendship have been written in the midst of civil wars. In these extreme political situations, the right impulse must surely be to say that if my friend did the unlawful deed, it is as if I had done it myself, and there is either a very good reason for it, or

This unpublished essay was written in 1987.

if not, then the claims of friendship are still so far greater than those of political duty that I must abide with my friend. And since most regimes are, after all, beneath contempt, that seems quite right. The illegal act whatever it may be is not usually genuinely reprehensible, and certainly not treachery at all. The other self is breaking the law of a criminal state, and one is obliged by both feeling and conviction to join her in her defiance. To love one's friends more than one's rulers may be morally and emotionally the only way to have a worthwhile life at all.

It is in free societies that the claims of friendship become politically ambiguous. It is not self-evident that friendship must in all cases have a greater call on our loyalty than our country and its elected government. Moreover, especially in decent states, it is not usually so dramatic a choice as having to decide between one's country and one's friend, but of thinking that a very dear friend may have joined a party or taken up a cause that one cannot support and indeed heartily detests. This is not a matter of moral man against an immoral society. Nor is it merely a conflict of personal ambitions. It is the tension of incompatible beliefs sincerely held that tears friends apart in countries where public and private lives are intricately woven together. The question then really is whether one should let politics destroy friendship like that. Should we not be able to defend our private affections against public disturbances? The finest of democratic thinkers have thought that we should certainly try, but they did not think that friendship meant spiritual unity, or the shared soul of the older classical view. Quite on the contrary, "better a nettle in the side of your friend than his echo . . . let him not cease an instant to be himself," wrote Emerson. When one is used to personal freedom and really cherishes it, unity and oneness do not seem inherently quite so valuable. It is the ability to love without demanding likeness or agreement, especially on political matters, that marks the friendship of free women and men. To be sure, there are always actions that overstep the boundaries of the tolerable, which may well end any friendship, but it is not very likely that one would be so utterly mistaken in a real friend's character. It is surely a rare failure that brings a friendship to an end because one or the other commits an act or acquires a belief that is too revolting to be borne. Politics, in short, normally ought not to divide friends. However, it often does, even among people who have a flexible sense of friendship and who live in a society that allows ample room for private relationships of every sort.

That is not all. There may be a special kind of friendship that is inherently political, and it is not entirely like personal affection. It is most usual among people who are deeply absorbed in political activity. Political friendship is the bond that unites them in a common cause. It is far more intense than a mere alliance or bargain, but it depends less on the personality than on the convictions of the friends, and it is peculiarly fragile. For political circumstances change very quickly. That is why most revolutionary comrades end up not just falling out with each other, but as often as not becoming bitter and violent enemies after their cause has triumphed. That does not mean that the original friendship was not genuine, but only that the political passion which inspired it easily turned to other objects when the battle was won. That is an extreme and notorious example, but it is no less true of those political friendships that border on coalitions and shared political interests in stable democratic political environments, and which are dissolved during contested elections. It is in fact possible that this may not be a bad thing, but on the contrary, to the public good. Political agents and officials should not have any real, enduring friendships. Government and political judgment require us to be impartial and just, and friendship is a perpetual temptation to favor those whom we love. Not only princes, but all those who are or strive to become responsible for the well-being of a people and who hold offices of public trust, must say goodbye to the claims of friendship. It is just something they cannot afford. And when one considers the corruptions and favoritism that prevail even among the officials of relatively open governments, not to mention the gifts handed out to the courtiers of kings and dictators, one can see why serious thinkers about politics have warned public men against friendship. There is a very noble stoic thought at work in this. "If a measure were good for me, but not for my friends, I would say no to it. If it were good for my friends, but not for my country, I would say no. And if it were good for my country, but bad for mankind, I would say no again." Justice can go no further, but one may well say against it that without friendship life is just not worth living. And why then not give way to the obvious temptation to get as far away from public life as possible, so that one can enjoy the pleasures of intimacy without any complicating political difficulties and conflicts? It is certainly a choice open to us, but it is, surely, not without its costs. To renounce citizenship in favor of a wholly personal life is to give up a great deal, half of a full life. It may not even be necessary. Why then not venture everything and try both friendship and politics?

There is in American history a unique example of all the vicissitudes of both personal and political friendship between two truly great men. The letters exchanged between John Adams and Thomas Jefferson are not only one of the great joys of American political literature; they are also a mirror of all the ups and downs of friendship between upright people. And it is particularly fitting that we should remember them in this year, the two-hundredth anniversary of the ratification of the United States Constitution. John Adams and Thomas Jefferson were not in America when that occurred (they were in Europe, representing their country in England and France respectively), but they were certainly part of the generation and, indeed, of the small group that forged the document. They were also present in spirit. The Constitutional Convention was in Jefferson's view "an assembly of demigods," which did not prevent him from criticizing them vigorously on many points and making his views known through letters to his young friend James Madison. The Constitution of Massachusetts, of which Adams had been the chief author, was in many ways the model for the federal one, so he was at the Convention indirectly as well. If ever there was a pair of Founding Fathers it was Adams and Jefferson, and they knew it, and their friendship was built on that enormous common achievement. But the history of that friendship was an unusual one, because it was not one, but two: one political, and later, a personal one. The first had its origin in the revolutionary project which they shared, and then in their joint diplomatic service abroad. It was broken off for a dozen years as a result of their electoral rivalry and ideological and party conflict, which reached its height when Jefferson succeeded Adams as president, after defeating him in the election. Then, after both had retired from public life and returned to their native states, and with the tactful prodding of a mutual friend, they took to writing each other again, and without ever meeting, became deeply affectionate, wholly personal friends until they died. In telling the story of these two friends and their two successive friendships I do not mean simply to remember them, but to celebrate friendship itself in all its phases. And unlike the classical authors, I do not exclude friendship between the two sexes.

Adams and Jefferson met in 1775 at the Continental Congress. Adams was thirty-nine and Jefferson thirty-two years old, and they found out quickly that they were among the few people there who wanted the thirteen colonies to unite and at once proclaim their independence from Great Britain. When at long last a five-man committee was appointed to draw up a declaration to that end, both were on it. As was to be their usual pattern of conduct, Jefferson tried to defer to Adams's greater political experience and suggested that he draw up the document, but Adams insisted that Jefferson do it, because he wrote ten times better. He never doubted that Jefferson had the greater literary talent. In return Jefferson claimed that it was Adams's brilliant and rousing speech in favor of independence that sent the delegates out of their seats and, of course, into war. They were to recollect that moment for the rest of their lives, and its memory illuminated their friendship to its last day. They constantly worried that the historians would not get it right. When had the Revolution really begun? they asked. It was as difficult to say, Jefferson thought, as finding "the exact moment when an embryo becomes an animal." Adams was upset that the Revolution and the War for Independence were being confused. "The Revolution was in the Minds of the People . . . in the course of fifteen years before a drop of blood was drawn at Lexington." Moreover, there was no false modesty here. Neither one was inclined to understate his own part in these events. Theirs was the Heroic age, Jefferson wrote in his last letter before his death, and they had been Argonauts. "It was the lot of our early years to witness nothing but the dull monotony of colonial subservience, and of our riper ones to breast the labors and perils of working out of it." He was sure that their descendants would never face a comparable challenge, nor achieve anything as grand.

In the event, they worked for the same political ends and came to depend on each other, at first during the stormy days of 1776, and then in the years during which Adams represented America in England and Jefferson was stationed in France. Their purpose there was to sign commercial treaties with as many countries as possible without getting entangled in European politics. Negotiations were always difficult, because America was a poor and weak country. From the first, Jefferson accepted Adams's judgment and relied on his advice, even when he did not agree. He was free in expressing his own opinions, but as a matter of course and without the slightest resentment he simply assumed that Adams's political knowledge was superior to his own. Yet as a diplomat he was more successful, because his manners and tact were perfect, while Adams was notoriously crotchety and hot-tempered. So on occasion the older man would ask the younger whether he had acted properly and, if not, how the damage was to be repaired. Jefferson would send a soothing letter back telling Adams that he had behaved quite appropriately and not to worry. Over and over one sees him being careful to avoid infringing on Adams's authority, stepping aside for his sensitive colleague, not just out of prudence, but with a sense of respect. Their one big policy disagreement came over the Barbary pirates, and that story has a sickeningly familiar ring. The pirates captured vessels off the North African coast and then demanded a ransom for their captives. All the European governments gave whatever was demanded in the hope that they, but not their commercial rivals, would be spared in the future. Adams thought this a completely disgusting policy, but saw no alternative and instructed Jefferson to pay up. Jefferson demurred. He thought that justice and honor demanded war. Moreover, "it will procure us respect in Europe and respect is a safe-guard to interest." In the long run, he thought, it would also be less expensive. The price tag for the hostages was $59,496 in addition to a huge sum for a treaty. It was an enormous amount of money. In closing, however, Jefferson wrote, "The same facts impress us differently," but that he would do whatever Adams and Congress thought best. He eventually appealed to the religious order that normally handled these deals, but they were dissolved during the French Revolution and it was ten years before the prisoners were freed.

The two men had other disagreements, but they were not on matters of immediate policy. Thus Adams was horrified by Shays's Rebellion in Massachusetts, while Jefferson thought an occasional popular uprising was a very good thing. It reminded governments that the consent of the people could not be taken for granted. They were at odds over the design of the Constitution. Jefferson feared a monarchical president, while Adams was afraid that the Constitution was not properly mixed and he worried about oligarchic tendencies. Clearly from the first also, Jefferson's inclinations were more democratic than Adams's, but neither their temperamental nor other differences in any way interfered in their close and courteous political friendship. It was, moreover, accompanied by a personal friendship between Jefferson and Mrs. Adams, with whom he had much in common. Abigail Adams looked after Jefferson's motherless daughters at various times and he delighted in doing little commissions for her. When the two men ran against each other for the presidency, it was she rather more than her husband who turned bitterly on Jefferson and could not get over her grievances against him. For her it was all insult and injury and betrayal. Jefferson did not want to quarrel at all and Adams tended to regain his temper as quickly as he lost it, which was frequently, but Abigail Adams was adamant. She wrote Jefferson a letter of condolence when his daughter died, but refused his request to resume their former friendship. In her case, politics were personalized and her friendship could not survive a serious clash of public opinions and ambitions. The actors directly involved in the political drama, especially Jefferson, found it much easier to live on different levels of feeling and activity.

The facts of the end of this political friendship are simple. The election of 1800 was the first one to be fought along straight party lines and bitterly so. Jefferson opposed every policy that Adams had pursued and Adams came to see his old friend as some sort of threatening Jacobin. To thwart him he made a mass of midnight appointments on his last day in office, which Jefferson greatly resented, and also said many foolish things about his rival. Jefferson, in turn, accused Adams of being backward-looking and indifferent to the progress of science, which was only half true. He also did exactly what he had said he would do, which was to release all the prisoners held under the Alien and Sedition Acts, which he quite rightly regarded as repressive and unconstitutional. Among those let out of jail was a thoroughly scurrilous character who had blackened Adams's name and who, as soon as he was sprung, turned with equal venom upon his liberator. Among his choicer remarks about Adams was that he was "a repulsive pedant, a gross hypocrite and an unprincipled oppressor . . . in private life one of the most egregious fools upon the continent . . . incapable of attracting tenderness or esteem." In time he accused Jefferson of being the father of the children of one of his slaves. It was the release of this wretch that infuriated Abigail Adams.

At first glance one might think that on the whole, Jefferson had more reasons to feel abused than the Adamses did, and that he behaved with a good deal more dignity. But his party had said many unfair things about Adams; and then he *was* the winner after all, and remained enormously popular, while Adams's reputation was never secure. Moreover, politics just were not that important to Jefferson. Eventually he admitted that he had been ambitious as a young man, but that politics had never pleased him nor fully absorbed his energies; at various times in his life he quit and went home to Monticello and his neighbors. When Adams, as vice president, sent him a learned book, as he often did, Jefferson wrote back that "it is on politics, a subject I never loved, and now hate. I will not therefore promise to read it carefully." When Adams was elected president, Jefferson retired to Virginia and wrote to him, "I have no ambition to govern men. It is a painful and thankless office." That may not have been more than half true, but it was far from being entirely false and Jefferson's purpose in saying it came at the end of the letter: he just wanted Adams to be less political and to remain his friend. "In the course of our voyage thro' life, various little incidents have happened or been contrived to separate us, [I retain] for you the solid esteem of the moments when we were working for our independence, and sentiments of respect and affectionate attachment." It was Jefferson's last futile effort to save a friendship that had its roots in and derived much of its value from the enormous political work they had done together, but he also tried to persuade Adams that politics should not dominate his entire life. That amounted to asking Adams to transform himself, to alter his personality for Jefferson's sake.

It was too much to ask of friendship. For Adams, politics was all of life, and so he could not do what Jefferson said he wanted, "to keep our difference of opinion to private conversation." Not the least of their disagreements was about the French Revolution. To the end of their days Adams could not help harping on the disaster he had foreseen and Jefferson had not grasped. Jefferson simply let these barbs pass in silence. It simply did not matter all that much to him, and that made it easier for him to overlook many of Adams's political obsessions which no longer interested him. So when many years later an enemy of the younger Adams published a set of letters that the father had written in 1799 accusing Jefferson of "a thirst for popularity, an immoderate ambition and want of sincerity," Jefferson told Adams not to worry. "The circumstances of the times, in which we have happened to live, and the partiality of our friends . . . placed us in a position of apparent opposition, which some might suppose to be personal also; and there might not be wanting those who wish'd to make it so, by filling our ears with malignant falsehoods . . . and [who] make us forget what we had known of each other for so many years and years of so much trial," he wrote. And he begged Adams not to let the old troubles disquiet him now, as both were in their eighties and had long since come to see things in their "true shape and colors." Adams had been mortified by the scandal at first, so when he got the letter he was delighted. "The best letter ever was written. How generous! How noble! How magnanimous!" he wrote back. If Adams had been able to control his bitterness in 1800, when he had written those mean-spirited lines, he might never have forfeited Jefferson's friendship at all. But he was every inch a political animal and he had behaved accordingly. And in the end he was the gainer, because in 1823 he did get that marvelous letter from his old friend.

When they had resumed their correspondence and their friendship both were in their eighties and had retired happily enough from public life. Jefferson was delighted to hear from Adams at last, and at once returned to the original source of their former friendship. "A letter from you calls up recollections very dear to my mind. It carries me back to the times when, beset with difficulties and dangers, we were fellow laborers in the same cause, struggling for what is most valuable to man, his right to self-government." In his retirement he had, however, given up politics forever. He read only Tacitus, Thucydides, Newton, and Euclid, which incidentally, helps to explain why his style was so pure, so clear, so perfectly classical. Adams had every reason to say that once Jefferson had told him, however briefly, what a book was about, there was no point in reading it, since he already knew exactly all there was to know about it. He had always acknowledged Jefferson's superior understanding of science and literature, and as their correspondence now was mostly about intellectual questions, their roles were rather reversed. Adams deferred to Jefferson, asking his opinion about the right translation of a Greek poem and the proper pronunciation of ancient Greek words.

What else did these two former presidents discuss in the dusk of their lives? Religion, moral philosophy, ancient history, education, and political philosophy. As one might expect, Adams tried to go over their old political quarrels, to justify himself, and even to ask for Jefferson's sympathy for the unpopularity which he still had to endure. Jefferson tended to evade all this in an effort, which was ultimately entirely successful, to build a wholly personal friendship, grounded in affection, common memories, shared experiences, and continued lively interest in books and ideas. He had no competitive spirit left. Yet one somehow feels that it was Adams who really loved Jefferson. "You and I," he wrote, "ought not to die before we have explained ourselves to each other." He wanted to have his friend see his life as he saw it himself. Jefferson tried as much as his habitual politeness permitted to stick to the happier days of their past and to the many subjects that had always interested him deeply. He felt little need to vindicate himself, not least because he took it for granted that each person must be unique and that differences of belief and opinion were inevitable and even a source of pleasure. But then his had been a more satisfying life. Adams was utterly dumbfounded when Jefferson wrote him that he would very much like to live his whole life over again. Nothing, Adams replied, could ever induce him to go through all that again!

One of the first things one notices about both the correspondents is how very restrained they are. Theirs were the best manners of the eighteenth century. After reporting on the numbers of their grand- and great-grandchildren we hear nothing of their nearest relatives, except when they die, visit, or in one case, are elected president. Yet these mattered to both enormously. Adams wondered how poor Mr. Madison could fill his life without children. Jefferson replied that public business and good works could in fact keep their younger friend quite occupied. The two aging men did complain of their physical infirmities to each other, but that was the limit to which intimate matters were discussed. Even though the last lines of each successive letter become more and more loving, there are no outpourings of the heart, no revelations, and no excesses of feeling. When Adams laments that "I cannot write a hundredth part of what I wish to say to you," he meant more of the same, which in his case were overwhelmingly ideas about politics and theology. Not that either one was religious—quite the contrary. They believed that there was a God who had created the world and that Christ had taught a sound moral doctrine. Adams believed in a life after death, but Jefferson maintained a discreet silence on that. Both detested priests and were inclined to blame most of the world's troubles on them. Adams particularly was horrified by the new and enormous revival of religiosity that he saw everywhere around him. He complained bitterly that religious intolerance and fanaticism resisted all reforming efforts in New England and that a conniving clergy was even behind the prevalence of oligarchy in Massachusetts. Jefferson wrote back that he was surprised. Could things really be so grim in New England? Surely Adams must be exaggerating. Conditions were certainly not as bad in Virginia. Even the sons of its most distinguished families had to prove their merit to get elected, and the clergy were not active. Jefferson went on to guess that having begun as members of a state establishment, the Virginia clergy were satisfied with their regular income and so showed no religious zeal or evangelical fervor at all, which was, of course, the only thing to be said in their favor. Both men were sure that the end of religious intolerance was the greatest benefit that their century had brought to mankind, even though priestcraft, as they always called it, and superstition seemed to be returning to the world. "We may say," Adams wrote, "that the Eighteenth Century, notwithstanding all its Errors and Vices has been of all that are past, the most honourable to human Nature. Knowledge and Virtues were increased and diffused, Arts, Sciences useful to Men, ameliorating their condition, were improved, more than in any former equal Period." It would not last, because "The Priests are at their Old Work again." Jefferson agreed that he had been too optimistic about the coming triumph of reason and freedom, especially at the beginning of the French Revolution. Perhaps floods of blood would have to be spilled before freedom and enlightenment would reign, but he believed that progress would steadily continue, thanks mostly to the advancement of scientific knowledge. As he admitted, "I am more sanguine than you," which is perhaps not saying all that much, since alarm and apprehension were Adams's normal state of mind. Still there was more than a temperamental difference here. Adams for all his loathing for the clergy thought that "without Religion this World would be Something not to be mentioned in polite Company, I mean Hell." He did not, he went on to say, believe in the total depravity of human nature, but conscience was somehow tied to religious belief. This, even though the history of religions was an abomination. Jefferson agreed with that, and about the importance of conscience, but he did not tie it to religious belief at all. All men are endowed with an instinctive moral sense and while it expresses itself differently in various times and cultures, it was all we needed to live well. What we did all need most was education, and lots of it.

As he devoted the last decade of his life to the University of Virginia, Jefferson was constantly preoccupied by the theory and practice of education, and Adams naturally heard all about it. To his dismay he had never thought much about the subject. "Education! Oh Education!" he wrote to Jefferson. "The greatest Grief of my heart, and the greatest Affliction of my Life! To my mortification I must confess, that I have never closely thought, or very deliberately reflected upon the Subject. . . . If I venture to give you any thoughts at all, they must be very crude." He need not have worried; Jefferson had enough ideas on the subject to keep both of them going for years. He wrote not only about the staffing and curriculum of the new university, but also about his dream, never to be put into effect, for a complete system of public education in Virginia. For Jefferson a university, like the encyclopedias of the eighteenth century, was meant to preserve the unity of the sciences. Its graduates would know something, and not superficially, about every branch of science, history, and philosophy. It was to be the pinnacle of a system of education which had political, rather than purely intellectual, aims. Education was to foster a "natural aristocracy" of talent to replace the artificial "pseudo-aristocracy" of wealth and privilege. At the most local ward level there were to be three years of universal primary education, which would not only make every citizen capable of running most of the governmental affairs affecting his life, but also give him the wits to outsmart anyone who might try to deprive him of his rights. From this pool the brightest scholars were to be sent, wholly at the public expense if necessary, to secondary district schools. The well-to-do would pay their own way. The finest minds who graduated from these high schools would then attend the University of Virginia, again free of charge unless they could afford to pay. From this elite would come the legislators, magistrates, and judges as well as the scientists of the future. Jefferson felt a considerable urgency about this, because he saw, no doubt correctly, that Americans had adopted an ideology of self-education and learning by intuition. They were not as well educated as he was, he noted sadly. In fact, they never would be. "Our post-revolutionary youth," he wrote sarcastically, "are born under happier stars than you and I were. They acquire all learning in their mothers' womb and bring it into the world ready-made. The information of books is no longer necessary; and all knowledge that is not innate, is in contempt, or neglect at least. Every folly must run its course, and so must that of self-learning, and self-sufficiency; of rejecting the knowledge acquired in past ages, and starting on the new ground of intuition. I hope when sobered by experience, our successors will turn their attention to the advantages of education." Adams for once did not feel a comparable anxiety, but that was only due to his not sharing his friend's hopes. There was no way of distinguishing natural from artificial aristocrats, and moreover, all were alike and equally dangerous politically. Any advantages, whether they be good looks, physical agility, a celebrated family name, money, education, or virtue, could and would be used to accumulate political power and influence in their possessors, who hardly had to make an effort to gain them. Indeed, the bedazzled citizenry were only too ready to give their votes and political rights away to these aristocrats. And whatever their talents, if they had unchecked political power they would abuse it. They always had and would go on doing so. "Checks and Ballances, Jefferson . . . are our only Security, for the progress of the Mind, as well as the Security of the Body." The history of Christianity, with its persecution, Adams wrote, in closing, was proof enough of this proposition. The solution in his view was to have a separate legislative chamber, in Massachusetts the Senate, to pen up all the rich representatives and keep an eye on them, so that they would not abuse their wealth politically. Jefferson did not care for that plan, at all: it simply gave the rich extra representation, which they did not need, because they already had more than their share of social power and security. Adams did not think so. He had, he wrote Jefferson, felt an absolute and unforgettable terror, especially during the Whiskey Rebellion, and he remained afraid of revolution. His considerable distrust of the rich was, however, not feigned, and he and Jefferson completely agreed that bankers were a menace.

Politics, in short, continued to divide the old gentlemen in many ways. Philosophy, however, was less of a bone of contention between them. Neither one had any use for Plato. Jefferson moreover only liked ideas that had some reasonably immediate application. He was an inventor and architect, rather than an experimental scientist. Adams had a greater inclination for speculative thought, but both preferred to think about direct human experiences. What is the use of grief? asked Jefferson. All our other passions, if kept in bounds, serve some useful purpose, but why are we forced to suffer, especially when those whom we love die, as his wife and daughter had died, both young? And we know that he was devastated each time. What good did grief do me or anyone else? he asked Adams in their old age. All Adams could offer was that grief teaches us the vanity of human wishes and to resign ourselves. It was just part of the metaphysical problem of Evil—and he then, characteristically, went on to politics. What really bothered him was the hypocrisy of exhibitions of public grief for political purposes, as the Federalists had used Hamilton's funeral to reorganize their party. Jefferson was not impressed. Adams's answers were "equivocal" at best; there was nothing to be said in favor of grief and the loss of those we love. It was not a rational world, and for a man of Jefferson's sanguine temper, the evidence of his own pointless suffering was not just a personal, but a cosmic outrage. "Only time and silence help," he wrote Abigail Adams. He was, of course an exceptionally self-controlled person. Adams did not, I think, understand what his friend was trying to say about the irrationality of our deepest emotions, just as Jefferson could not follow Adams in taking religion seriously. Nor could he understand why the past continued to haunt Adams so bitterly. "I leave to others to judge of what I have done, and to give me exactly that place which they shall think I have occupied," and he clearly hoped that Adams would do the same. Nor did he want to go over their past feelings. They were not of any historical significance. "About facts, you and I cannot differ; because truth is our mutual guide," he wrote to Adams, and if they had different opinions they must receive them "with liberality and indulgence," because of the "affectionate respect" they felt for each other. Opinions were a private matter between friends. Intellectually it was important that the facts be put down truthfully, but that was their only public obligation and he felt that they had discharged it well. And in time Adams came to agree with him.

The pride both felt in their own accomplishments and those of their country did much to soften the dour temper of one, while the recognition of the political failures of post-Napoleonic Europe did much to subdue the ebullience of the other. So that in the end, they were not so dissimilar. Neither one suffered from historical nostalgia. The ancient republics did not excite their admiration at all. Rome had made a desert of the world, while the older Greek republics had no political sense. America was the only good republic and the only free nation, and they were thrilled to have lived to see it mature. Both thought that on the whole the present world was better than that of the past.

With the years their letters became fonder and fonder. They now had only each other to share their memories, and as both were perfectly ready to die they became detached from everything except perhaps from their only friend. However, to recall Emerson's metaphors, at no time were they echoes of each other, even if they were not quite the nettles they had once been. In their diversity they had built a perfect friendship. They died on the same day, the Fourth of July, 1826, exactly fifty years after their finest hour, the signing of the Declaration of Independence.

CHAPTER THREE

Hawthorne in Utopia

Readers of Frank Manuel's work will wonder how one could have tracked down so many utopians. Their number and variety seem almost inexhaustible, but we at least have a clear idea of the significant manifestations of the utopian mentality now. What, however, of the anti-utopian mind? Are those who reject utopia all alike? Are they all ultra-realistic revolutionaries or complacent pragmatists, incapable of any imaginative effort or even of hope? The enemies of utopia are generally recognized to be wise, but dangerous, or at the very least lacking in generosity and sympathy. These animadversions are by no means baseless, but they do not exhaust the more subtle possibilities of a moral consciousness that takes evil, especially cruelty, both physical and moral, seriously. Nathaniel Hawthorne was undeniably a devastating critic of utopia in all its forms, but this in no way reconciled him to the prevailing order. He fully shared and grasped the disgust which moved so many Americans of his generation to form what we would now call alternative societies or communes. Indeed, he briefly joined and heavily invested in Brook Farm. When he eventually turned his back on its aspirations and pretensions, he did not complacently rejoin the more comfortable members of society. On the contrary, he illuminated both the ambiguity of utopia and the faults of its foes.

Hawthorne's position was especially complicated since he was con-

"Hawthorne in Utopia" is reprinted from R. T. Bienvenu and M. Feingold (eds.), *In the Presence of the Past* (Boston: Kluwer Academic Publishers, 1991), pp. 215–31, with kind permission from Kluwer Academic Publishers. © 1991 Kluwer Academic Publishers.

fronted by more than one kind of utopianism. He was in many ways close to the last of the Jacksonian democrats who saw America as a redeeming nation, without a history to soil it, unique in its purity and thus unlike all the others. America as a nation was to be a vast utopia, to be made all but perfect, thanks to its exceptional character and good fortune. Providentially destined to be a beacon and a haven for all the peoples of the earth, America had only to fulfill the promise of the Declaration of Independence. These hopes were very different from those of the Blithedalers who had given up on American politics. This was the ideology of the far more popular radicalism of ultra-democratic Young America and more generally of a republican self-image that was to be shattered only by the Civil War. Hawthorne was in no way at odds with the democratic, egalitarian aspects of Young America, but he was as caustic about its extravagant expectations as he was about the dreamers at Brook Farm.[1] To really reject utopia in the decades before the Civil War, and to do so not only out of petty partiality, but in moral skepticism and anguish, was therefore not an easy task. For it meant a double denial if it was to be consistent; a rejection of both the social perfectionism of Emersonian New England reformers, more ardent than their master, and of the radical democrats who toiled on behalf of a more genuinely popular sovereignty.

The Brook Farmers tended to be single-minded, liberal and dedicated to the spiritual transformation of a grossly materialistic society. Hawthorne knew them all and had hoped to be one of them, though he never quite accepted all their views. But when he spoke of himself as the "loco-foco surveyor" of the Salem Custom House he was also entirely candid. The friend of that apostle of democratic nationalism, the journalist John O'Sullivan, the champion of the rights of white workers, the biographer of Franklin Pierce and the sworn enemy of the Massachusetts Whigs was an obvious democrat. He was certainly not untouched by their intense patriotism and he never doubted that America's republican institutions were superior to, and the best future model for, those of old aristocratic England. The difficulty was that he did not believe in progress, but only in a permanent balance between good and evil, with the scales weighted in favor of the latter. He could be as eager for a native democratic American literary culture as the editor of *The United States Magazine and Democratic Review,* to which he contributed frequently and for very small rewards. But he was not able to believe that America, though different, was an inherently and incomparably superior nation. That was not because of any aristocratic yearnings. There was not even a hint of an Emersonian individuality crushed by the crowd in Hawthorne. He simply could not accept the fantasy that collectivities would rise above the usual limits of their individual members. This knowledge did not come easily to him, and his three American novels are all hazardous voyages of exploration into areas of his own spiritual world—a world that had been unalterably shaped by his Puritan ancestors. Indeed, for all their overwhelming sense of sin and perdition, the Puritans' quest for righteousness was the first and deepest of America's utopian efforts, the one from which all the others had directly or indirectly grown. Even the democratic rebellion which was meant to free America from its Puritan past was marked and enfeebled by the original and indelible character of New England.

Hawthorne's first and purest journey to utopia was to provide him with some, but by no means all, of the elements of *The Blithedale Romance.* Nothing particularly painful or dramatic happened to him at Brook Farm, and the ideas which structure the novel had many other sources as well. Nevertheless, even if Coverdale, as narrator, is not Hawthorne, he also is an artist and a participating observer of a utopian community. It is difficult not to take his voice as Hawthorne's own, perhaps especially so because it is very self-critical. A man so revolted by hypocrisy, and so determined to avoid infatuation, could hardly fail to be ironical in observing himself. "Man's conscience was his theme," Henry James was to say in his intelligent but condescending essay on Hawthorne. It was not just other men's consciences, however, that were to be uncovered. His own, the artist's, the observer's, the perennial aloof outsider's moral structure was also revealed. The supra-utopian author here reviews his own state at the same time as his hero and alter-ego reveals all the absurdities of the utopians, no less than the meanness of the world from which they have tried to escape.

Was a utopia possible at all? The Blithedalers scorned the label as denigrating, and indeed long before Engels the word itself had acquired a decidedly derogatory sound. More serious than its name was its remoteness from history. Was it really "a blessed state of brotherhood and sisterhood" created in half a day? Its members appeared to believe that they had been "transported a world-wide distance from the system of society that shackled us at breakfast time" as soon as they arrived at Blithedale. All was cosy in their new kitchen, just like the ones the Pilgrims might have used. We are not warmed by that recollection, but we are left in no doubt about the earnestness of those gathered there. Nevertheless, this is merely "an oasis" and they all suffer from profound self-deceptions about themselves and their relations to the society into which they were born and where they were educated. This was for Hawthorne a relatively mild foible, and while it made Blithedale both ridiculous and impossible, it was not its most destructive aspect. The survival of the human passions may be more threatening in a closed community. They are not, however, in themselves the real danger, if they are openly recognized. Hawthorne was no Puritan; he believed neither in original sin nor in the sinfulness of natural passion. Sex and pride should not be shunned or moralized away. They are not inherently destructive, even though they do open every tragic possibility for us. Passion is certainly dangerous, but it does not weaken us individually or socially. Utopia does not require denatured men and women, but it cannot protect its members against the sufferings of the heart, as the imperious and sexually intense Zenobia discovers. A community can survive the war between the sexes and the willfulness of the proud, but it will not and cannot be the calm haven that most utopians expect in their utter simplicity.

The real ruin of a utopian community is not caused by unruly passions, but by cynicism and fanaticism which exploit and play upon these emotions. The disasters that tear utopia apart are all the more terrible because they come not only in the form of commercial greed, but also in the guise of philanthropic zeal. In either case a conscienceless, cruel egotism is at work. "Self, self, self, you embodied yourself in a project," Zenobia finally cries out at the philanthropic blacksmith, Hollingsworth. And it is he, no less than his con man rival, who destroys utopia. Even though it was the economic folly of Fourier's scheme that ultimately shut Blithedale down, its heart stopped beating when Zenobia, "awaker, disenchanted, disenthralled" killed herself. It would, therefore, be far too facile to ascribe the failures of Blithedale simply to human nature generally. It is to be found in quite specific psychological dispositions, not in a general fear of physical passion or pride.

Unlike other critics of utopia, moreover, Hawthorne did not prefer more conventional social arrangements, economic theories, or communal orders. He had no traditional or radical scheme of his own, and did not, therefore, blame the Blithedalers for following another path. He took no pleasure in their failures, even though he understood them with a chilling clarity. His scepticism was, indeed, rooted in psychology and he found social and moral imbecility not so much among those who simply meant well, but in those who were obsessed by a passion for perfection. Dr. Rappacini, who poisonously protects his daughter against all danger, and Ethan Brand, who seeks the "Unpardonable Sin," are both demons of destruction, a danger to themselves and to others. These urges made the Puritans cruel and their successors no better. To this must be added oppression and the cruelty of the strong toward the weak, horrible especially as it is generally well covered by hypocrisy. And hypocrisy is not only the Puritans' very own speciality, it is also the most characteristic vice of the democratic politicians who succeeded them. Between them, in short, the fanatic and the hypocrite defeat both the utopian reformer and the democrat—and not only from without, but also because these inherited psychological traits lurk within their own hearts and make them especially vulnerable. Neither Blithedale nor the Salem of *The House of the Seven Gables* could escape these threats, much to the regret of their most distinguished citizen.

Psychological weakness is not like sin and our wickedness may not even be indelible. As the narrator of *Earth's Holocaust* exclaims,

> How sad a truth, if true it were, that man's age-long endeavor for perfection had served only to render him the mockery of the evil principle, from the fatal circumstance of an error at the very root of the matter! The heart, the heart,—there was the little yet boundless sphere wherein existed the original wrong of which the crime and misery of this outward world were merely types. Purify that inward sphere, and the many shapes of evil that haunt the outward, and which now seem almost our only realities, will turn to shadowy phantoms and vanish of their own accord; but if we go no deeper than the intellect, and strive, with merely that feeble instrument, to discern and rectify what is wrong, our whole accomplishment will be a dream.

What is it in the heart that conscience should extirpate? It is not the seven deadly sins of Christianity. Sex and pride sustain us. They save Hester Prynne in *The Scarlet Letter* and make her a radiant moral heroine. It is the failure of pride and sex that kills Zenobia. Even dotty old Hepzibah in *The House of the Seven Gables* is well-served by her pride. There was in Hawthorne's moral world only one supreme vice: cruelty. Almost any occasion can give rise to it, and "there are few uglier traits of human nature than this tendency—to grow cruel, merely because [of] the power of inflicting harm." Cruelty, physical and psychic, is what makes "the heart" the seat of evil, for we need hardly learn to be cruel. Even children, indeed especially that "brood of baby friends . . . (displays) an instinct of destruction," far more loathsome than the blood-thirstiness of adult mankind. Every child enjoys tormenting the little Quaker in *The Gentle Boy*. But then all the adult fanatics are also without pity. Even his mother is too busy evangelizing to love her child. The Blithedale utopians were not such helpless victims of fanaticism and exploitation. They were, however, not well protected against these, and the attendant cruelties, because they lacked self-understanding. Utopians succumb so readily to external forces because they are so self-infatuated. The Blithedalers were enfeebled because they really thought that "they had left the rusty iron-frame work of society" behind them. The past was to be forsaken, and its bitter lesson was forgotten. Blithedale did not choose to remember the first annals of New England, where

> the founders of a new colony, whatever Utopia of human virtue and happiness they might originally project, have invariably recognized it among their earliest practical necessities to allot a portion of the virgin soil as a cemetery, and another portion as the site of a prison. In accordance with this rule, it may safely be assumed that the forefathers of Boston had built the first prison-house, somewhere in the vicinity of Cornhill, almost as seasonably as they marked out the first burial-ground, on Isaac Johnson's lot.

The Blithedalers would not allow themselves to be depressed by "old, desolate, distrustful phantoms." They

> had broken through many hindrances that are powerful enough to keep most people on the weary tread-mill of the established system, even while they feel its irksomeness almost as intolerable as we did. We had stept down from the pulpit; we had flung aside the pen; we had shut up the ledger; we had thrown off that sweet, bewitching, enervating indolence, which is better, after all, than most of the enjoyments within mortal grasp. It was our purpose—a generous one certainly, and absurd, no doubt, in full proportion with its generosity—to give up whatever we had heretofore attained, for the sake of showing mankind the example of a life governed by other than the false and cruel principles on which human society has all along been based . . .
> And, first of all, we had divorced ourselves from pride, and were striving to supply its place with familiar love. We meant to lessen the laboring man's great burthen of toil, by performing our due share of it at the cost of our own thews and sinews. We sought our profit of mutual aid, instead of wresting it by the strong hand from an enemy, or filching it craftily from those less shrewd than ourselves (if, indeed,

there were any such in New England), or winning it by selfish competition with a neighbor; in one or another of which fashions every son
of woman both perpetrates and suffers his share of the common evil,
whether he chooses it or no. And, as the basis of our institution, we
purposed to offer up the earnest toil of our bodies, as a prayer no
less than an effort for the advancement of our race.

The members of this society were "persons of marked individuality,
and they were very tolerant of each other's diverse opinions." But their
union was marked by many ambiguities. It was negative, not affirma-
tive. Blithedale was really 'an oasis,' a fertile spot to which they had
escaped from the world that each one had for some reason found to
be a desert. That not only did not make their bond a positive one, but
"as regarded society at large we stood in a position of a new hostility,
rather than a new brotherhood," as Coverdale noted. How were they
to set a model to others with such attitudes? Their contempt for those
whom they professed to serve was, moreover, not the only doubtful
aspect of their enterprise. Blithedale's determination to overcome the
degradations of the division of labor by combining physical and intellectual work had its share of delusions. Working-class men and
women are obliged to work for their daily bread. The intellectual es-
capees from the world of competition and privilege, on the contrary,
"cherished" the consciousness that "it was not by necessity, but by
choice" that they dug the soil. They knew that at any moment they
could throw away their mugs and return to porcelain and silver cut-
lery. At worst they ostentatiously strove to prove themselves the equals
of the local farm laborers.

Reprehensible as that was, it was not all. There was finally the belief
that hard physical labor redeems the soul, that work was to be spiritu-
alized. "Each stroke of the hoe was to uncover some aromatic sort of
wisdom, heretofore hidden from the sun." But they soon discovered
that "our labor symbolized nothing, and left us mentally sluggish."
Coverdale found quite soon that he was not doing himself or anyone
else any good by becoming "the Chambermaid of two yoke of oxen
and a dozen cows." Sooner or later they would all learn that work
does not ennoble us and that the spectacle of physically exhausted
poets and preachers was not likely to convert the real rustics to the
advantages of the Fourierist organization of labor. The turn to that
fantasy, which ended Blithedale completely, was, one may guess,
merely the last nail in its coffin of self-deception and moral extravagance. The artist was merely the first to be put off by the self-admiring

airs of the utopians and prepared to admit that no man can long remain sane who lives "exclusively among reformers." Eventually Hawthorne said of himself that even the grossest, mindless animal of a man could be a relief "to a man who had known Alcott." Nevertheless, he never regretted that he had gone to Blithedale, nor did he deny the generosity of purpose that had moved him and his friends to create it. At the very least, it was an instructive experiment.

The flaw in the midst of utopia is the perfecting temper. And Hawthorne never forgot its dangers. *Young Goodman Brown* remains an awful reminder of the misanthropy and joylessness that will haunt the man who cannot tolerate natural faults. In the economy of our passions it is not the life-giving and life-sustaining ones, whether sex, pride, physical vanity, or the love of beauty and luxury, that undo us. It is zeal. And there was no doubt in Hawthorne's mind that in America, Puritanism was the fountain of this disfiguring urge. In the world at large and at other times there were, of course, other ways of seeking bliss, such as magic and art. But in all its forms the drive to perfection is a will to power and it is generally a masculine, rather than a feminine, vice, though not always. There is in *The Gentle Boy* a memorable portrait of a woman fanatic. By and large, however, women are the victim of male perfectionism, precisely because they represent all the natural passions. Hollingsworth, immensely attractive to both women and men, comes to Blithedale for no other purpose than to exploit its members for his own social cause, the reform of criminals and prisons. In pursuit of this end he is utterly single-minded. It is his one and only concern and he cannot entertain any other feeling or interest. In this he is not only a representative of all single-minded reformers, but also of all those who give their entire energies to the removal of some moral or aesthetic flaw. These are wholly negative people. In *The Birthmark* a man marries a perfectly beautiful woman who has a tiny mark on her face. He becomes so obsessed by the miniscule blot that he cannot think of anything but some way of removing it. Finally, after many scientific experiments he finds a way of getting it off, but the medicine kills her. He had "rejected the best the earth could offer," because he would not endure even "that sole token of human imperfection" and so had "flung away" all the happiness that life has to offer. It is not nature, or natural knowledge, but the alchemical hope of stepping outside passion, natural knowledge and probability that ruins everything.

A utopian community is obviously likely to attract fanatics. Hollingsworth, the self-educated reformer, had absolutely no interest in the ideology of the Blithedalers and considered Fourier's visions disgustingly selfish. In his eyes only his own cause was a triumph over egotism and injustice. We must assume that it was abolitionism. It was the only reform movement that could and did arouse such political intensity. And Hollingsworth also had apparently no personal acquaintance with the objects of his benevolence. We never hear of him actually talking to criminals or the like. What he does know is how to give spell-binding speeches which enthrall Zenobia and her timid half-sister, Priscilla. It is not difficult to see how hypnotizing a mixture of sexual and moral energy might be. In any ordinary natural way Hollingsworth was selfless. He had become his cause. This artificial passion had replaced all the natural ones. "He was not altogether human" any longer:

> This is always true of those men who have surrendered themselves to an overruling purpose. It does not so much impel them from without, nor even operate as a motive power within, but grows incorporate with all that they think and feel, and finally converts them into little else save that one principle. When such begins to be the predicament, it is not cowardice, but wisdom, to avoid these victims. They have no heart, no sympathy, no reason, no conscience. They will keep no friend, unless he make himself the mirror of their purpose; they will smite and slay you, and trample your dead corpse under foot, all the more readily, if you take the first step with them, and cannot take the second, and the third, and every other step of their terribly straight path. They have an idol, to which they consecrate themselves high-priest, and deem it holy work to offer sacrifices of whatever is most precious; and never once seem to suspect—so cunning has the devil been with them—that this false deity, in whose iron features, immitigable to all the rest of mankind, they see only benignity and love, is but a spectrum of the very priest himself, projected upon the surrounding darkness. And the higher and purer the original object, and the more unselfishly it may have been taken up, the slighter is the probability that they can be led to recognize the process by which godlike benevolence has been debased into all-devouring egotism. The besetting sin of a philanthropist, it appears to me, is apt to be a moral obliquity. His sense of honor ceases to be the sense of other honorable men. At some point of his course—I know not exactly when or where—he is tempted to palter with the right, and can scarcely forbear persuading himself that the importance of his public ends renders it allowable to throw aside his private conscience.

The abstractness of Hollingsworth's prison reforms makes him not merely intolerant; he is blind to the actual emotions and sufferings of the people closest to him. They exist for him only as aids or hindrances to his project. He was not even conscious of sacrificing them, since he could not acknowledge any personal claims. When it is finally brought home to him that his cold indifference has driven Zenobia to her death, he loses his convictions and is reduced to a helpless imbecility.

No one is liberated by Hollingsworth, but those who are drawn to him are deeply injured. Like the philanthropist in *The Christmas Banquet* he was so busy with the ills of distant millions that he would not do "what little good lay immediately within his power." His futility, indeed that of all Blithedalers, was in any case predictable. They had not read Puritan history intelligently and knew nothing of the real cost of overrating one's moral prowess. Hollingsworth preached to his little band from a rock that was reputed to have served John Eliot as a pulpit. As a measure of success that apostle to the Indians was only a warning. If his successors were to free as many men as he had converted Indians their prospects were utterly discouraging. But since they took intentions for achievements, they were incapable of doing anything but repeating in various degrees of awfulness the failures of the Puritans whose spirit lived on in their frames.

Hollingsworth was not Blithedale's only enemy. All utopias suffer from internal disruptions, each one a sign and proof of the failure to be an example to the unregenerate. But the outside world itself not only fails to respond to the message of utopia, but is extremely hostile to it. Hollingsworth for all his public mania can, in an extremity, help a victim and act on behalf of a weak friend. His is by no means the worst presence in Blithedale. The real enemy to its survival is the world that its members think that they have abandoned, but which has not necessarily forgotten them. It appears in the person of Zenobia's presumed ex-lover, Westerveldt, that is, the Western world or history in general. The villain of Blithedale is a figure as old as he is new, a modern necromancer. Westerveldt is a sham, a charlatan, a mesmerist, a snob, cruel, dishonest and extremely attractive to women. His cynicism is as deep and complete as Hollingsworth's fanaticism, but unlike the latter, Westerveldt has not a single redeeming virtue and he probably will never have the slightest occasion to regret the suffering he has caused, while Hollingsworth does repent. We need never doubt that there is a vast difference between the kinds of men who destroy out of moral zeal, and those who, like Westerveldt, simply deceive and steal for their personal gain. For Westerveldt is every real or potential enslaver, seducing the two sisters into joining his lurid hypnotic exhibitions. Hollingsworth at least saves one of them from the clutches of this confidence man. That does not mitigate the misery that Hollingsworth inflicts, but it does distinguish both its scope and character from the unending extortions of Westerveldt, who represents the sham and deceit that dominate everyday, ordinary social life. Westerveldt—who is worldliness personified—cannot be evaded and it is he who defeats Zenobia "on the broad battlefield of life." His indifference to her death or to any suffering is the sign of his power and that of the actual world. And such coldness also lives within "the oasis" of Blithedale. Even the man who observes and records, the poet Coverdale, is implicated in her death, since he does nothing to prevent disasters which at the very least were not unthinkable.

Hawthorne never regretted his stay at Brook Farm and did not in the least care whether he had seemed ridiculous in trying the experiment.[2] His review of his far more conventional term in the Salem Custom House was much more venomous than his memories of the young dwellers in utopia. He may have been thrown out of his job as surveyor for being a "loco-foco" democrat, but it was there that he seems to have lost some of his Jacksonian faith in the future of America. The Custom House is a relic of the American Revolution.[3] "Over the entrance hovers an enormous specimen of the American eagle," which Hawthorne noted with wry humor was "an unhappy fowl," given its vile temper and vixenly looks, but which, nevertheless, was supposed to offer shelter to every job-seeker. As he discovered, she could not be relied on to protect these citizens. Nevertheless, in his and their eyes she is a figure of fun because she stands for nothing else but the fragile hopes of spoilsmen, himself among them. These were the spiritual leftovers from the Revolutionary, republican soldiers, gone to seed. The very sight of these remnants of the Revolutionary hope made it clear that "neither the front nor the back entrance of the Custom House opens on the road to Paradise." Neither America's past nor its future would measure up to the expectations of the republican imagination. Its house of customs, its habits and aspirations, were petty and commercial now, and likely to remain so. Its inhabitants had neither the virtues of their ancestors nor their phenomenal faults. And more immediately they were not the bearers of the politically transforming energies of the Declaration of Independence.

Hawthorne's friend John O'Sullivan had in several celebrated articles announced not only that the American Revolution was the greatest of experiments, but that its aim was to achieve democracy and that this was "the cause of Humanity" which young Americans were destined to fulfill. The dynamism of the democratic idea had indeed only begun its career, and it was America's task to spread and nurture it so that mankind might eventually achieve it. To that end, America must ward off its own oligarchic and conservative tendencies, and forge a genuinely democratic national ethos, beginning with a truly national literature that would owe nothing to England or to any past at all. "America is destined for better deeds" than any of its predecessor; the "boundless future will be the era of American greatness," for "we are the nation of progress, of individual freedom, of universal enfranchisement," indeed "the great nation of futurity."[4] Hawthorne had no quarrel with much of this. He certainly detested the oligarchic politics of the Judge Pyncheons of Salem, and he did more than merely call for a native literature. What he did reject was the belief that America was on the way to paradise, that the Revolution was the beginning of the millennium and that America could free itself from the past. America was in fact not unique; it also had its past and a limited future, like all the other nations.

The evidence of the past is everywhere, and it is not always encouraging. It is in the surveyor himself, who is driven by instinct to remain in his native town where his awful Puritan ancestors were famous as persecutors of Quakers. Yet even these men in their great dignity and severity only revealed the feeble inconsequence of their successors who display "the half-dog look of a republican official, who, as the servant of the people, feels himself less than the least, and below the lowest, of his masters." Hawthorne did not think that he was an improvement upon his terrifying ancestors, and he thought the other specimens of republican virtue who inherited the Custom House were much worse; even the young men among them were "wearisome old souls." The oldest, the inspector son of a Revolutionary hero, was a mere stomach, food his only thought. The Collector, himself a military hero of a later encounter, was more or less a mental ruin, as ponderous as Old Ticonderoga, but at least very good natured. It is not with such as these that America would conquer the future, obviously. Indeed, the Custom House was sapping even his energies. He had at first been happy to remember that Chaucer and Burns had also been customs house officials, but he discovered that their service had not injured them as his was diminishing him.

An effect—which I believe to be observable, more or less, in every individual who has occupied the position—is, that, while he leans on the mighty arm of the Republic, his own proper strength departs from him. He loses, in an extent proportioned to the weakness or force of his original nature, the capability of self-support. If he possess an unusual share of native energy, or the enervating magic of place do not operate too long upon him, his forfeited powers may be redeemable. The ejected officer—fortunate in the unkindly shove that sends him forth betimes, to struggle amid a struggling world—may return to himself, and become all that he has ever been. But this seldom happens. He usually keeps his ground just long enough for his own ruin, and is then thrust out, with sinews all unstrung, to totter along the difficult footpath of life as he best may.

Salem's, indeed America's House of Customs, was not one likely to encourage heroes of the public life. The great eagle does not summon political warriors, Revolutionary heroes of republican virtue, ready to spread the message of the Declaration of Independence around the world. That ill-disposed bird merely shelters incompetents. Salem itself had little to offer—except a past for which one could not possibly feel any nostalgia. If utopia was not in the future of America, it was certainly not in its past. The Revolution did not open a door to anything very marvelous. To be sure, England also was unregenerate. After he had lived there for several years, Hawthorne was convinced that England must soon become more democratic, and that politically America should set a republican example to the world. Unlike O'Sullivan, however, he had no intention of forgetting his literary past. His pilgrimage to Dr. Johnson's Litchfield renewed a deeply felt spiritual attachment. And he, again unlike his Jacksonian friends, feared that America's institutions might never fulfill their possibilities. The promise of democracy was for him, in any case, crystallized into one virtue, simplicity, an absence of distinctions and pretensions.[5] In its way, that is not an unambitious ideal, but it is not utopian. It explains why Hawthorne went to Blithedale, left it, and continued to find the Custom House, that epitome of the actual world, so disappointing. Its doors not only did not lead to a paradise, they did not even lead to the democratic vistas of which his fellow Jacksonians dreamed. America might never achieve those "deeds of simple greatness" which he valued far more than any grandiose visions. Simplicity was a possibility within our psychological powers.

Although neither nostalgia nor Anglophilia troubled Hawthorne's view of the past, he was constantly aware of its presence. The past was not dead in the Custom House where he found the tattered scarlet letter nor was it dead in Salem. The past simply has the present in its grip. That meant not only that the future would not be perfect, that utopia was impossible, but also, that one could see the present in terms of the past and judge it from a distance, with perspective, rather than with mindless enthusiasm or loathing. *The House of the Seven Gables* is the tale of the past in its re-incarnation and *The Scarlet Letter* a measure of its survivors.[6] The past bears down on New England as a double burden. Its Puritan founders left it a legacy of fanaticism and a powerful passion for wealth and power. Hollingsworth is clearly their heir, but by no means as dreadful a man as an original Puritan, such as Colonel Pyncheon, the first of a long line of Salem grandees. Born in England, he was as grasping as he was relentless in his persecutions.

> Endowed with common sense, as massive and hard as blocks of granite, fastened together by stern rigidity of purpose, as with iron clamps, he followed out his original design, probably without so much as imagining an objection to it. On the score of delicacy, or any scrupulousness which a finer sensibility might have taught him, the Colonel, like most of his breed and generation, was impenetrable.

These qualities are not without advantage in a ruling class if they could be joined by imperturbable passions, but that is not the case, and Hawthorne's preference for democratic government rested substantially on his considered insight into the character of the New England oligarchy since its earliest days. Their participation in the witch-hunts of Salem should teach us

> among its other morals, that the influential classes, and those who take upon themselves to be leaders of the people, are fully liable to all the passionate error that has ever characterized the maddest mob. Clergyman, judges, statesmen—the wisest, calmest, holiest persons of their day—stood in the inner circle round about the gallows, loudest to applaud the work of blood, latest to confess themselves miserably deceived. If any one part of their proceedings can be said to deserve less blame than another, it was the singular indiscrimination with which they persecuted, not merely the poor and aged, as in former judicial massacres, but people of all ranks; their own equals, brethren, and wives.

Among the contemporary Pyncheons, there was at least one descendant of the Colonel who resembled him both physically and morally, and his position in Salem was still that of a member of the "influential classes." For the Pyncheons represent the most undemocratic of all political principles, hereditary social privilege. This is also the vehicle which conveys much of what is worst in the past to the present. Hawthorne had no doubt "of the folly of tumbling down an avalanche of ill-gotten gold, or real estate, on the heads of an unfortunate posterity, thereby to maim and crush them" and the entire public. One cannot help sympathizing with Holgrave, the young Jacksonian artist, when he exclaims "shall we never, never get rid of this Past," as he observes both the genteel helplessness of some of the Pyncheons and the ruthless power of other Pyncheons. He is after all the descendant of the old wizard whom the original Pyncheon had wronged so cruelly. Hawthorne did not share his young hero's scorn for history entirely: "Life is made up of marble and mud." Politically, however, Holgrave's point was well taken. The supremacy of the living people over the dead is the authentic claim of democracy. Tom Paine's and Jefferson's view that each generation must be free from the dead hand of its predecessors was certainly not foreign to "the loco-foco" surveyor. No majority should be hindered by inherited powers or legacies. The world of democracy is the world of the eternal present. It imposes no burdens upon the future, and it refuses to suffer restrictions that the past might try to inflict upon it.

Holgrave's hope that "we shall live to see the day . . . when no man builds his house for posterity," when he rails against "that odious and abominable Past," is the faith of republican equality. "To plant a family! This idea is at the bottom of most of the wrong and mischief which men do." That is so for Holgrave not because it is a mark of pride, but because he distrusts everything fixed and unchanging. Hawthorne presents us not only with Holgrave's opinions, but also with his character and experiences. He is in constant flux. Democratic man escapes class and caste by moving from place to place and from job to job. Holgrave "had begun to be self-dependent while yet a boy," had supported himself by every means from peddling to dentistry, and was now a daguerreotypist. He had been all over Europe and America, but

> what was the most remarkable, and, perhaps, showed a more than common poise in the young man, was the fact that, amid all these personal vicissitudes, he had never lost his identity. Homeless as he had been—continually changing his whereabout, and, therefore, responsible neither to public opinion nor to individuals—putting off

one exterior, and snatching up another, to be soon shifted for a third—he had never violated the innermost man, but had carried his conscience along with him.

Holgrave has strong opinions and does tend to rave and rant, especially about the continuing power of dead men, but this is the normal enthusiasm of youth, not fanaticism. His conscience and inner balance would protect him against that, and allow him to become "the champion of some practicable cause." His magnanimity, though without faith or culture, was well grounded in a certain moral solidity and in this Hawthorne thought he "represented many compeers in his native land." Hawthorne himself looked upon him with far too much irony to take him quite seriously. For although Holgrave thinks that he will never "plant a family," his author knew better. The young radical matures, falls in love with the last of the Pyncheons, marries her and accepts their common past and future. Soon he also plans "to build a house for another generation." He will not, we are led to believe, become just like the Pyncheons, but he will not strive to undo the past entirely, or to build America all over again.

The story of Phoebe and Holgrave is a very Jacksonian romance of spontaneous democratization. Phoebe, although a Pyncheon and eventually an heiress, has grown up in modest circumstances without any of the Pyncheon vices. She is the perfect example of that noble simplicity that Hawthorne hoped would replace genteel manners in America. She is not to be a lady, but a practical, intelligent woman who can cheerfully perform any task at hand. But she, unlike the heir of the Maules whom she marries, has a sense of place and time. She at first distrusts Holgrave's extravagances, and it is only when he accepts the past as it appears in her that he abandons them to settle down—again under the ironic mocking eye of his creator.

Why should Holgrave not accept Phoebe's legacy and reconcile the resentful heirs of the victims to the chastened descendants of the old oligarchy? Social harmony was also a Jacksonian hope. There are, nevertheless, aspects of Holgrave's character and of Salem generally, with its awful Custom House, that are politically and morally inferior to their Puritan predecessors. Holgrave is unsteady. The later Pyncheons, excepting Phoebe, are feeble wrecks or unmitigated scoundrels. The denizens of the Custom House, the public servants of the republic, can charitably be described as clowns. In all this they not only put the long-range future consequences of the Revolution in doubt, they also suffer from comparisons with the remote Colonial past. The Puritans did have qualities that were far from contemptible, and Holgrave lacks their tough integrity. Not that they were to be venerated. The present was in many ways better. Hawthorne did not claim that his America was as cruel as the New England of his ancestors, even though he saw a good deal of cruelty around him. But somehow the moral balance between good and evil remains fairly constant. The past that had taught Hawthorne so much was not to be valued as a tradition, as valuable in itself, but strictly as a point of reference. The back door of the Custom House led to no utopia either, but to memories of a prison house and pillory. The Bostonians of *The Scarlet Letter* are not likely to induce ancestor worship, even if they were not without admirable qualities.

It was in fact a matter of political importance for Hawthorne not to present the Puritan world as a utopia or to overestimate his ancestors in any way. Such myths had become the ideological speciality of the Whigs. Indeed, one might well speak of an American Whig interpretation of history that may already be perceived in John Adams, and which burst into full flower in the orations of Rufus Choate, Hawthorne's contemporary. It was in Salem in 1833 that Choate delivered an address on "The Importance of Illustrating New England History by a Service of Romances like the Waverly Novels." The burden of this lecture and of several others dealing with the "heroic period" of America was that the Puritans were the source of everything fine and free in American public and private life. The Revolutionary generation and the Founding Fathers were merely the beneficiaries of inherited values. Nowhere in the history of mankind was "such a specimen of character as this" produced, nor will there ever be one like it. Only poetry, not prosaic, fact-bound history, can truly illuminate "such moral sublimity as this." One must celebrate not just the tragic epic of King Philip's War, but also the Puritans' achievement in setting up republican, representative government and the provisions they made for "the mental and moral culture of the rising nation." Above all the love of liberty was brought along with a sublime religion to flourish in the harsh climate of New England. Clearly Choate preferred the Colonial Puritans to any later generation of ancestors, even hoping that their memory, recalled with exciting fantasies, might serve to preserve the Union. As for such incidents as "the persecution of the Quakers, the controversies with Roger Williams and Mrs. Hutchinson . . . a great deal of this is too tedious to be read, or it offends and alienates you. It is truth, fact; but it is just what you do not want to know and are none the wiser for knowing." [7]

Choate certainly got his romances, and they did owe something to Sir Walter Scott, although Hawthorne surely wrote in a style of his own. His answer to Choate is Roger Williams's smile in *Endicott and the Red Cross*, as he watches the Puritan governor defend only his own religious liberty. And then there is the more universal truth of *The Scarlet Letter*, which re-enrolls the Puritans in the ranks of mankind.

The great quality of the Puritans, especially as Hawthorne pictured them in *The Scarlet Letter*, was dignity. Hester Prynne on the platform of the Boston pillory was at least not subjected to frivolous "mocking infamy and ridicule." On the contrary, as she stood there,

> The scene was not without a mixture of awe, such as must always invest the spectacle of guilt and shame in a fellow-creature, before society shall have grown corrupt enough to smile, instead of shuddering, at it. The witnesses of Hester Prynne's disgrace had not yet passed beyond their simplicity. They were stern enough to look upon her death, had that been the sentence, without a murmur at its severity, but had none of the heartlessness of another social state, which would find only a theme for jest in an exhibition like the present. Even had there been a disposition to turn the matter into ridicule, it must have been repressed and overpowered by the solemn presence of men no less dignified than the Governor, and several of his counsellors, a judge, a general, and the ministers of the town; all of whom sat or stood in a balcony of the meeting-house, looking down upon the platform. When such personages could constitute a part of the spectacle, without risking the majesty or reverence of rank and office, it was safely to be inferred that the infliction of a legal sentence would have an earnest and effectual meaning. Accordingly, the crowd was sombre and grave.

There was of course a great price to be paid for this religious solemnity: "we have yet to learn the forgotten art of gayity" which they so thoroughly eliminated. There was moreover the Puritans' constant and daily cruelty to the sinner in their midst. "Quiet malice" as well as "coarser expressions" gave Hester daily pain; the clergy exhorted her at every opportunity; and worst of all, there were the "shrill cries" of children schooled in cruelty. Somewhere "little urchins" were always ready to sling mud at her. That and violent intolerance were one side of the moral scale. The other side was not without political weight, however. The rulers of Boston were wise and virtuous, stern and sagacious, "accomplishing so much, precisely because (they) imagined and hoped so little." They invested "the simple framework" of government with every dignity and stability of character.

> It was an age when what we call talent had far less consideration than now, but the massive materials which produce stability and dignity of character a great deal more. The people possessed, by hereditary right, the quality of reverence; which, in their descendants, if it survive at all, exists in smaller proportion, and with a vastly diminished force in the selection and estimate of public men. The change may be for good or ill, and is partly, perhaps, for both. These primitive statesmen, therefore, Bradstreet, Endicott, Dudley, Bellingham, and their compeers,—who were elevated to power by the early choice of the people, seem to have been not often brilliant, but distinguished by a ponderous sobriety, rather than activity of intellect. They had fortitude and self-reliance, and, in time of difficulty or peril, stood up for the welfare of the state like a line of cliffs against a tempestuous tide. So far as a demeanour of natural authority was concerned, the mother country need not have been ashamed to see these foremost men of an actual democracy adopted into the House of Peers, or made the Privy Council of the sovereign.

These statesmen did not suffer from the avarice of Colonel Pyncheon, and so their public virtues stand out quite clearly. They were not able to transmit them to future generations of politicians, but then their equally enormous vices had also been abandoned to be replaced with less violent forms of cruelty. One could not really speak of progress, but merely of change. Compared to the Puritan past Hawthorne found his own age enfeebled and insubstantial, both in virtue and in vice. Holgrave had much to recommend him, but he clearly did not have the moral stamina of the old Puritans. He was not likely to have the qualities needed to really perfect America's social institutions. "The higher mode of simplicity than has been known to past ages" found its only representative in Phoebe, the last and the best of the Pyncheons. She at least was a purified legacy from the Puritan past. If Blithedale's simplicity had been false and pretentious, hers was perfectly genuine. It was not to be put at the service of a utopia, but of a family. The burden of America's hopes rests on her. Villainous Jeffrey Pyncheon and Holgrave are not likely to make American democracy realize all its possibilities, and certainly they would not have redeemed oppressed mankind. Both were in some bondage to a past that could not be evaded or forgotten. It was present as a force and as a judgment in every custom and every house. It accompanied every utopian community and it was reincarnated in every Salem family—even that of a democrat.

In these respects, America was just like the rest of humanity. It was not to be a great utopia, and it would not be composed of, or transformed by, little ones. It is the political achievement of Hawthorne's art that he makes us understand why this must be so without exaggerated regret, contempt, or indifference. He was not prepared to answer the radical democrats' call for a new American literature that "would breathe the spirit of our republican institutions" and sing of "the matchless sublimity of our position amongst the nations of the world."[8] He had more affection for these aspirations than for the myths of the Whigs, but he was too wise for any political illusions. There was no reason to suppose that the citizens of Salem were fit for vast political enterprises. Those who did attempt them were dangerous zealots. The little utopia and "the great nation of futurity" would not be realized, just as the righteous Puritan order had faded. If its heirs would not fail in the old way, they would only fail in another manner, but fail they undoubtedly must.

Notes

This is in no sense a complete reading of Hawthorne's novels. There is always a danger in thinking of imaginative fiction of the first order as if it were merely political. Hawthorne's art went far beyond the political themes which are discussed in this essay. That does not imply an unawareness of the more universal moral, aesthetic and psychological range of Hawthorne's art. Utopia does, however, play a sufficiently important part in all three of his American novels to warrant a separate study, and it is not wholly artificial to consider this one theme in isolation from its larger sphere, because it is sufficiently significant, both in its own right and for the America of the years preceding the Civil War.

1. For Hawthorne's relations to Young America and democratic radicalism, as well as for his rejection of the abolitionists, see Lawrence Sargent Hall, *Hawthorne, Critic of Society* (New Haven: Yale University Press, 1944). F. O. Mathiessen (ed.), *American Renaissance* (London: Oxford University Press, 1941), 316–37, presents an acute though slightly condescending analysis of Hawthorne's politics, arguing that Hawthorne could see evil in the world but not an evil world—in short, that neither original sin nor revolutionary ideology informed his novels. The absence of these grandiose systems may at present constitute one of Hawthorne's greatest merits.

2. A valuable comparison of Hawthorne with Cooper shows just how little the former gloated over utopia's failure. See Taylor Stocher, "Art *vs* Utopia: The Case of Nathaniel Hawthorne and Brook Farm," *Antioch Review* 36 (1978): 89–102. See A. N. Kaul (ed.), *Hawthorne* (Englewood Cliffs: Prentice-Hall, 1966), 153–

63, for a different view of *Blithedale,* which however, also sees it as not a complete rejection of the utopian enterprise.

3. For a brilliant essay that reveals many other dimensions of "The Custom House" see Larzer Ziff, "The Ethical Dimension of the Customs House," in A. N. Kaul, op. cit., 123–28.

4. *The United States and Democratic Review* 1 (1837): 1–15; and 6 (1839): 426–30.

5. *Our Old Home: Centenary Edition of the Works of Nathaniel Hawthorne* (Columbus: Ohio State University Press, 1970), vol. 5, pp. 119, 286.

6. The following is obviously not a full account of the *Scarlet Letter,* but merely a minor aspect of the whole.

7. Samuel Gilman Brown (ed.), *The Works of Rufus Choate* (Boston: Little, Brown and Co., 1862), vol. 1, pp. 319–46; and also "The Age of the Pilgrims: The Heroic Period of Our History," pp. 370–93.

8. "The Great Nation of Futurity," *United States Magazine and Democratic Review* 6 (1839): 426–30.

CHAPTER FOUR

Emerson and the Inhibitions
of Democracy

Emerson may not have been what is conventionally called a political philosopher, but political considerations played a more subtle part in his thinking than mere expressions of opinion on public affairs would suggest. For Emerson, the beliefs and practices of American representative democracy constituted an integral moral barrier which he could neither ignore nor cross. It brought him up short, like a stop sign at a junction. This inhibition was not, however, something externally imposed on him against his will or better judgment. He was not giving in to something he could not overcome. Not only did democratic political experiences offer him an ample source of illustration but they quite often gave his essays their intellectual purpose and direction. That could never be said of Nietzsche, and it is a great part of the difference in the very substance of what they wrote. What are the democratic convictions and habits that are so relevant to Emerson's writings? They are the most obvious ones. The most important is that we are "created equal" and that the qualities that truly distinguish us are not those that are available only to exceptional individuals but those which we can all potentially achieve. Neither inherited nor accidentally acquired advantages can have any moral standing. Last, the consent of the governed is one of the necessary marks, though not the only one, of the just powers of governments. With that, there is, most important of all, an intuitive respect

This chapter was previously published as "Emerson and the Inhibitions of Democracy," in *Political Theory* 18, no. 4 (Nov. 1990): 601–14. © 1990 Sage Publications, Inc. Reprinted by permission of Sage Publications, Inc.

for one's fellow citizens, felt not as an obligation but as a given. At a more reflective level, democratic government also entails its own genre of political criticism, and this was also part of Emerson's system of complaints. Since Madison, the tyranny of the majority has been seen as a major threat to republican liberty. And since Tocqueville, no one has forgotten the dangerous pressure of public opinion on free individual expression and development. Mill may have been right to regard timidity and social conformity as the burdens of middle-class civilization rather than of democratic government, but that hardly improves America's prospects. In either case, to fret about equality is an enduring act of democratic American self-criticism as well as to lament that democratic class society is more hostile to individuality than a society of castes. It was certainly part of Emerson's democratic inheritance to accept these democratic discontents. To these he added a no less usual suspiciousness of the probity of all parties and elected officials.

It is not simply the presence of some or all of these political dispositions in Emerson's various essays that is, in itself, interesting, but also the way in which they control the flow of his thought generally. That is particularly revealing in those cases where politics is not the overt topic, as in *Self-Reliance*.[1] It is, in any event, not an essay one can ignore, but is also one in which the boundaries of democracy would appear to be crossed by the call to each of us to create our own world and to acknowledge our isolation. Here, Emerson seems quite prepared to flout the democratic creed in his enthusiasm for the self-reliant individual, but, in fact, he avoids a full assault and backs off from it. Early on in *Self-Reliance* we are told very firmly that "society everywhere is in conspiracy against the manhood of every one of its members" (p. 261). One does not, therefore, given the danger, have to offer reasons for refusing any association or acts of convention. "I shun father and mother and wife and brother, when my genius calls me." Why should he be generous to the needy? *"Are they my poor?"* He will go to prison for a cause that is his, but not for Christianity's poor. And not a dime will he give to ordinary socially, democratically approved charities. There must be some "spiritual affinity" to move him to act for another. Dissociation could hardly go further. He certainly means to shock his readers. He also does so in order to demonstrate his indifference to any obligation that is not self-made. The impact is, however, softened at once by irony. He confesses with shame and regret that, in fact, he is too weak to refuse a dollar to the poor.

The principle remains intact, the joke is on him, but he has not withdrawn himself from fellowship after all. It is easy to turn one's back on parties, churches, and a "dead Bible society," but on the poor? That is only to be proclaimed; it cannot be done (pp. 262–63). As for genius, we hear the names of all the greatest men and the misunderstanding that society has always vented on them. Greatness, however, radiated its bounty in spite of that. And again we retreat. Greatness is a genuine quality that is not really a matter of extraordinary talent and rare acts. We can all be great when we are called to it, and so Emerson ends with the fable of the poor sot who was dressed up and treated like a duke in his sleep, and who, on awakening, used his wits and behaved like a true prince (p. 267). This is not the genius as destroyer-creator, second Prometheus, or the superman of a more desperate imagination. Self-creation without the signposts of normality needs to be asserted, but not at the expense of every person.

What, then, is self-reliance to achieve? It is not a call to reject the usual bonds of family life but to take them on as one's own discovery. Making one's own rules is a new life and, indeed, the only remaining possibility for constructing a law out of that transforming experience of nature. Nature, to be sure, might be a universal territory of exploration. Supposing that it were, then there is no reason to exclude anyone who did not turn one's back on self-reliance as an adventure, at the very least. This would be possible even if "it demands something godlike in him who has cast off the common motives of humanity" (p. 274). Most people are simply too timid and too dependent to try, especially in the big cities. The god-like qualities are not, however, a matter of locality or class or genius in a vulgar sense. The model of self-reliance is the Yankee farmer. There are untutored yeomen in Vermont and in New Hampshire who were for Emerson, no less than for Jefferson before him, the embodiment of democratic ideals. The Yankee lad moves from social role to social role with no difficulty. He always lands on his feet. He farms, peddles, teaches school, gets elected to Congress, and then tries something else. He is always competent, and, above all, he never *is* his job or social definition. Clearly, "greater self-reliance must work a revolution in all the offices and relations of men," if this is what it would mean in daily terms (p. 275). This man has no past and, indeed, no social baggage to encumber him at all. No aggregate can contain him. And "is not a man better than a town?" (p. 282). That allows Emerson to leave democratic man on his pinnacle, without having to make any compromises with those features of democratic life that were not compatible with self-reliance. He could scorn the parties and their members, indeed membership as such, without falling into the cant of a quasi-aristocratic individualism.

There remains, nevertheless, a real difficulty. *Self-Reliance* is a veritable roll call of great men. Explorers, scientists, poets, and even philosophers are invoked to show what a self-reliant, unimitating character can be and do. And they are great, surely, not because they were first scorned and later copied by other men. Yet Emerson cannot face them directly. He notes depths and energies but swerves off to worry about the impact of greatness on the rest of us. All disciples infuriate Emerson, but he cannot simply look away and let the great man be. The genius, whose light, after all, does illuminate those intimations of unmediated contact with pure nature, cannot be left to his greatness. "The great genius returns to essential man" (p. 280). That is not entirely what that extraordinary litany of names, each one the creator of a new religion, the discoverer of a continent, or an incomparable artist, means. It may well be that society does not improve, thanks to their deeds. It may even be true that lesser men fall into passive admiration when they contemplate them. They may not invigorate people who resist vitality, but that is not and cannot be the whole purpose of recalling the great, who were each and every one of them original to a superlative degree. It is as if Emerson could not bring himself to decide openly whether the difference between them and the Yankee lad either does or does not exist. Is it a matter of scale, or does genius constitute an unbridgeable gulf? In fact, he meant both. There is a space between all self-reliant men. Their awareness of that uncrossable division is what renders them self-relying persons in the first place. What Emerson could not get himself to say was that the great are absolutely different and better within their sphere. That was the inhibition of democracy. The great speak to us without barriers of time or class or space. The Yankee lad may or may not hear them. As long as he also is in his every act and feeling dissociated in that same way, he is not an inferior.

Emerson's great neither destroy nor recreate worlds. They do not eliminate human obstacles to do their will. That is very comforting, but are we to avoid admiring them as well? We may ask: What use are they at all? It is, indeed, the very question Emerson was forced to ask himself. *Representative Men* is Emerson's effort to answer the question about human greatness which he had posed for himself most of all. That was not, however, the only incentive to return to the matter. There was also his friend Carlyle's *Heroes and Hero-Worship* to confront him with a way of thinking about the relations between great and small men that he could not ignore. Carlyle had few problems. He merely recorded the already well-worn themes of a conventional romanticism. The hero was indeed a force of nature, who created universal history. That there might be a vast gap between the energies of nature and the course of human history did not appear to occur to Carlyle. That thought was left to Marx, although a quick reading of Rousseau might have given even Carlyle pause. In any event, "they are the leaders of men, these great ones . . . in a wide sense creators of whatever the wide mass of mankind do or attain." To worship such heroes is the only path to any sort of spiritual life open to all other persons. Indeed, the failure to do so is the cause of the degeneracy of the age. Emerson's own account of the mind's passage to oneness with nature made such a scenario quite plausible, though not inevitable. It was certainly important for him to avoid Carlyle's summons to fall humbly silent as we listen to the single heroic voice of the nation, just as if it were the call of the universe, addressing us in poetry, prose, and military orders. Emerson would not obey, but what was he to do instead?

Emerson's first move was simply to refuse to talk about heroes or great men at all. Plato, Swedenborg, Montaigne, Shakespeare, Napoleon, and Goethe are *representative men,* not, by definition, therefore, objects of worship. Even this was not enough and he remained uneasy:

> Many after thoughts, as usual, . . . and my book seems to lose all value from their omission. Plainly one is the justice that should have been done to the unexpressed greatness of the common farmer and laborer. A hundred times have I felt the superiority of George and Edmund and Barrows, and yet I continue to parrot echoes of the names of literary notabilities and mediocrities.[2]

This piece of self-criticism, put into his *Journal,* can come as no surprise to readers of *Self-Reliance,* but it is important nonetheless. For it reveals that Emerson completely understood the divisions within the essay, his own convictions, and that the impulses of democracy were not something he merely had to take into account but were a part of himself. The evident difficulty was that they were not without rivals in his mind. Who was he to deny that the great men on his roster were, indeed, great? If most political great men were charlatans, destroyers, and certainly a deadly threat to any of the more decent forms of government, what of the other greats? Was he to accept that they had names, while all the rest of his neighbors were to be known only as statistics? What became of "created equal" in that case? Even the universal accessibility of nature might be threatened. But to deny that Shakespeare or Mozart was wholly apart, wholly superior? Emerson was acutely aware of the decisions that he would have to make. And so, in his effort to navigate between these conflicts, he resorted to a very political metaphor, the representative, the central figure of American political practice, the elected spokesperson of one's constituency.

The whole movement of "Uses of Great Men," the essay which opens *Representative Men,* is a zig-zag. Nature exists for excellence (up), but anyone who is good among us qualifies (down). Do the great raise our sights? Yes, they do (up), but they are a part of all humanity, else they could not reach us (down). If they see things more quickly and before others do (up), we all can see eventually (down). To be sure, they are so absorbed in and by nature that they can interpret it for us and make it intelligible to us. That is what great scientists do for us (up), but this power is not to be construed as a personal quality. These men are vessels of an idea, conveyors as it were (down). Even as messengers, however, do the great not alter mankind significantly (up)? And do we not gain encouragement from reading the biographies of great people (up)? Maybe. A wise man in our village would do more for us on all counts (down). And the deepest encouragement that can ever come to us is from a true friend (down). Genius does guide us to a "supersensible region" and takes us out of the pettiness and monotony of everyday life (up). That is also the source of its dangers. It tempts us to passivity and idolatry (down). The antidote to that is supplied by the fact that great people replace their predecessors and so reveal the relativity of all greatness, its passing character. It is all time-bound, as every successor puts one's predecessor in the shadow and so keeps things alive and moving (down and up). The trouble with this last remark is that it is so obviously untrue that it must have been a prescription for how to treat greatness rather than an even remotely plausible statement about it. Just who, after all, has put Plato, Montaigne and, say, Mozart, in a shadow? The notion is ridiculous. Emerson's best and preferred argument is that without an audience, there is effectually no genius, and that while knowledge is revealed to us, no one can know it for us. We, small men and women, must also act. Without Plato, we would not have known that rational discourse was possible (up). Without it, all would have been complacency and self-satisfaction. However, were we not able to respond to him, he would not have been great (down). Indeed, Emerson distrusted even his own occasional paternalism, his care for the independence of ordinary people. They will not be lost forever in an excess of admiration for great people. Sooner or later they will regain their balance.

We need others to know ourselves and great people, especially, are measures, but we can eventually attain a true sense of our being and dispense with that overpowering otherness. Only moral grandeur endures, and that is not a socially recognized form of greatness. The moral genius abolishes oneself and leaves a lasting resonance. The acts survive the person, and refresh us. Even so, let us be bold. If we must remember famous names, let us learn to say from time to time, "Damn George Washington." This roller-coaster of weights and measures is less a revelation of a mind's discomfort than a proof of Emerson's unswerving determination to reject the political implications of a romanticism, which, in most other respects, was his own. He was not going to replace God with genius. He would not permit any person to say "I am that I am" and to be wholly unaccountable to humanity for one's oppressive power. Nevertheless, he would not simply pretend that greatness did not matter at all. The very possibility of a supersensible sphere, of transcendence, is more accessible to great individuals' eyes and more open to the rest of us because genius brings its intimations to us. That not only admits a vast gap between the two kinds of people but offers all possible grounds for admiring the great and their works. The absolute necessity of great men for revealing the possibilities of reason, imagination, discovery, and beauty is implicit in everything Emerson said about them. He had no way around that. Nevertheless, he grudged the great their glory, not because he was small-minded but because an uncritical belief in great people was not compatible with his democratic convictions. The way he coped with it was nothing if not ingenious. The masses of humanity certainly do not exist in order to allow a great person to emerge from their depth to lead and mold them. The great person serves them. And that service is described in the language of democratic politics. The way out of the tension between the sense of the apartness of the great and the claims of humanity was, as in constitutional states, to resort to representation. It is the only way out of the seesaw between anarchy and oppression. Nothing could illustrate more vividly the hold that democratic norms had on Emerson's intellectual imagination.

In what way do great people act as representatives? They may serve us directly by giving us something, be it material or metaphysical, but that is not representation. They also do something for us that is "pictorial," that is, they make something present that is absent. In this representation, a great person puts before our eyes some part of nature that is peculiarly one's own and makes us aware of it, makes it present to us. Dalton's atoms are "his" and he pictures them for us, so that we can eventually say, "Now I see it" (p. 618). It is easier for him than for us, but we are not altogether passive. It is not a matter of some neo-Platonic overflowing of spiritual energy from a pinnacle downward. Moreover, Emerson quickly drops the pictorial analogy and turns to political representation. That is not a matter of aristocratic generosity:

> The constituency decides the vote of the representative. He is not only representative, but participant. Like can only be known by like. The reason he knows about them is, that he is of them; he has just come out of nature, or from being a part of that thing. (P. 619)

As he is chosen by nature to be great, he represents it to us. For one always represents to someone. The congressperson speaks on behalf of one's district (nature) to Congress, the nation's assembled representatives (the world of others, of humanity at large, lesser people, ourselves). And as such, we are not consumers of their activity. Assemblies are deliberative bodies, and we become vigorous as we talk to the other delegates. "We are entitled to these enlargements." They save us from domesticity through multiplied extended relations and to be a delegate is to inspire trust, not subservience, moreover. We are drawn out, not bullied. Certainly, nature's attorney is no demonic force. The imagery, if not political, is nautical. The great person is a "mapmaker," easily the most useful, practical form of pictorial representation. Still, the point is for us to actively use that map and take to the road ourselves. The way by which the great individual liberates us is that this person does not stay around forever. Like all public servants, one's term comes to an end—and none too soon. What is important is the process of "rotation," again a word from the vocabulary of democracy. In fact, rotation in office was *the* great watchword of Jacksonian democracy; it meant that, since anyone could perform the modest tasks of the civil servant, no one should occupy an office for too long or monopolize it or think that one had some sort of proprietary right to it. When Emerson said that "rotation is the law of nature" (p. 623), he was clearly speaking of the social no less than of the physical laws of change. Each great person is a separate class and can have no clones. Jefferson and Franklin will be succeeded by a "great salesman; then a road-contractor, then a student of fishes." Clearly, Emerson was no culture snob. What unites these disparate types is that they are all servants of an idea. And though they alone glow with it, they share the light with the rest of us. Theirs is not the vulgarity that exploits our imbecility to dazzle us. "If a wise man should appear in our village, he would create, in those who conversed with him, a new consciousness of wealth, by opening their eyes to unobserved advantages; he would establish a sense of immovable equality." He would defend us against our worst impulse, the passion for worshipping great people. He would, in short, liberate us.

The great one who introduces us to the "qualities of primary nature" (p. 624) may also rescue us from the tedium and futility of political contests, the normal process of democratic politics. A stranger to parties who, coming from a higher sphere, gets to the heart of "the equity" of any policy also liberates us. In politics, the great person is not the winner but the self-liquidating hero, who leaves not a name but a just law behind. Public opinion devoid of intellect was also in need of service from the great (p. 625). They put a drop of acid on complacency and sentimentality, "on maudlin agglutinations" and on the insanity of our frenzied cities. It is their "foreign" quality, their distance from us, after all, that is the source of their gifts (pp. 626–27). Emerson could not, however, leave it at that. He must immediately warn us against the dangers of submission to the great, lest we become "underlings and intellectual suicides." The constitutional, free state depends on a "seesaw" between radicals who defy the past and its great men and those who will go right on admiring George Washington and the rest of their ancestors (pp. 627–28). It is no disgrace. As individuals, we might afford a degree of trust in the old great men, because ultimately we too will regain the balance of an independent, critical state. No sooner said than Emerson's irony asserts itself, and the rug is pulled out from the reader who might have been lulled into self-satisfaction. "But *great men*: the word is injurious" (p. 629). Great people are not good for us, because we are small. We are unstable in our moods, moving haltlessly "from dignity to dependence." We do not allow rotation to occur. We are *not* democratic enough. Instead, we talk meanly of masses and common people; "there are no common men. All men are of a size" (p. 630). If we mean business with "created equal," we will have to change our entire way of thinking about history. Is it just us he is warning or is he teetering back and forth himself—drawn by his two poles? In a dismissive moment, we leave the great behind us.

Heroes are relative to their time and place. Great today and gone tomorrow. Only humanity goes on. "The genius of humanity" should be the subject of biography. The spirit of the genius is absorbed in the flow of humanity's passage through time. We ought to think of great people in social and impersonal terms, as messengers from an idea that they represent to us, or really to all humanity. Then, they should get lost as fast as possible. "We have never come to the true and best benefit of genius, so long as we believe him an original force" (p. 631). There could not be a more complete rejection of the romantic notion of genius than that. Great individuals have only one claim on our attention: to help us grow up and do without them, except that there are many reasons to believe that this is not the whole story.

It would be wrong to think that Emerson was just dispensing wholesome milk and cookies to his fellow citizens. First of all, he spends most of his energy on excoriating their social pettiness and competitiveness and their mental torpor. Moreover, not all the incoherence of the essay is due to democratic pathos. Emerson is illuminating the two very different and incompatible faces of human greatness. Along with the rest of us, he knew that great people were in touch with forces that transform the realms of experience; let us again say, Mozart. It is not we who elect them, they are delegated to us, to unite us with the powers that have chosen them. They *are* the elect. That is not all, however. Great people are historical figures. Without their followers, their disciples, and their audiences, they would remain unknown and unrecognized. It is as absurd to speak of a hidden great person as of an ungifted genius. That is, surely, Emerson's chief point. To assert all its implications against Carlyle and the politically obtuse longing for hero-leaders and to reassert his loyalty to democratic men and women, however, required more, far more, than an account of the dual nature of human greatness. It required a choice between the two sides, and Emerson, in the language of democratic politics, came down heavily on the side of the democratic ethos. What is needed, once the choice has been made, is a more generous sense of appreciation, a larger vision of human worth and achievement, so that there will be more honor for uncommon, but universally possible, acts of ordinary decency.

It cannot be said that Emerson really tells us how to think about Plato and his other representative men. He does give us an idea of what he thought about them. And as one might expect, he is very carping. Only Montaigne comes off fairly well. We are told in *Montaigne; or the Skeptic* that he was gross in the way that he talked about sex, but that was in keeping with the manners of his time. He was the "prince of egotists" and an "admirable gossip" (pp. 697–98). These sentiments do not do Emerson much honor, but they are not grounded in spite or envy. It was really a mild form of self-criticism. For he also tells us that when he first read Cotton's translation of the *Essays,* he felt that he had written them himself (p. 697). He had become, and in many ways remained, Montaigne. What was the skepticism that Montaigne represented like? It was not the skepticism of the *Apology for Raimond Sebond,* but that of *Of Cannibals,* social rather than philosophical. And its audience is defined psychologically. Most people find skepticism intolerable. They cannot endure it. It is a matter of temperament (pp. 706–7). Some people do take to it spontaneously, however, as did Montaigne, and he speaks for them and for their great truth: *There are doubts.*

One cannot easily imagine Emerson accepting the religion of his country simply because it was there and the alternatives were not really any better, but possibly worse, as novelties are likely to be. Montaigne's resignation to religious custom was not compatible with the agonies of Protestantism. So deep an indifference to the content, to the specifics of religious belief, or unbelief for that matter, was not within Emerson's range of possibilities. His skepticism was limited to the social world where it was enhanced rather than constrained by democracy. The social case for skepticism was overwhelming. On one side, there is the arrogance of the intellectuals, who look on the rest of humankind as rats and mice (pp. 691–93). Between the pretensions of the intellectuals and the cynicism of the business person, the skeptic is a breath of fresh air who blows the dogmatizers away. He is not going to affirm or deny; one can survive without proclamations or judgments. Emerson did not think that this implied complete unbelief or "scoffing and profligate jeering at all that is stable and good." The genuine skeptic is a spectator whom one can trust, for aloofness is not incompatible with conventional probity. Far from it (pp. 695–96). Montaigne, who represents this skepticism, was the most honest and frank and sincere man who ever lived. Honesty, fastidious and self-contained, is the skeptic's virtue, and Emerson did not grudge it his admiration (pp. 698–700). We may find such honesty repulsive, for we are all natural believers, but one cannot overlook its results. Not only is skepticism the scourge of bigots and blockheads, the skeptic has the strength to be a very bad citizen and is just the dose of salts that democracy needs. The skeptic is neither a conservative nor a reformer and is not a joiner of any sort. No club, party, or cause can claim the skeptic as its own (pp. 702–3). This person is just the cure for both the crude materialism and the cloying religiosity that democratic societies seem to encourage. The conventional case against skepticism, therefore, leaves Emerson cold. Only a childish religiosity will suffer from it: nothing to regret in that. As for asserting the instability of human opinion, who can deny the record of history? What is permanent except human selfishness? We cannot blame skepticism for the facts of life. They may upset us, but that is not the skeptic's fault. Will we feel defeated in our pursuits if we suspect that all is illusion? Why should we react that way? Doubt is more likely to inspire courage and determination than credulity (pp. 703–6). And Montaigne and the skepticism he represented were not wholly without belief, however tentative. He held onto, or at least practiced, honesty. The difficulty is that honesty puts one at odds with the world. But what is skepticism without its claim to that state of mind which we call honest?

Having said so much on behalf of his one and only hero, Emerson did, in the end, feel compelled to withdraw. "The final solution in which skepticism is lost, is in the moral sentiment, which never forfeits its supremacy." Dissolving or resolving, in our time, "the final solution" is a phrase that evokes other resonances. It makes a mockery of Emerson's pieties. They were needed even then only to reconcile him to the chasm between hope and experience. Did he really believe that sentimentality? At the social level, there is some reason to believe that this was a quiet acceptance of conventional belief, not unlike Montaigne's peace with public manners, rituals, and conventions, but more creedal and less provisional. The moral sense assures us "that appearance is immoral; the result is moral." The whole absorbs and purifies its parts. The public religion of Emerson's America was the faith in progress, real moral and political advance. Democracy depended on it. Emerson could not dismiss that faith. And so we are told that every successive government may only be a parade of knaves and fools, but in the end, "a great and beneficent tendency irresistibly streams." Having just poured scorn on Charles Fourier, who really did believe that sort of thing, Emerson was not in the best position to endorse a historical myth against which his entire essay rebelled. To have rejected it out of honesty might, however, have removed him from his community to an intolerable degree. So like Montaigne, he respected the prevailing religion, but unlike the great skeptic he did not do so openly. It was not democratically possible, and then he *did* believe in something more, in an Eternal Cause, a supersensible Nature, an intimation of another World.

Whatever the limits of Emerson's skepticism were, whether they were political or mystical, he gave his doubts a free rein when he thought about social reformers. Neither *Self-Reliance* nor *Representative Men* is about politics, which is why the constant intrusion of political language, illustrations, and preoccupations is so striking. In *New England Reformers,* Emerson is talking about the political conduct of his friends, and as he says "we," one must suppose his own as well. In one sense, Emerson thought that we were all reformers, because we all want to improve ourselves in some way. That is not, however, what he means in this, his most ironic and self-deprecating essay. Here, he is defending democratic people against the moral-reform societies that were the most conspicuous feature of Jacksonian New England: utopian communities, temperance, prison reform, educational experiments, and, of course, more seriously, abolitionism. Most of the young men and women who undertook to devote their lives to these causes had been moved by Emerson, a point of which he was aware. His responsibility was obvious; therefore, it is "we," not "you." Moreover, the scorn does not have to be softened in that case. One need not spare oneself for the sake of tact or prudence. It is here that we can find out why skepticism and democracy were jointed in Emerson's mind. To be mindful of the people of one's town, to respect their opinions may well force "us" to doubt our most cherished political dreams. We may have to give up utopian enterprises, because our neighbors think that they are ridiculous and the townspeople just may be right. So there *are* doubts. The pursuit of the perfect city is an insult to the actual town, and that is a very questionable political action. To look at the reform of other people from their point of view, to consider their consent, is democratic, and it must introduce doubts of the most severe sort into the mind of the reforming agent. Skepticism about reform was what Emerson thought he owed his town. It was a debt to be paid to democracy, not only as something out there but as it existed in half of his own mind and as part of his own moral sense for which he, as part of "we," had to apologize.

The Church, that is, the truly religious party, is leaving the "church nominal." That is the way of Protestant piety, of course. The quest for perfect purity means sectarianism. The established congregation has again been rejected in "a spirit of protest and detachment." That sounds pretty serious and dignified, but before we are fooled for too long, irony removes our blinkers. "What a fertility of projects for the salvation of the world! . . . [A] society for the protection of ground worms, slugs and mosquitoes was to be incorporated without delay" (pp. 591–92). It was a replay of the antinomianism of "the elder puritans." As an assertion of the independence of private citizens, this is fine, but it loses all value when it is copied, when it is a matter of group life. There is, moreover, something inherently absurd about the projection of the purity of conscience into the public glare. "Hands off! Let there be no control and no interference in the administration of this kingdom of me." The verbal imbecility reflects the confusion of intentions. The result is predictable. The independence of conscience once it enters the public domain is exploited by less scrupulous political agents. So freedom quickly is translated into free trade, as reformers and regular politicians soon are engaged in a ritual dance. Groups are all alike. Emerson had no intention of whitewashing the established institutions. Education, especially, was futile, cynical, and indifferent to the development of individual children. He did not support slavery but did not choose to act until the passage of the Fugitive Slave Law. He thought that the efforts of reformers who were not themselves reformed were no better than their awful adversaries. They were, indeed, particularly obtuse. When their domestic life was a mess, they thought that everything could be solved by joining a utopian commune on the assumption that collective activity was the equivalent of a psychological self-transformation. In fact, the tax levied by radical conformity was no less heavy than that extracted by official associations. The ardent do-gooders were not for "my poor" after all. Emerson was not going to allow philanthropy to pressure him or to deflect him from his will to act only on his grounds. No part of society was really better than any other. And the radical "groupie" was just a rebellious conformist in his view. The only way to reform is to begin with oneself and then to deal only with others as discrete individuals, not "causes."

There is, to begin with, far less inequality between individuals than we pretend, so we may not need to reform each other. Everyone is good at something. Moreover, they are as keen to do their best for their town as one could wish. So we might refrain from preaching to them. When they vote, they try to choose the better candidate, and all prefer the company of people whom they regard as their superiors. The desire to improve is universal. It is thoughtless and also cynical to see pure malignity among those with whom we disagree or who may indeed be utterly wrong. To organize others is to demote them in advance. The town is better than it may seem, and it is ready to alter when it is approached patiently and appreciatively—democratically, in fact. The alternative is a deserved failure:

> We wish to escape from subjection, and a sense of inferiority, and we make self-denying ordinances, we drink water, we eat grass, we refuse the laws, we go to jail, it is all in vain. (P. 608)

All this public display of virtue neither liberates the reformer nor impresses the town. If you want to do something about education, teach a child. If you want to change the local laws, talk to the citizens. Everyone can be free, and no one can rise to any height by stepping on the Yankee lad.

Emerson did not claim that he had the key to public or private success: "Every discourse is an approximate answer." To the end, however, there were simply two immovable propositions from which he never departed. The first was that the approach to truth could be made only in complete solitude. If it is unspoken, it is, after all, beyond doubt and dogma. The second was that if there was a moral law, it was democratic. He might choose to be alone, but he would not look down on the ploughboy. He would scorn the New England reformers, the great men, and even his own impulse to antinomian assertion because he could not, and would not, turn his back on the townspeople. And in the end, it was for their sake that he chose only bearable doubts and to be a skeptical bad citizen, who would resist both the enthusiasms of radicalism and the matey thuggery of all established parties. He was just not going to talk that way. We are all better than we think and a lot better than we are usually told we are. In its way, this wry affirmation is deeply democratic. And it inspired Emerson's philosophy, as often as it inhibited him from following his mind's impulse to explore those darkest moments of contempt from which one cannot redeem oneself or others.

Notes

Author's note: This article was originally given as part of a celebration of the sixtieth birthday of Stanley Cavell and is scheduled for inclusion in *Pursuits of*

Reason: Essays in Honor of Stanley Cavell, edited by Ted Cohen, Paul Guyer, and Hilary Putnam (Texas Tech University Press, 1993).

1. All references are to Ralph Waldo Emerson, *Essays and Lectures* (New York: Library of America, 1983).

2. *Emerson in His Journals,* edited by Joel Porte (Cambridge, MA: Harvard University Press, 1982), p. 408.

CHAPTER FIVE

An Education for America:
Tocqueville, Hawthorne, Emerson

D
o we really know what sort of schooling is most likely to make students into good citizens? Is a liberal arts curriculum best, or should we emphasize the social and natural sciences? We all know far too many wonderfully well educated scoundrels to be in a position to answer the question with any degree of certainty. Fanatics and free riders seem to come from every sort of school. Instead of lamenting the current state of education, therefore, one might begin by asking what sort of character American democracy might encourage to achieve its hopes. And because our finest minds have, in fact, thought about it for a long time, one way to come to grips with the question, even to begin to understand it, is to come to a balanced view of our past, especially our intellectual history.

How does American democracy educate its citizens or help them to educate themselves? That was certainly Tocqueville's question, and, as he came to America at a time of great intellectual ferment, it is particularly useful to begin with him. It is also worth asking whether we have always made the best possible use of his great book, especially when we cite him in bemoaning our present condition.

Democracy in America is a work of social science in one of its most complex forms, comparative history. Like any such work, it formulates general propositions and puts aside those local differences that are irrelevant to the subject at hand. Moreover, it treats specific institutions and informal social phenomena functionally. Do they sustain democratic government? What does and does not support this politi-

This undated essay was not previously published.

cal system? These are the sort of questions that political science, ancient and modern, asks. If we want a complete picture we must, however, also look at what anthropologists call "the native's point of view." We must ask Tocqueville's contemporaries, such as Hawthorne and Emerson, to tell us what the experiences that observers described felt like, how they interpreted their world. For they "lived" what Tocqueville observed and so complete the record.

Not only is a reading of Tocqueville not enough to give us a sense of the American character in the Jacksonian era, it is a mistake to use him in our own polemics. The two errors are, indeed, related. A too partial reading of our history is a positive inducement to its mindless exploitation. Since the Second World War, there have been at least two phases of the misuse of *Democracy in America*, both equally fatuous. In the fifties McCarthyism was creating a great deal of justifiable anxiety, not least because it followed so closely upon the heels of European fascism. One response was an upsurge of fear of "conformism," of a society of "outer-directed," consensus-seeking, mindless imitators. These were the American mass-men, the hordes who had so recently roared their approval of dictatorship in Europe. Was not Tocqueville, with his fear of the tyranny of the majority, the herald of this bad news? Had he not warned us that this was where we were headed? Was not our ideological history just one long "irrational Lockeanism," devoid of critical intelligence? Was not our educational system without the vigor needed for real culture and freedom as well? Had not Tocqueville already noted that without a feudal past, there was no struggle and strife here, so that we were prone to forget the demands of a liberty we had attained too easily? In this light, America was ready to let a McCarthy play havoc with dissenters. America was about to go to ruin as Europe had.

Ample empirical works on European history have shown by now that mass-man was not the cause of the rise of fascism and that notions such as mass culture have no explanatory power. As for McCarthy, nasty as he was, he was not a sign of the ageless darkness of the American psyche or of the inherent feebleness of liberal politics, but a passing phenomenon. It is important to be vigilant; liberty needs to be attended. But do we really need this kind of self-flagellation?

Time passed, and fear of tyrannical mass-man was replaced by worry about egalitarian radicalism and violent dissent. Was this not proof of the feebleness of our educational system, and had not

Tocqueville warned us of these dangers? Had he not told us that "equality of conditions" posed a mortal danger to our liberty?

First of all, economic redistribution was not what he had in mind at all. The phrase "equality of conditions" did not mean economic equality for him. It meant the end of the society of orders, of castes with hereditary political and social ranks, such as the ancien régime in France. America had, of course, never been such a society. Nor did Tocqueville think that there was the slightest danger to private property in the United States, and, in any case, he thought economic equality impossible. The absence of intermediary bodies that stood between the individual and the democratic state did concern him, but he had considerable confidence in the ability of voluntary associations to take the place of the orders and ranks of aristocratic societies. The educational effect of democracy, he believed, was to isolate individuals and make them too dependent on public opinion, but it also made them enterprising and quick to act together to promote political ends. That most of these voluntary associations were very radical at that time did not seem to upset him in the least. It was their function in the system that concerned him.

How did this sober historian come to be used as a source of prophecies of doom? If one wants to look for warnings and disregard everything else, they are there. To do so is, moreover, the purpose of a very old and traditional form of educational rhetoric: the American jeremiad. Beginning with the Puritans in the seventeenth century, preachers and teachers have seen nothing but "declension," a falling away from earlier standards, in American life.[1]

The American jeremiad is not just any reproach and imprecation. It has a very definite meaning and structure. Covenant theology, which had sent them on their "errand into the wilderness," had given the Puritans a powerful sense of being both the best and the worst of mankind. They were the best because they had made a covenant with God and were his chosen people, summoned to act as a beacon for the rest of humanity and to complete the great Reformation. They were also the worst, for when they erred, they were guiltier than the rest of sinning mankind. They had abandoned the mission that they, and they alone, had received from God. Thus, they were always doubly failing. The only people with whom their experiences could be compared were the biblical people of Israel, whom they had succeeded and whose fate was a dreadful warning to them. The other nations of the world really had nothing to say to them and did not interest them at all. However, even as they lamented their sins and recalled the anger of the Lord, the Puritan preachers also reminded their listeners of how very special they were and how close to God.

The jeremiad was "a ritual designed to join social criticism to spiritual renewal."[2] Even when it became clear that the Reformation was not going to be completed soon, and as later Puritans compared themselves to their more heroic and faithful ancestors, they did not lose hope. They had declined since the first generation of the saints, and they had often betrayed God, but they were still the chosen people, and their sense of uniqueness did not abate. Especially in the nineteenth century, as the movement westward began in earnest, Protestant preachers reminded Americans that they were a redeemer nation with a mission. The mantle of Israel was on their shoulders, and they must play their part in the providential design.

Exaltation through lamentation is the essence of the jeremiad, and its hold on our social and political rhetoric has never been loosened. Tocqueville simply was drawn into it. He became, through no fault of his own, an inexhaustible source of quotations for illustrating our declension, as dreadful now as it has ever been, even when its religious moorings are forgotten. What is especially enduring is the indifference to the ways and problems of other nations.

To forget that in *Democracy in America* Tocqueville wrote entirely for France and, very often, about it, is in itself a mark of the continuity of the jeremiadical form. Who among his American readers showed the slightest interest in the comparison with France and the many pages overtly addressed to French readers? Yet Tocqueville made it plain enough that he had come to America to report back to his own people. He explicitly put aside those things that were due entirely to American circumstances and concentrated only on what was universally democratic. The whole point was to tell his French readers that democracy was inevitable and that it was not incompatible with their religion or with freedom. Only one chapter is wholly American, the one dealing with the three races; all the others have an eye on France.[3] Even the introduction is a quick tour through French history. He had no doubt that France's passage to democracy would be far more hazardous and difficult than that of the United States, and he dwelled at special length on those points that he expected to be the most difficult.[4] Tocqueville's questions to the people whom he interviewed were those bound to interest most a democratically inclined Frenchman.

An Education for America   69

Thus, he paid an inordinate amount of attention to American Catholics, then very few in number compared to Protestants.[5] France, however, had few Protestants, and to convince his fellow Catholics that
democracy and the separation of church and state would be good for
them spiritually as well as morally and politically was one of his chief
objects. The American arrangement was not just the best one possible;
it was good in itself in its effect on the purity of morals and the genuine faith of the general population. On the other hand, Tocqueville
worried inordinately about the possible political ambitions of the non-
commissioned officers of the United States Army, which does seem a
bit bizarre, considering their exemplary loyalty to the constitutional
order.[6] It is, however, just what would trouble a Frenchman writing a
mere fifteen years after the fall of Napoleon.

These are but two of a long series of considerations that Tocqueville
raised with his French audience in mind. He was an outsider, and that
gave him both his impartiality and his insight, but it also limited the
scope of his interests. To forget the French half of the book is a peculiar act of historical self-absorption in any case. It is the mark of minds
indifferent to the external world, intent entirely upon their own present preoccupations.

It was not only Tocqueville's concern with France that made him an
outsider. His stance as a political scientist had the same effect. As a
political observer he tried to explain, compare, and interpret manifest
political institutions of government in their social setting. He was not
nearly as interested in the experiences of individuals and their own
interpretations of their lives. Thus, we find him very interested in the
domestic and social impact of Protestant religiosity.[7] He was particularly struck by the way sectarianism released social energies and
spilled over into all kinds of social causes and associations. Its functions fascinated him, but he had little, if any, time for the inner life of
Protestants or for their doctrines and psychology. It was for him, quite
properly, a social phenomenon.

So, also, in his discussions of literature, he concentrated on the size
and character of the audience, the supply and demand for books of
various kinds, and similar externalities, but not on its integral character.[8] He did not expect America as a democracy to produce much in
the way of literature. Nor did he have much hope for France. Had he
been able to recognize the inner torments of Protestantism and
thought about where great writing really comes from, he might have
left that chapter unwritten. Social science simply has its limitations.

The fact is that the greatest of American writers were just starting out as he so confidently predicted their impossibility.

Tocqueville thought of education as sociologically as he thought of religion and of literature. What was its function in a democratic age? Greek and Latin should be taught only to future authors, for the classical authors were masters of style. Their political doctrines were less than useless for contemporary democracy. The schools should prepare young people for practical life. He liked the empirical cast of mind of democratic citizens and compared it very favorably with the arid abstractions of the aristocratic past.[9] He did worry about a loss of genuine interest in history.

Such, then, briefly, were Tocqueville's thoughts on schooling and, more broadly, the education of democratic men and women. The one thing he did not write was a jeremiad. Both his fears and hopes were balanced. If one looks only at him, one would still not know all one might want to know about the America of his age, but one would certainly be better served by reading all of him than by picking out passages to construct yet another jeremiad.

What can the greatest American writers of that time add to this picture? Unlike Tocqueville, Hawthorne and Emerson were not interested in defining a single national democratic character. Tocqueville, looking at democratic characteristics in America from a distance, painted a political model. Here were people with peculiar domestic and public habits that could be traced to the democratic conditions in which they had always lived. They tended to be overly preoccupied with making money at the expense of public affairs, but they were quick to get involved in voluntary associations that served public purposes. In an egalitarian spirit, they tended to fear and resent exceptional individuals but were quite able to appreciate merit when they saw it.

For someone who lives in this society and thinks about it as an insider, the tensions and differences among groups and individuals are bound to seem far more significant. Political generalizations are less significant to the local critic than, for instance, the conflict between the impulse to reform and self-satisfaction among their fellow citizens.

In these as in other respects, both Hawthorne and Emerson should be examples to us, not least because both, each in his own way, protested against the jeremiad. Neither was given to thinking of our history as a mixture of decay and missionary calling. Both were deeply concerned with the sort of education, not just schooling, that America could offer its people and what sort of human beings might emerge from it, especially in New England. Both, also, thought about how we might best consider our own past and present efforts at improvement—realistically, even tragically, and with a sense of limitations, though without cynicism.

Even if one cannot discuss the entire work of two constantly developing geniuses, one can look at some of their most striking writings. "The Custom House" is the essay that introduces Hawthorne's *The Scarlet Letter*, and, in a concentrated form, it expresses most of what he thought about his people. Emerson's *New England Reformers* is no less intense a view of his corner of America. This is America seen from within, and, in Hawthorne's case, it is a tragic vision; in Emerson's, an ironic one. Both give us a psychology for always rethinking our past and present prospects so that we may arrive at a sane view of what kinds of character we have and may expect to have. For both, the only education that matters is self-education. Lamenting and boasting would get us nowhere. It is only by mastering the collective past in a cool spirit that we can hope to arrive at some degree of self-understanding. Without that, we are not likely to have a clear sense of direction or to find our path collectively or as individuals. Moral psychology was for both Hawthorne and Emerson the master science that would help us escape from the various kinds of illusion that they saw flourishing in their midst and saw in greater diversity and detail than a visiting social scientist, even a genius like Tocqueville, was likely to observe.

Hawthorne had worked as a surveyor in the Salem Custom House. He knew it and its inhabitants extremely well. Salem was his ancestral home. Oddly, he was an ardent Jacksonian, a "loco-foco democrat" by his own description. His was a patronage appointment, and, when the Whigs came into office, he was fired. Like many another dismissed employee, he was enraged, but, unlike most, he was able to turn his fury into a work of art, and we may be grateful that thanks to bad political luck, he did not spend much time in the Custom House weighing cargoes and keeping records.

"The Custom House" has many meanings. It is the house of our customs, of our habits, our manners, our education, and our usages. It is also the place where new goods from abroad arrive and are measured and weighed. We think about change there. It is both a commercial and political place and was such even before the Revolution. And since records are preserved there, it is a place where our past and present meet. In sum, it is the place where we discover all the complexities of our actual condition.

Now Hawthorne was a "surveyor" there in more senses than one; he was certainly taking the measure of the place, but he did not do so as a stranger. He did not think of himself as an alien, but as a participating observer. He was tied to Salem, he tells us, by "instinct," but he hoped that his children would leave it and that even he might move. Thus, "whenever a new change of custom should be essential to my good, a change would come."[10] In America customs are not fated; individuals choose to come and go, change or remain the same. Hawthorne can be a detached surveyor, and his children can strike their roots wherever they wish. Yet he does feel an "affection" for the old town, and when he walks its streets, there is "a sort of home-feeling with the past," even though it is "the mere sensuous sympathy of dust for dust." He means to be friends with the past, but very much on his own terms. He remembers that his Puritan ancestors would have despised him as a mere scribbler and idler and that he was very far from being proud of them. His own ancestor had been a witch-burner, a persecutor of Quakers, and a zealot. The past is a problem and a challenge, not something to be forgotten or uncritically accepted.[11]

There are, in fact, two pasts in "The Custom House," one recent and the other remote. The remote past has to be recovered with considerable effort for there "the Actual and the Imaginary may meet."[12] It is because it is so different from the present that it enlightens us about our actual selves, here and now, about our possibilities, our beliefs, and our conduct. It is an education for the present moment.

So as he walked back and forth inside the Custom House, he recognized that perfection was nowhere to be found. "Neither the front nor the back entrance of the Custom House opens on the road to Paradise."[13] Utopia is neither in the past nor in the future of America. That is why Hawthorne reminds us on the very first page of the novel itself that however utopian a community thinks itself, it still must begin by building a prison and a graveyard. It is by walking between the two doors, neither one of which leads to Paradise, that our education begins.

What of those who do not care to learn from the past, but merely consume it passively? They look back and comfortably go to sleep. The majority of the customsmen are merely the heirs of the men who fought the Revolution and the War of 1812. Thanks to them, Salem is declining in "the glow of decaying wood."

Over the entrance hovers an enormous specimen of the American eagle, with outspread wings, a shield before her breast, and, if I recollect aright, a bunch of intermingled thunderbolts and barbed arrows in each claw. With the customary infirmity of temper that characterizes this unhappy fowl, she appears, by the fierceness of her beak and eye, and the general truculency of her attitude, to threaten mischief to the inoffensive community; and especially to warn all citizens, careful of their safety, against intruding on the premises which she overshadows with her wings. Nevertheless, vixenly as she looks, many people are seeking, at this very moment, to shelter themselves under the wing of the federal eagle; imagining, I presume, that her bosom has all the softness and snugness of an eider-down pillow.[14]

Huddled under the wings of this heroic federal "fowl" are several antiques feathering their beds. These are the men of the Custom House, and Hawthorne describes them in detail. The patriarch of the establishment is the permanent Inspector, "the son of the revenue system." His place was provided for him by his father, a Revolutionary War colonel, who had been the collector of the port. The Inspector is a walking stomach, an "absolute nonentity." This man simply lives off the past, especially the memory of the Revolution. He has ancestors and feels no need to think of the present or the future. Mindlessness can go no further. Such are all who derive their spiritual and material sustenance by resting on the work of "the Founders" and neglecting the work they have been called to do here and now. The back door leads to a utopian past, the inheritance of which they can now enjoy without more effort than it takes to look back and praise the past now long gone. That is what getting fat on memories is like as an education.

The second man of the Custom House is the Collector, an old general from the War of 1812. He is "dim," though not "imbecile," a human ruin like the ruined fortress, Ticonderoga. Like many retired soldiers, he loves flowers. That is the extent of the energy which past military exertion has left him and his like.

Both of these characters represent not only a mindless traditionalism, but also an essentially undemocratic belief that they have inherited or earned a permanent place in the civil service. The Republic owes them a living.

While he leans on the mighty arm of the Republic, his own proper strength departs from him. He loses, in an extent proportioned to the weakness or force of his original nature, the capability of self-support. If he possess an unusual share of native energy, or the enervating magic of place do not operate too long upon him, his forfeited powers may be redeemable.[15]

Hawthorne himself presumably was able to escape the moral decay that dependency upon the government induces, but most people are not that hardy. Yet these have become our customs, and the education offered by both a passive traditionalism and an effortless acceptance of its gifts is not wholesome. Still, Hawthorne was fair. Even these two ruins were better company than some of the New England radicals with whom he had recently lived.

There was a third man in the Custom House. He was bred there from boyhood, and he gave Hawthorne "a new idea of talent." This man was the ideal young American, and he shows up in most of Hawthorne's novels. He is self-made within a democratic order to which he has completely adapted. His are our best customs, for he is the perfect Yankee.

> His gifts were emphatically those of a man of business; prompt, acute, clear-minded; with an eye that saw through all perplexities, and a faculty of arrangement that made them vanish. . . . In my contemplation, he stood as the ideal of his class. He was, indeed, the Custom House in himself. . . . His integrity was perfect; it was a law of nature with him, rather than a choice or a principle. . . . A stain on his conscience, as to any thing that came within the range of his vocation, would trouble such a man very much in the same way, though to a far greater degree, than an error in the balance of an account.[16]

This is the character democracy requires. It is not a matter of schooling, but of competence, openness, and integrity, and Hawthorne thought that our customs were by no means incapable of rearing such people. One of the things that they ought to receive was a realistic and energizing sense of their own history, one without illusions or inducements to indolence. They ought to be surveyors, neither utopians nor nostalgic traditionalists, but poised between past and future with self-confident and open minds.

It is thus that Hawthorne himself goes to the cupboard that holds a message for him from the remote past. When the Surveyor opens the door to the Puritan past, he finds that awful scarlet letter. He also discovers the portrait of one of his English, pre-Revolutionary predecessors, Surveyor Pue. The face of this royal official is proud and self-confident, so unlike the "hang-dog expression" of republican officials. "Do this," says the face, and Hawthorne obeys, looking hard and long at the contents of the closet, which tell the story of the Puritan past, with all its dark as well as shining sides.[17] There they were: persecutors, burners, cruel and pitiless, and, in their aspirations, utopians, determined upon reaching perfection. Nor is it possible to blame the vast inhumanities on an ignorant populace. The clergy, judges, statesmen—all stood by the gallows and the stocks.

It was, however, a part of Hawthorne's maturity to be able to be fair even to his own ancestors. He admired their sagacity, their probity, and their utter fairness, sparing no one, certainly not themselves. The women who jeered at Hester, the heroine, and her baby, born out of wedlock, are at least not frivolous. Neither the Puritan nor the royal officials were subject to the weaknesses that afflict republican civil servants. The virtues of the remote past were great, but so were the cruelties and oppression. If virtue is more modest now, so is evil. The moral balance, in sum, remains constant. To learn to think like that about the past and the most probable future is to be fortified against both the idleness of tradition and the rage of utopian hope.

In the present, living here and now for attainable moral and political goods, is the practical Yankee, Hawthorne's moral hero, free from attachment to place and time, immensely competent at many jobs and marked by one virtue above all others: personal integrity. It is not clear that schools can inculcate such virtue, though they can help the young toward it by giving them a genuine, tragic sense of history. That is not what educational reformers usually have in mind, and one can see why Hawthorne was bored and irritated by those among the reformers who believed that they could transform mankind by changing the way grade schools are organized.

Hawthorne was not alone in being skeptical about the efforts of all educational reformers. Emerson was also doubtful of what they could accomplish, but, unlike Hawthorne, he could not simply turn his back on them. When he wrote *New England Reformers* in 1844, he consistently spoke of "we" and "us."[18] It was very much an act of searing self-criticism and irony directed at himself. In a way, that is what Emerson meant by genuine reform. It was always self-improvement, something we were all capable of and which did require that we look at our own lives before we scrutinized those of our neighbors.

Emerson was certainly also a social reformer in the most usual sense of the word and a great inspiration to many an ardent young New Englander. He thought the official reason for public education cynical. It was argued that with universal suffrage, even the lower classes

needed education to turn them into reasonable, property-loving voters. The character and needs and hopes and possibilities of individual
children were of no concern. Those attributes would not help their
development or powers of self-education or help them to become self-
reliant individuals with minds of their own. To Emerson an education
that did not attempt more than to constrain was no education at all;
it was a betrayal.

When he turned to the reformers who shared his ideas, however,
his heart sank. Were these self-reforming, self-critical men and women
or just a group of self-righteous joiners? In Tocqueville's view these
people, who were so ready to come together to promote causes, were
public-spirited people who were essential to the maintenance of liberty and civic vigor in a democracy otherwise too easily given to private concerns. Their place in the democratic scheme as a whole was,
therefore, entirely admirable. What, however, did they directly and
actually achieve? Were they personally improved, educated, by their
activity? Were their causes wise, acceptable, and likely to strengthen
their immediate communities?

To the insider who, like Emerson, did not just observe the political
functions of these voluntary associations, but lived within their orbit,
such questions are necessary. We should not overlook them either.
New England Reformers begins very grandly. "The Church," that is,
the real spiritual energy of society, had left the "church nominal," that
is, the establishment. That was, of course, the normal movement of
Protestantism. Congregations constantly split, and, by calling the reformers a church, Emerson is reminding us of the enduring character
of these ways. And then he ironically pulls the rug out from under
these pretensions and the reader's equally serious expectations. "What
a fertility of projects for the salvation of the world! . . . Even . . . a
society for the protection of groundworms, slugs, and mosquitoes."[19]

To what purpose were people organized? If they sought purity of
conscience, that was noble, but why join an association for that? A
moral awakening in the course of a protest was fine, but politics was
not the realm for purity. "Hands off! No interference with the kingdom of me!" Such was the cry of the reformer who thought that his
personal project was beyond reproach and that it was only others who
needed reforming. This sort of egoism quickly became very conventional. The arguments of the reforming individualist could be adapted
to every self-regarding economic policy by the newspapers. In the end
the reforming association simply entered into a ritualistic, back-and-

forth dance with its opponents because they were not as unlike each other as they claimed.

To Emerson, all associations were morally similar. Organizations tended to be imitative. Moreover, most associations were stifling. A reform movement that was not able to alter the members who joined it was not, in the long run, reforming. And groups, in Emerson's eyes, were not conducive to self-improvement. No one was really better off simply by joining a club. A crooked political candidate was not going to become honest when he became a member of Congress. If one's domestic life was a mess, he should not expect it to improve if he joined a utopian commune, as so many of Emerson's young contemporaries were doing. Indeed, even Hawthorne had spent a while at Brook Farm.

Emerson was not telling his readers that one ought to be complacent. He dreaded the inner death that comes with a passive acceptance of the way things are. He did not suggest that one give up hopes for a generous rather than a mean-spirited schooling for the young.

To achieve anything, however, one must take a more respectful look at "the town" and inquire into its real beliefs. The town was not an invalid beyond hope. And no democrat could proceed on the assumption that one's fellow citizens were purely malignant. To scorn them, to show off one's purity of intention, and to act the angel, was not acceptable. Rather, tell the town what it plausibly might be, and it would listen. Forget about yourself in public, and the public may help to improve you indirectly. "We wish to escape from subjugation, and a sense of inferiority,—and we make self-denying ordinances, we drink water, we eat grass, we refuse the laws, we go to jail: it is all in vain." [20] It is important to note that he was saying *we*, not *you*. Emerson was in danger of forgetting that the only political belief worth holding is one that is believable to one's town. Reform is a two way street. One is reformed by those whom one tries to reform. That also is education. If you think the schools are ruining children, become a teacher and inspire a child. You too will be improved by it.

Reform in Emerson's vision *was* education. Clearly, Emerson cared more about the democratic habits of individuals than did Tocqueville. He was also more aware of a lot of futility, folly, and pretension in those voluntary associations that the latter admired so much for their systemic value. They may have been good for democracy, but were they also good for the people engaged in them and for their neighbors? Emerson thought them superficial in that they encouraged their members to move "from zeal to laxity," rather than to be steadfast in the pursuit of local goals. In his very different way, he distrusted the utopian temper just as much as Hawthorne, not just because of the content of the projects, but because the moral stance in and of itself hampered the education in reality that the best sort of townsman needs and so rarely gets. He was caught between the fears and small-mindedness of convention and the alien extravagance of the reformer. Neither one really wished him well. In the end Emerson believed most in the force of example as the only genuine education we can offer each other.

What, then, do Hawthorne and Emerson add to Tocqueville in considering the education of democratic men and women? They saw just why it was important that Americans acquire a balanced view of their past, to overcome both the utopian and the conventional excesses to which they were prone. Out of that sober sense of moral limitations, they would emerge, not cynical, but energetic, practical, efficient, living in the present, and with personal integrity and self-reliance as their chief moral aspirations. This is important ultimately not just for democracy, but for democratic man as an admirable human being. That education turn to this hope rather than to collective and improbable schemes of salvation-through-schooling is as important for us as it was for them.

Notes

1. Sacvan Bercovitch, *The American Jeremiad* (Madison: University of Wisconsin Press, 1978). Readers interested in the topic should consult this work.
2. Ibid., p. xi.
3. Alexis de Tocqueville, *Democracy in America,* trans. George Lawrence, ed. J. P. Mayer (Garden City, NY: Doubleday and Co., 1969), pp. 316–407.
4. Ibid., pp. 9–20, 87–98, 122–25, 220–21, 314–15, 639–40.
5. Ibid., pp. 287–301, 442–51.
6. Ibid., pp. 651–54.
7. Ibid., pp. 189–95, 513–17, 534–85.
8. Ibid., pp. 454–75, 482–96.
9. Ibid., pp. 475–77, 429–33.
10. Nathaniel Hawthorne, *The Scarlet Letter,* in *Novels* (New York: Literary Classics of the United States: distributed by the Viking Press; The Library of America, 1983), p. 141.
11. Ibid., pp. 125–28.
12. Ibid., p. 149.
13. Ibid., p. 130.
14. Ibid., p. 122–23.

15. Ibid., p. 151–52.

16. Ibid., p. 139–40.

17. Ibid., p. 147.

18. Ralph Waldo Emerson, "New England Reformers," in *Essays and Lectures* (New York: Literary Classics of the United States: distributed by the Viking Press; The Library of America, 1983), pp. 591–609.

19. Ibid., pp. 591–92.

20. Ibid., p. 608.

CHAPTER SIX

The Education of Henry Adams, by Henry Adams

A utobiographies are not always meant to be self-revealing or even personal. Indeed, "antimemoirs" are quite common. It is an obvious impulse of the historicist mind to place even its own life within the stream of public events and look at it as might some future historian. The passion for objectivity can be so strong that it imposes impersonality even upon the memory of a past self. To write a public autobiography one must have a public life of general intellectual concern, and a rich public scene in which to lose the self. It is not difficult to compose such memoirs if one stands in the shadow of a Mao or a de Gaulle and is engulfed by great causes. In the absence of great men and enormous upheavals, however, the recreation of a public self is impossible. This is not the least of the lessons taught by *The Education of Henry Adams*.

The writer who looks upon himself as a public actor is generally quite overtly hostile to the egoism of those who choose to present their deepest feelings and most intimate relationships to public scrutiny. When measured by a purely public and especially political standard, such revelations count for no more than the most petty trivialities of daily life. He is also remote from the confessing self, which looks for expiation through the exposure of its sins and crimes. Confessions are at least partially didactic in intent and are therefore rather less private than autobiographies of pure self-remembrance. However,

Reprinted with permission of *Daedalus,* Journal of the American Academy of Arts and Sciences, from the issue entitled, "Twentieth-Century Classics Revisited," Winter 1974, vol. 103, no. 1.

they also depend for their interest entirely on the genius and intelligence of the author.[1]

Henry Adams certainly set out to write a public autobiography, a book as different from Rousseau's *Confessions* as possible. However, his only public experience was his "education," his effort to find and grasp a significant public place in post–Civil War America. Education is inevitably personal, since it involves not only the teaching world, but also a learning individual. Adams, despite all his contempt for egotism, was driven to write a thoroughly self-centered book. Among other things, it was in fact a confession. And he had much to confess. He was a failure: he had, at least in his own eyes, committed the worst of American sins. Not only had he failed to meet the standards of public eminence set by his ancestors, but he had not achieved his own intellectual ends either. To be sure he set himself astronomical goals. With these in mind, he was able to concentrate all his immense Puritan energies on his own worthlessness. The result is a matchless contribution to the literature of pure sadness. For there was, in his world, no redemption, no posterity, and no God to forgive or condemn him. There was nothing but regret.

Henry Adams understood all this perfectly. As a boy he too "should have been like his grandfather, a protégé of George Washington, a statesman designated by destiny, with nothing to do but look directly ahead, follow orders, and march." Instead he was an exile from politics, not only because he was not anchored to a great man or a noble cause, but because he was a born spectator. His character was his real fate. Probably no child born in 1838 "held better cards than he," but he never played the game at all; "he lost himself in study of it." The one path that never occurred to him when he graduated from Harvard was "going West and growing with the country." If he had no preparation for such an adventure, neither had anyone else, but he lacked in addition, daring and imagination. Unlike some of his classmates he did not have to think about making a name for himself. His social position was so good it could not be improved, but it made him afraid of risks. "He took to the pen. He wrote." In short, he was inescapably intellectual—aloof and critical. Education, certain knowledge, was what he really needed, and his quest for it proved interminable. For a man with his forebears such a situation had its ironies. They had certainly been learned men, scholar-statesmen, as well as active politicians, yet, as he looked back upon them with a historian's eyes, he saw that he knew far more than they could ever have guessed. But what was the use of all his accumulated wisdom if it only made him futile, baffled, and passive?

Irony hovers over every page of *The Education*. It begins with the declared purpose of showing young men what sort of education might be useful to them, at least what sorts of "tools" they ought to be given for dealing with the future. However, it is at once clear that no example, certainly not Adams', can be of any value. Youth does not need models, and he is certainly a warning at best, since he was never fit for life. That is why he begins by referring to himself disparagingly as a mere "manikin." He goes on, however, to reveal an even greater irony. His final discovery was that not only his education but all education was pointless, whether it was his own obsolete eighteenth-century one or an up-to-date version. No one could be shown how to cope with an inscrutable, ever-changing world. He did not find a science that could predict the social future accurately and without that no one could really be taught how to adapt. The very idea of an education that prepared young people for success was a delusion. That is his ultimate message and he begins by hinting at it.

Self-deprecation and irony were not Henry Adams' sole purposes in writing this book. He also had a quite independent, perhaps never fully admitted, aesthetic design. Memory is capable not only of every mood, but also of creativity. Adams had an immensely constructive memory. He was not really interested in accurate recollection at all. If he had seriously intended to help train young men, he would, of course, have had to make every effort to reveal the exact chain of causes and effects by which he had been educated. In fact, however, his promise of a manual is an ironic joke. What signifies here is not the past as such, but its remembrance as a free activity of the present imagination. The actual journey, he wrote of his first boyhood trip to Washington, was probably quite different from the one he remembered, but "only the memory matters." The memory had to have a meaning; the old man had to add a great deal to the original, often vividly recalled experiences of the boy. Each recollection has a double bearing: a primary sensation and a transforming reflection. The book as a whole is constructed to achieve this effect. Its first half takes us up to the end of youth; the second deals with the speculations of the prematurely old man twenty years later. The old Adams, the creator of the young one, is present on every page from the beginning, until he finally appears openly in his own person, the man he has become and now judges. By juxtaposing the two selves, the remembered youth and the remembering old man, the evoked memories and the cumulative reflections, Adams was able to sustain the mood of sadness without a break. No reader can escape the atmosphere of disappointment and sorrow. It is utterly depressing.

Even if Adams had been a cheerful soul, his would have been painful memories. The Civil War was at the core of his young manhood, the point toward and from which everything led. He did not see it as a tragedy. He, who often claimed that his countrymen lacked a sense of the tragic, was in this respect, as in all else, distinctly American. Three presidential assassinations, Adams noticed, could not raise the specter of the Eumenides before eyes that looked upon death as a neurosis. But one may well ask whether those assassinations really were tragic. Only Lincoln's was part of a tragic drama. To Adams, however, the Civil War was the result partly of ignorance, partly of treason. As he saw it, some Southerners plotted rebellion, but most of America's political leaders were simply too incompetent to avert a war that no one wanted. As for the issues at stake, in his simple Puritan vision, they were simply right against wrong: slavery was an evil and the sole purpose of life was to fight evil. It never occurred to Adams that slavery was more than a wrong to be undone once and for all, that it was an ineradicable curse that would not be ended in a battle but would haunt future generations and poison the body politic. That is why, for the most part, the aftermath of the carnage seemed puzzling to him. The Civil War appeared as an inexplicable, accidental destruction of the old America into which he had been born. He spoke of that former world, especially of New England, as Cromwellian in spirit and Ciceronian in politics. Who during Grant's administration could still believe that there would be a new Jerusalem and a new Roman Republic in America's green and pleasant land? Who has believed it since? For Adams the memory of what America had been, in hope, if not in actuality, gave the Civil War its ambiguity and sadness. He saw it as a just war that had unfortunate, but not really tragic, results.

The Civil War left Henry Adams with an overwhelming sense of historical paradox which colored all the memories of his youth. The dirty disordered roads of the South with the horror of slavery everywhere terrified the twelve-year-old boy on his first visit to Washington. He only wanted to run away from it, but the Senate and Mount Vernon impressed the boy. The old man added a reflective memory: the evil of slavery somehow led to Mount Vernon, the symbol of American virtue, and the two were apparently inextricably tied together.

Long before the story of the war begins, it is already present. The old man's memory rearranges time and feelings to reveal that the war that abolished slavery also destroyed the America for which Mount Vernon stood. Complexity of this order is a sort of lament. Again, as a schoolboy, Henry had found the big snowball fights on Boston Common exhilarating; old Adams could still remember the names of the bravest of his school fellows. Was it there, he wondered, that they had learned how to die in battle? Young Henry did not learn much at Harvard, but he was evidently very popular and enjoyed his years there. Old Adams saw what a disaster that self-satisfaction had been. It meant that Harvard only confirmed the quiet, well-bred sons of New England in a docility which would soon sweep them all into war. The Southerners, like Robert E. Lee's son Rooney, were not civilized at Harvard. They were animals when they arrived and they were still animals when they graduated and returned to the South. Harvard changed no one. It failed to create a new American elite or to teach the old one how to survive. That is why, in memory, old Adams came to hate old schools, especially his own. They had failed to educate his generation in the art of survival. The pleasures of his actual years at Harvard were covered by the memory of the war. So was his account of his first trip to Rome, which he, like all young people of "either sex and every race—passionately, perversely, wickedly loved." But the old historian recalled also how often he sat on the steps of the Church of Santa Maria di Ara Coeli where Gibbon had first thought of writing about the decline and fall of Rome. He too asked the eternal question: Why? "Substitute the word America for Rome and the question became personal."

When the war finally broke out Henry Adams went to London to help his father, who was Lincoln's Minister to England. What met him there was the undeviating hostility of the government and ruling classes to the North and general sympathy for the South. Dealing with Her Majesty's Government turned out to be extremely difficult, but Minister Adams and his son thought that they came to understand the motives and policies of its individual members. Old Henry Adams could recall every move and countermove in the diplomatic duel, but he saw that all his certainties had been fantasies when he read the published papers of his erstwhile opponents. The Adamses had both been wrong about almost everyone. Even the diplomacy of the Civil War turned out, in retrospect, to have been paradoxical, a series of misunderstandings. Indeed, the ambiguity of the war had been brought home to him long before these historical revelations. When he returned to America after seven years in England he found, as did those of his contemporaries who had spent those years in the Army, that he had no place in his own country. No one could settle down or find a career. In Adams' case the resulting uneasiness was aggravated by the realization that his unfitness was due not only to the social and political transformation of America, but to his own temperament. Nevertheless, his most striking memory is that of returning to the world of Grant's administration, of Jay Gould, of railroads and expansion everywhere. Adams' reaction was one of helpless revulsion. Yet, even as he ranted and raged against the social outcome of the war, he hastened to add that he was not fit to set it right.

Post-war America was not the first glimpse that Adams had of this new order of capitalism and industrial development. Years before the war he had seen the Black District of the Midlands and reacted to it as he had to his first sight of slavery, with fear and dismay. He ran away. Old Adams, however, remembered the man who had stayed to look, and whose doctrines troubled all his later years. The boy did not know it, but Karl Marx "was standing there waiting for him." After the war, when he was confronted by the Industrial Revolution at home, he should, by rights, have been a Marxist, "but some narrow trait of New England nature seemed to blight socialism, and he tried in vain to make himself a convert." It is not at all clear what it was in the New England mind that Adams was thinking of. Surely New England has produced more than its share of radicals, and many a socialist among them. It is not difficult, however, to discover what it was in Henry Adams that inhibited him from taking such a step. He simply feared and hated the men and women whose physical labor was building industrial America. As a boy he had been afraid of the rough youngsters from the other side of Boston Common. Now he looked upon that extreme example of the European immigrant—"the Polish Jew fresh from Warsaw or Cracow . . . reeking of the Ghetto, snarling a weird Yiddish"—and felt defeated. The sheer energy of these repellent creatures made them far more fit for the new America than he was as an "American of Americans with Heaven knows how many Puritans and Patriots behind him and an education that cost a civil war." That education and that war had rendered him as obsolete as the Indian and the buffalo "who had been ejected from their heritage" by his ancestors. The old man saw the paradox even in his own, to him wholly unfair, situation.

To a man with such predispositions, socialism was clearly an impossible ideology, however right Marx may have been about capitalism and the economic interpretation of history. But a hatred of capitalism need not lead to socialism; it can take other political directions. Adams did not follow any of them; he simply withdrew from politics. That had been implicit all along. He was morally too fastidious and regarded the prospect of "Machiavelli translated to America" as something to be generally avoided as part of the wicked Old World. Even the normal course of party politics was too much for him. His father and his Free Soil friends did not disdain the managerial talent of Thurloe Weed. Even Henry Adams came to like him personally, although he continued to find the lessons he taught indigestible. If these were the laws of party politics Adams wanted none of it. He had "hitched his star" to the cause of reform, but he was not willing to do anything to bring it about. A job in the State Department would have suited him very well, but no one offered him one, and he consoled himself, in a fashion, by reflecting that nothing could be done in Grant's administration by anyone anyway. It all proved that the moral system and the political order of 1789 were dead and past salvation. The Constitution was no longer adequate, any more than other remnants of the eighteenth century, including himself. We are not told what changes and reforms he contemplated. The truth is that he was too skeptical and too uncompromising for any kind of political action. Even a late fling at "Silver" was only an exercise in eighteenth-century nostalgia. When he spoke of himself as an anarchist, he meant merely that he was dissociated.

The final chapter of old Adams' memories of his youth has the simple title "Failure." It tells of his leaving Washington, all his political hopes expired, to become a professor of medieval history at Harvard. This flight to the academy was no disgrace; he called it "the only honorable service" possible in America. Why then was it failure? It was a failure partly because he did not believe in academic education, and partly because he came to see his experiences at Harvard as foreshadowing all the sadness he was to feel as an old man. It was a matter both of political disappointment, and of intellectual despair. Henry Adams was clearly an excellent teacher and he knew that his students often worked hard. To be sure, medieval history was not his field, but he mastered it. Like most good teachers, he was tormented by worry about his impact upon his students. Was he doing them any good? He feared that he was useless to them. Moreover, he found faculty life a bore. After seven years he had had enough and left the university. The no longer youthful Adams now had to face himself. He was an intellectual, not a statesman; he had no social role and was not at all confident that his vocation had any value. He who needed an education could not bring himself to sell one to others. A man so flawed could not be a teacher. He had failed in his one attempt at a career, and could not find any merit in his true calling: to be the historian of his country.

What would success be like? Old Henry Adams was not at all sure that he knew. It required social position and polish, as well as wealth. One without the others would not suffice. He himself clearly craved something more: political power gained on his own terms. He was caught in that recurrent crisis of aristocratization that marked his own generation and is endemic in periods of economic expansion in America. Essentially, this is a crisis of people who have gained everything America has to offer, who continue to feel a deep native drive to achieve ever more, but who cannot find anything at home still worthy of the effort. Some feel that, as members of distinguished and wealthy families, they should be treated with automatic deference. Such feelings combined with social ambition led the wives of new millionaires to marry off their daughters quite brutally to the redundant members of the European aristocracy. Others went to live in England and France where the wealthy could enjoy a more leisurely, stylish, and effortless sort of life. Some men, unwilling to continue in the businesses or professions of their fathers, but not ready to leave America, looked to politics as a new arena. Especially when America became a world power, at the end of the century, foreign affairs here became, as it always had been in Europe, an occupation fit for gentlemen. And some, like Henry Adams, felt victimized by their position and became either very reactionary or very radical or both by turns.

Henry Adams was completely aware of these tendencies in himself and among his contemporaries, and he was far too reflective and intelligent to lapse into any of the more common forms of social pretentiousness. Lothrop Motley, who succeeded Henry Adams' father in London, thought the English country house "the height of civilization," but Adams knew it to be a silly bore. He was utterly contemptuous of those Bostonians who "knelt in self-abasement before the majesty of English standards," or who, like Charles Sumner, boasted of their friendships among English earls and dukes. Adams' father, much to his credit, had no trace of snobbery and no sense of social distinctions at all. He thought that Europe corrupted young Americans and looked upon the English as the perpetual enemies of America and his family. The son admired the father and agreed. He saw the French as immoral and superficial, and the English as stupid, coarse, and eccentric. The central experience of his youth was the uniform hostility of the British upper classes to the cause of the Union. He never forgot it, and all his old feelings of outrage rose in him again during the Boer War. The only Englishmen who had supported the Northern side were Cobden and Bright and he continued to admire the latter for his tireless hatred of sham in all its guises. Henry Adams was proud of his family and he did not wish to cease being an American. He understood England too well, in any case, to suffer from the illusion that an American expatriate might become a genuine part of English society. Adams had many friends in England and loved London, but he was too smart to become a pseudo-Englishman. A literary genius like his friend Henry James is always in and out of any society and must suit his residence to the demands of his art. A historian is in a different situation and Adams made his mark as an American historian. Nevertheless, for all his pride in his ancestors, he had aristocratic aspirations that were foreign to them. He also wanted to be a statesman, but not a democratic one. His father had not been too proud to be a Congressman and his grandfather, a veritable Cincinnatus, had returned modestly to the House of Representatives after having been President. Henry Adams never thought of such a career. If he had been offered the opportunity, he would have entered the State Department at the top in order to frustrate, as best he could, the provincial, petty designs of the subhumans who now populated the Senate. Ill luck and personal deficiencies combined to thwart this idea of success. Unhappily, Adams took to sour grapes. As he watched the rise of his closest friend, John Hay, to the pinnacle of public eminence, it became impossible to blame his age or his countrymen for his failures. He declared that he was really most useful to his country as a private citizen and fulminated more and more against the dreadful corruptions of political power as such. Office, he said, ruined character and destroyed all friendships.

The embittering experience of always missing office was not the only source of Adams' discontent. There was intellectual misery as well. Society offers historians only one social function: teaching. Adams could not accept it. He could afford just to write, which he did very well and enjoyed, even if he noted that Americans had no interest in the past and that he had no more than perhaps three adequate readers. At least he did not envy his English opposite numbers. He was aware that the Oxford graduate was in the same boat as the Harvard man. Indeed, unlike many American intellectuals, Adams realized that there was no lack of first-rate minds in America. He knew who Willard Gibbs was and recognized the quality of his achievement. His self-doubt went deeper. The old Puritan wanted to be useful, and he did not think history a useful vocation. It did not yield certain knowledge, nor did it help one to predict the future. Since his days at Harvard, he had, like many another literary man, suffered at the sight of the economist, the physicist, and the chemist, who knew exactly what they were doing and why they did it. The Chicago Exhibition of 1893 was the final shock. Utterly shaken, Henry Adams tried to master mathematics and physics. The only outcome was his disastrous decision to fashion a science of history on these models. History was to reveal laws of social change. He had read his Comte, Spencer, and Buckle carefully, and knew that they had failed. That did not deter him. He took to using metaphors drawn from physics, and analogies to it, in writing history. *Mass, energy, motion, acceleration,* and words like these now dominated his vocabulary as he tried to show how European society had moved from the unity of the Middle Ages to the disintegration and diversity of the present. For in the end Henry Adams had to return to Europe, spiritually at least. That, after all, is where America began and the attempt to understand its present degradation led him back to the age of the cathedrals. But in spite of all his efforts to do so, he could not believe in Christianity, and theology was beyond him. His twin symbols, the Virgin and the dynamo, tell us more about his psyche than about medieval Europe. No unifying vision emerged and in spite of the words he borrowed from Newton, history remained incoherent. Finally Henry Adams realized that the sciences did not even offer a road to cosmic order and unity. He found some satisfaction in the thought that at least confusion reigned everywhere, not only in the minds of American historians.

These multiple failures, political and intellectual, turned old Henry Adams, in his own words, into "a crank" and "a tiresome superannuated pedagogue." He also became commonplace as he "drifted in the dead-water of the *fin-de-siècle.*" When the age discovered sex, race, and religion, so did Henry Adams, both as a historian and as an ill-tempered bigot. Without a real calling, intellectual or religious, this last Puritan withered amid the roaring energies of his age and country.

He had failed to govern, or even to know America, and he had spent a lifetime observing himself fail. He knew as clearly as anyone that he should have ended his life a better and happier man. Unlike him, however, we can see that his *Education* was not a failure, that his confession redeemed his life, and that, in spite of his irony, he has taught his readers much.

Notes

1. The writer may choose to instruct or to entertain, but his success in either enterprise depends on the personality he presents. The private character revealed in a public autobiography matters a great deal less.

CHAPTER SEVEN

Redeeming American Political Theory

As is evident, I am in some ways an unusual president of this association; and I feel my responsibilities tonight particularly deeply, both as a woman and as a political theorist.

What I plan to do in this talk is therefore quite ambitious, namely, redeem American political theory, in order to bring out both its intrinsic intellectual importance and its significance for American political science. Far from being demeaning and scientifically superfluous, I would like to show that we have much to gain from seeing our present work as a continuation of the history of political thought in America. Such an outlook would serve to integrate political theory into political science, where it belongs; and it would also offer mainstream political science the self-understanding that only a historically grounded analysis can give it.

Such an effort is necessary, I believe, because American political theory has long been neglected. It has been charged with an obsessive and unconscious commitment to a liberal faith that prevents it from asking profound and critical questions. Incapable of envisaging alternatives, American political thought is said to be mired in the legacy of John Locke and a mindless optimism. The fact that there have always been many lively controversies, moreover, does nothing to dispel this bland uniformity, because all parties are at some level said to be liberal. In any event our petty intellectual squabbles are mere shadow-boxing compared to the *real thing*, the kind of ideological combat that feudalism and class war generated in Europe.

Reprinted from the *American Political Science Review* 85, no. 1 (March, 1991).

I do not think that American political thought is a compulsive repetition of the same theme. Nor did it suffer a single fall from grace, as some now claim, when it abandoned a premodern republicanism in favor of an amoral, atomized individualism. Nor, finally, need we continue that endless Jeremiad about the absence of socialism and conservatism. I believe that when we take a good look at our actual tradition of political theory, we will find something better than a drab and cheerless heritage, a poor thing, but our own.

On close examination American political theory is not, in fact, just our own; for it has not been hermetically sealed off from European thought. Isolating it in order to illuminate its peculiarities is bound to reduce it to charmless uniformity. We do have special political traits; but from Locke to Social Darwinism, from the negative to the positive state, from Montesquieu to the Chicago School of political sociology, the controversies and the agreements have been shared, even if not shared identically by both sides of the big puddle. One should not overlook the local circumstances that give a special color to American political ideas, but there is no reason at all to treat them either in quarantine or contemptuously.

At least four obvious political phenomena have contributed to distinguishing American political thought from its cultural neighbors: the early and painless acceptance of white adult male suffrage, federalism, judicial review, and most deeply, the prevalence of chattel slavery long after it had disappeared in the rest of the European world. Not racism—which is universal—but *slavery* in a modern constitutional state is truly unique. Until the Civil War amendments America was neither a liberal nor a democratic country, whatever its citizens might have believed. Yet it did have in place a set of institutions that were capable of becoming so and to an unequaled degree. This country had embarked upon two experiments simultaneously: one in democracy, the other in tyranny. This list of the characteristics of our political development is hardly complete (I would add our unique university establishments), but it does point to features that have set American political institutions apart and have had a decisive impact upon its most reflective citizens.

Of all aspects of this political culture none might seem more peculiarly local than political science, in all its many manifestations and eclecticism. To be sure, political science is only one of the modern social sciences; but it is the one that has flourished most in America, where it has also lately become notably democratic. At the deepest level all the social sciences are part of a process of intellectual democratization. For only recently (in the last two centuries) has either the inclination or the political need to think seriously about the lives of ordinary people as intrinsically significant emerged at all. The history, remote or contemporary, of great men and dramatic events has only very lately made a place for people who are absent from the annals of monumental history. These lives can never be more than statistics; but they have come to matter, partly because social scientists became convinced that they were important in and of themselves and partly because the many began to assert themselves as urban citizens, as voters, as strikers, and as members of increasingly diverse and lay-oriented religious denominations.

All the social sciences are submerged biographies of the silent majority of humanity: the peasant, the artisan, the immigrant, the slave, women, and (in our case) that basic irreducible unit of representative politics, the voter. All of them, even as mere numbers, have surfaced in the human sciences as part of a long and slow democratization of values in a period whose ideologies were often in every degree hostile to these aspirations. This is the historical context that makes the fact-mindedness of the social sciences different from that of those ancient bureaucratic regimes that also liked to keep minute records about their subjects. At their purest, the social sciences are knowledge for its own sake about everyone, because everyone is interesting as a social being.

We should not be surprised that this expansiveness has not been a continuous movement in either America or Europe. It would also be far too facile to attribute either the ups or the downs of scientific concern only to ideological commitments. Some of the finest social scientists from Alexander Hamilton to Vilfredo Pareto have been utterly opposed to democracy. Others have been ardently democratic. The democratization of values that is implicit in the social sciences in general is entirely compatible with a great variety of political beliefs and theories, including some of the most destructive and cruel. Nevertheless, I do want to argue that within a welter of diverse ideas the social sciences are fundamentally inclusive in their orientation and that given the institutions of American government, a democratic political science was eventually to be expected. It need hardly be mentioned that this trend was in no way incompatible with a rich tradition of flailing every aspect of America's political culture.

I see no homogeneity and no straight line in our history at all; but

I do think that our end was in our beginning, and that those who originally framed our institutions can be seen in retrospect to have given us, in embryonic form, the elements of a science that would best correspond to our political institutions and the social circumstances within which they arose. The works of Jefferson, Madison, and Hamilton display the intellectual germs of several kinds of political science, all responding integrally to the government that they created and understood.

The authors of the *Federalist Papers* and Jefferson belonged to a fact-minded and science-oriented cosmopolitan culture. In the brief experience of democracy that the French enjoyed after the Revolution, Jefferson's close friend, Condorcet, went well beyond anything that had been done in America by applying advanced mathematics to voting in legislative bodies. The older administrative science of the Colbertian tradition was Alexander Hamilton's acknowledged inspiration. And Madison admired Montesquieu as the master of the new science of politics.

There were, from the first, three political sciences in America. Jefferson's was speculative and physiological. Madison's was institutional and historical, and Hamilton's was empirical and behavioral. None was perfect, all were prophetic. Let me begin with Jefferson's occasional writings. He had an undeniably scientific mind in the sense that he had fully absorbed the advances in the natural sciences of his age and that he took a scientist's interest in the physical characteristics of the New World and its inhabitants, especially in order to refute Buffon's slanders upon our flora and fauna. He also accepted Locke's cognitive psychology, which encouraged the empirical study of humanity within its many social and natural environments. As an observer of the human species, he examined his objects exactly as a naturalist would study the beasts and vegetation of an area. The extent to which this set him apart from them is worth noting because Jefferson, who was ideologically by far the most democratic of our intellectual ancestors, was enormously elitist as a scientist and educator. I stress the point and its implications in order to insist that ideology does not determine scientific work nearly as simply or as completely as has been assumed.

Jefferson was sure that our beliefs and preferences were not a matter of choice but that each one of us had been quite differently endowed by nature. We are also the creatures of our environment, which impinges upon us as we try to form a cognitive picture of our experiences. It follows that any effort to impose a single belief system upon us was as futile as it was psychologically unscientific. What we needed was an education to protect us against false associations of ideas imposed upon us by superstitions, traditions, and other errors. Free government was to be sustained by public education from compulsory primary school to the university. An educated meritocracy, open to all talented citizens, was to prevail, as natural aristocrats were annually "raked from the rubbish" to become the political and scientific leaders of Virginia. Public education was not a random public good for Jefferson; it was based on a scientific theory of learning with obvious political implications. If more democracy was the cure for political ills (as he certainly believed), it was because all governments were to be distrusted. The prosperity of the new nation could not be left to governments, but would depend on the educational system.

These attitudes point to an extraordinary faith in the social and practical value of learning. Schools may, of course, also become constricting institutions—a point that Condorcet understood better than Jefferson, who had no interest in the study of how educational institutions function both to enhance and restrict freedom. He was simply sure that the arts and sciences would underpin liberal democracy.

There were other implications in this anthropology. If Jefferson looked at his fellow citizens as educable subjects, the Native American was just part of the scenery. It was his great regret that "they had never been viewed by us as subjects of natural history." He was also sorry that their languages had not been recorded in time in the service of linguistics, a science in which he was deeply interested. It comes as no surprise, then, that in his dealings with the Native American population he was in some respects even less just than with his slaves. At least he acknowledged guilt and shame in the latter case. The Indians were told to behave like the Anglo-Americans; and if they could not do so, they must expect to be exploited. He consistently treated them as children and openly boasted of his intention to bribe them into submission.

The truth of the matter is that it is not social science as such but the kind of inquiries we choose that are often questionable. Jefferson wanted to assimilate social science to natural history. Current psychology permitted him to believe in progress through education for his own kind and to treat the native populations as subjects of physiological speculation and manipulation. Having remained, as it were, natural rather than political beings, they were to be scrutinized and classified, as if they had no rights. This had nothing to do with Jefferson's consistently democratic ideology; he certainly trusted those yeomen, but we should recall that most of the ethical objections to the sciences of man have been rooted in the perception that no human beings should be treated like laboratory animals.

What of Jefferson's friend and loyal associate, James Madison? No man was ever more conscious of public unsteadiness, of change and mutability. He had a historian's mind, which was a great intellectual advantage. It enabled him to penetrate to the logic of collective action even when on the surface there seemed to be nothing but random irrationality and partisan wrangling. By reflecting upon previous occurrences and experiences he was always able to see a pattern amid the confusion of men and events. Consider his papers on representation and the likely conduct of legislators under various rules. Too large an assembly puts Michel's law of oligarchy into effect. The group that sets the agenda is bound to dominate the whole. How long should terms of office last? Long enough for the representatives to learn their jobs, not so long as to make them forget the voters and the fact that they would soon be private citizens again, obliged to live under the laws they had passed. Here, too, size and the interactions of parties and factions are considered. Or take his response to Jefferson's suggestion that the Constitution be rewritten every twenty years to allow every generation to decide its own fate. Against this daft proposal, Madison offered two arguments, one psychological, the second prudential. First, there is a need for habit and emotional attachment to institutions if they are to function. Second, deinstitutionalization creates intolerable economic and political instability. No credit will be extended to such a country and there is no guarantee that some future generation might not be swayed to abolish republican government and ruin the system permanently.

Madison devised a profound theory of political rationality that recognized that individuals must be expected to bring limited and self-directed policies to the public arena but that in a constitutional system not only do they become collectively more rational as a whole people, but they also learn to appreciate the necessity of limiting their interests in response to the rights of others (as well as the best possible outcome for the country as a whole). The critics of procedural republicanism have often misread Madison and the institutions he championed. The individual political agent learns to adapt and is forced to become more public-spirited as he accepts and follows the procedures that institutions compel him to follow.

When the question of universal white adult male suffrage came up in Virginia, he cut right through the rhetoric of both parties. If the majority of landless citizens were disenfranchised, they would have every reason to rise up against the freeholders, he warned. In a republic the inequality of property depends upon the consent of the majority. That is its only security. Here was a deeply functional view of democracy, which held that even some political rights might be institutionally validated. Thus, Madison did not expect the freedom of the press or "the right to aminadversion" to promote truth or learning. Nevertheless, they were the only way to keep the citizens informed about what the government was doing; and republican government depended on an electorate that could check up on its representatives.

Madison was intellectually not only remote from Jefferson, he was also very unlike his one-time coauthor, Hamilton. I must confess to an intense admiration for Alexander Hamilton as a political scientist but also because he proves how shallow ideological analysis can be. Hamilton was not a democratic or even a liberal politician, but he was quite capable of giving a sophisticated and unbiased account of how electoral politics worked in New York and subordinating his immediate political concerns to his scientific ambitions. His friend Chancellor Kent said of him that he had contemplated "a full investigation of the history and science of civil government . . . and to have the subject treated in reference to past experience upon Lord Bacon's inductive philosophy." And it is with this in mind that all of us here can share Hamilton's distress when he wrote to Robert Morris in 1782 about New York's balance of trade, "These calculations cannot absolutely be relied on because the data are necessarily uncertain, but they are the result of the best information I can obtain." Here is a fact-minded thinker who fully knows the difference between basing one's policies on always-incomplete information and lusting after certainty.

To understand republican government—which Hamilton accepted as necessarily based on the consent of the majority—he looked to its irreducible unit, the individual voter. The first thing that impressed him was "the alarming indifference discoverable in the exercise of so valuable a privilege as voting." When the citizens do exert themselves, however, they behave quite rationally. Mechanics and manufacturers will always be inclined, with a few exceptions, to give their votes to a merchant in preference to a person of their own profession because they see a friend and patron in him (since he trades in their products) and so are quite ready to trust him to promote their interests. They vote not identity but agency, in short. Hamilton also thought that the electoral chances of "the learned professions"—by which I think he meant lawyers—were good by virtue of their education and presumed impartiality. Voters certainly do want candidates "to understand their feelings and interests," Hamilton noted; but they also want reliable brokers to bring diverse preferences together, which calls for the skills of the lawyer.

Hamilton's greatest contribution to a disaggregating science of political economy was surely his *Report on Manufactures,* in which he displays as much of an interest in individual producers and the incentives to which they might respond, as his political reflections centered on voters. This inclination may well have been fueled by his frantic efforts to make America a strong and active state. Such a structure would demonstrate (even as the frail and miserable Constitution of 1787, which he despised, might fail to demonstrate) that good government can be established by societies of men "from reflection and choice" rather than being driven by "accident and force." The modern state that he envisaged depended on information as no older regime had to, because it must regulate, indirectly, not only a single, unified military, administrative, and productive system but a system based on the rule of law and the consent of its citizens. Its government needed to know exactly not only what should be done but what its citizens would agree to do, individually and collectively.

Starved for sovereignty, Hamilton put his hopes into the Supreme Court; but it was not what he had really wanted. What he got was a far from centralized or coherent state, but it did require information just as much as his administrative model. Representative democracy also needs information. Hence, the Constitution mandates a national census every ten years, and there is a built-in interest among elective officials in the actual interests and beliefs of the voters. Constitutional democracy is inherently a fact hungry political system, in which both those who govern and those who are governed yearn for solid information.

So far, I have tried to show only how diverse and complex American political theory has been from its very origins. Not all periods in our history have been as creative as the Enlightenment. We have in our bitter century learned again to appreciate their ideals of freedom, human rights, and justice. The founders have left us not only several ways of trying to make sense of American politics but also an enduring public ethos.

In one important respect all three also illustrate the limits of political science. Not one could even suggest a plausible solution to America's greatest single failure, black chattel slavery. History, institutional analysis, and economic calculation were all equally useless. For all their confidence in political knowledge and in their own ability to determine the fate of a nation, they were unable to imagine a multiracial citizenry. No one saw the likelihood of a sectional conflict more clearly than Madison did, yet no one temporized more disastrously than he did when he came up with the federal ratio. The narrowness of the politics of rational compromise confront us starkly (as do those of merely accurate knowledge) when we recall the drift to the Civil War.

Nevertheless, for the study of democratization few eras in American history are more revealing than the first four decades of the last century. This is not only because of the enduring political changes that emerged at that time but also because the vocabulary of American political controversy was transformed. President Jackson's use of the language of his most radical supporters in the course of his war against the Bank of the United States really justifies the phrase "Jacksonian democracy." This new political style was forged in the state constitutional conventions called to establish white adult male suffrage as a right and not as a limited privilege. No less significant was a new and radically democratic journalism that stressed the dignity of work, equal rights, and free public education not as a means to create a natural aristocracy but as the ground upon which equality of opportunity and self-respect would be built. If economic inequality appeared natural to these democrats, political inequality was excoriated. From the first, fairness was the very essence of their notion of justice. And *rights* was a word that appeared in every democratic sentence. For they were threatened by "aristocrats"—citizens who used wealth to acquire an unfair share of political influence and corrupted the laws. They were the tarnished remnants of Europe and a cultural and a political menace. The European past should be forgotten.

The sense of political isolation from Europe was not felt as a deprivation, but it did raise enduring and perhaps insoluble questions about the proper education for a democratic people. History is not a useful subject. It was all about undemocratic practices and ideologies, and it stuffed young minds with inappropriate fantasies. The sciences, natural and social, were safer. They were also more edifying, reminding the young of the contribution that the inventions of artisans had made to civilization. Madison's plea for reverence as a politically positive state of mind had no appeal for these democrats, but they longed for a usable past of their own. The study of the unsung many is as much a demand for recognition by the democratized public as it is an object of interest to scientific observers. Unhappily, both were so self-absorbed that they simply ignored what did not touch them immediately. Fearing and hating both slavery and the slave, they looked the other way until they were forced to consider both.

The democrats' ferocious attack on aristocracy could, however, not go unchallenged. One response was to rewrite American history relegating the Revolution to the background and stressing the disciplined Puritans as the fathers of America's free, but hardly egalitarian, political institutions. Literary Whigs, such as Rufus Choate of Massachusetts, offered a disgruntled upper class just such a reading of the past. Tocqueville was one among several visitors who were disturbed by this commercial aristocracy, who disdained the free institutions of their country. These commentators received a perceptive answer from Frederick Grimké, who, in his remarkably dispassionate study of American government, *The Nature and Tendency of Free Institutions*, noted that these elites had no hereditary caste features and no distinct military ethos.

It was also among Whig opponents of democracy that one can discern the beginnings of a political sociology with a special interest in the functions of elites. Choate quite agreed with Tocqueville that the bench and bar had an extraordinary position in the United States. He saw them as bringing tradition, continuity, and stability to the political system. They tied the generations together. Not legislation, but the accretion of judicial precedents must determine the rules; and they develop inarticulately as a slow process, comprehensible only to a few. The law is a single moral unit; but significantly, it did not, for Choate, exist in a social vacuum. It was the creation of a special group that operated within a political system and was meant to impose itself upon wayward majorities and elected governments. Fortified by this view of the primacy of law as an unchanging inheritance and by the constitutional jurisprudence of Kent and Storey, the operative ideology of the courts became that they were meant to protect every form of property by building an infrangible wall against the threat of democratic legislation.

These conservative thinkers, with their sense of society as a fragile structure, were not opposed to slavery. It was part of the historical inheritance. Nevertheless, political sociology could also serve the few abolitionists who were not moved by religion. Richard Hildreth's truly remarkable book, *Despotism in America,* was, as its title indicates, partly an answer to Tocqueville but also a close analysis of the entire plantation system of the South. Hildreth was no Jacksonian democrat. He defended democracy as the most stable of political systems and the one most likely to promote economic prosperity. All his work on comparative government and on slavery was deeply indebted to Montesquieu's *Spirit of the Laws,* both in the analysis of equilibrium and disorder in various forms of government and of despotism as a distinct political system. That is what he saw in the South, where fear was the active principle of rule and where the ruling class possessed no discernible political virtue or will to improve. They were not Tocqueville's decadent aristocrats but despots on their plantations, and democracy could not compromise with them. Also like his master, Montesquieu, he saw much that was vital, as well as much that was crushed, in the lives of the enslaved. Finally, Hildreth tried to demonstrate that the bench and bar could use their authority and the existing law to abolish slavery in the United States. Mercifully, he died some years before the Civil War.

One cannot think of Emerson as either a Jacksonian democrat or an aristocratic Whig. No label could do him justice. He remains, after all, *the* American philosopher. And it was as such that he tried to grasp and represent the entire world in which he lived. He not only responded intensely to the stirrings around him, but he also tried to show his enormous public what they meant. The two warring parties were not really the few and the many, they were the party of memory and the party of hope; and America needed both. If Emerson found memory as hard to bear as his democratic neighbors, he also met the reformers with an irony that was truly devastating. They were not at all self-reliant, just self-centered and futile. Nevertheless, his "American Scholar" is all hope, a scientists' Declaration of Independence. It is not just a Jacksonian rejection of the European past but a passionate affirmation of the spirit of discovery. And his essay "Young America" is a hymn to the independent Yankee lad and to the democratic ethos of the age.

Emerson was, however, not only repelled by the frivolity of radical gestures; he was also haunted by memory, especially of the great men of the past. He might believe that we *should* say, "Damn George Washington" every morning; but he was not up to it. Instead, he remembered those who were truly great and tried to integrate them into a democratic faith. *Representative Men* was Emerson's answer to Carlyle's hero worship. The term *representative* was deliberately political. Great men could not be great unless they were able to move, and to be moved by, their public. Greatness was a transaction in which we all had a part. Aristocracy was tamed.

It was a way to encapsule the age in a vision of social interaction in which the normal and the rare could live with each other on democratic, if isolated, terms, bound by a direct, unmediated understanding. Thus, also, science and common sense had for Emerson an equal dignity, not because they yielded any certain knowledge but because both were acts of personal and public creativity. Scientific knowledge was not merely Baconian power but an adventure and a door to the new. Though he was utterly skeptical and solitary, Emerson's generous ambition was the same as Lincoln's: to sum up and renew the promise of pre–Civil War America. And they still remind us of it.

If Emerson and his New England disciples defined themselves in contrast to Europe, many Southerners came to think of themselves as a culture distinctly opposed to that of the North. It may well be that political sociology flourishes amid conflict. The defenders of the "peculiar institution," no less than the abolitionists, perceived that they were defending two different ways of life, not just two incompatible labor systems. The Civil War was not only a monumental bloodbath and the first modern war, it was also an ideological struggle that had raged for decades before the first shot was fired.

I wish I could do full justice to the intricacies of Southern political thought; but as I cannot, I will just point to its more lasting characteristics. One was an emphasis on the ethical primacy of society as an organism. The second was a celebration of its elite. And finally, there was the affirmation of personal authority as both inevitable and inherently good. In most cases these notions were couched in the language of social science. Baconian fact-mindedness was very much an overt feature of secular Southern political thought. Malthus and Comte were the accepted authorities. Demographic pessimism and the sociology of hierarchical integrity had an instant appeal. Jefferson's natural rights were abandoned, but not his scientific inclinations.

To any careful reader of pre–Civil War Southern political theory, it is perfectly obvious that this mixture of ideas constituted an indigenous authoritarian ideology that was as utterly unique as the slavery it encompassed. The secular defense of Southern society took three forms. Slavery might not be just in the abstract, it was conceded, but the idea of the right was not primary. Communal, shared values rooted in the very structure of society really defined the social good. Slavery was woven into the fabric of Southern life, which, as a whole, was well worth defending. It was a bastion of republican values. Generosity, civic duty, honor, a lively sense of the public good, and a martial spirit—all the essence of republican virtue—marked the planters, in contrast to their mercenary and rights-oriented Yankee opponents. Jefferson, who lamented the effects of slavery on the masters, had been wrong. Solidarity and public virtue were rooted in slavery and more than justified it.

Southern political science also supported this view. A good deal of it was exceptionally neologistic. The invention of new words to give readers the impression that they were absorbing an objective, nonevaluative, systematic treatise was a marked trait of its most Baconian writers. Henry Hughes's *Treatise on Sociology* is a particularly intelligent example of this style. Society was divided into *warrantors* and *warrantees* in the South. The warrantees had a peculiar ethnic character but were not slaves, since, as in all societies, the warrantors were limited by obligations and restraints. They had to provide safety and comfort, as well as public hygiene, already a matter of much social concern.

Third and last, there was the sociology of the ineffable George Fitzhugh's *Cannibals All*, which has received more attention now than it did when it was written. His argument was that free labor was pure exploitation, since the laborers lacked the paternal benefits enjoyed by slaves, who, as the planters' capital, were valuable assets. Even more interesting was his claim that this was indeed a despotic regime but that despotism was really a benign system, because it gave the weak a whole range of informal ways of asserting themselves within a society in which each one had a suitable niche. Given that all political regimes were exploitative, despotism was quite tolerable. So much for Montesquieu and Hildreth.

These political theories were heralds of things to come. In a way the South won the war of ideas. Northern social scientists certainly did not come to approve of slavery, but after the Civil War they adopted the sociological fatalism that had been so notable a mark of Southern thought. Moral pessimism was nothing new in America. It had its roots in Calvinism, and both John Adams and John Calhoun shared its overwhelming sense of human depravity. Ambition, avarice, violence, and guile marked the few no less than the many, and both feared for the fate of the republic. Yet in very different ways, both put their minds to devising governmental institutions that might withstand the inevitable onslaught of corruption. Adams looked to checks and balances, Calhoun to an intricate system of vetoes; but both took it for granted that institutions could and should stem the tide of political decay. The fatalism of the post–Civil War period was quite different. It was not moral but biologistic and was indifferent to political initiative, which seemed irrelevant in an overdetermined social world.

The intellectual tone of the veterans was often coarse and aggressive. One can find it in the letters of Justice Holmes to Sir Frederick Pollock no less than in the writings of William Graham Sumner. Facts are always hard and insuperable. They function as weapons against the "sentimental," the "humanitarian" and presumably feeble. The hopes that had rung in the essays and speeches of Frederick Douglass during the struggle for the Fifteenth Amendment were soon dispersed. Indeed, rights were said to be meaningless, except as acts of force. The end of Reconstruction, especially, had a deadening impact. Both Burgess and Dunning, the founders of academic political science, wrote books on it, applauding the nationalization of politics that Reconstruction had achieved and deeply deploring the effort to secure the rights of the freedmen. Their equality was impossible for Burgess because of racial reasons, for Dunning because blacks were socially backward and only military force could ever impose them on their former masters. Peace and justice required their exclusion from Southern politics. Sumner, to be sure, was no racist; but Reconstruction was his favorite example to illustrate the power of custom and the impotence of the state. Southern black and white mores were simply too different to be joined. A total separation of the two populations would thus quickly reestablish harmony. This, we might recall, was the social science written into *Plessy versus Ferguson* of unlamented memory.

The end of Reconstruction was only one inducement to sociological fatalism. A baffled inability to understand the world that followed the Civil War had the same effect. Social scientists felt overwhelmed by changes that reminded them of the forces of natural necessity. This sometimes served as an alibi for inaction; but it was also a pathway to a new science, one that would at last uncover the interactions of all the human elements that compose society and order them according to comprehensive laws. If only the underlying causes of change could be grasped, then certainty and even predictability might restore a measure of intellectual control. Southern sociological fatalism—now amply fortified by new race sciences, Social Darwinism, and classical economics—revealed regulative impersonal forces, which would explain the effect of new immigrants, urbanization, and the new technological industrialism. Every conceivable biological and geological theory was snapped up and ground to fit what passed for "hard" facts and to assuage the need for intellectual certainty.

With this in mind, one ought to read *The Education of Henry Adams* with some respect. He took the message of evolution and perpetual social change to its logical end. Given that nothing endured, education was simply impossible. Every lesson learned in youth was false and burdensome in one's mature years. The America he had left before the Civil War was gone forever and all its doctrines had been shown to be absurd. There was no point in trying to teach anyone anything, except perhaps history, since it was settled (though merely ornamental). In politics all was vanity.

But if Adams was the extreme that illuminates, William Graham Sumner and Lester Ward were the norm that defined an intellectual generation. They really put Spencer and social evolution on the intellectual map as they labored to give the social sciences the same prestige that the natural sciences enjoyed. At first Sumner had used the vocabulary of natural selection to justify the new captains of industry but also to hammer in such facts to prove that political action was futile. When he came to write *Folkways,* he had, however, given up biological analogies. It is in many ways a very remarkable book. Nothing endures, and nothing can be done. Even scientific knowledge is temporary. We are all the blind prisoners of the mores of our time and place. In America democracy is above being questioned, and evolution is the fad of the age. Sumner was the real inventor of the paradoxes of the sociology of knowledge. *Folkways* is both dogmatic and skeptical. We may know nothing, but he was sure that Hamilton had been wrong in believing that will, rather than fate and force, could determine the government of a people.

Ideologically, Sumner's most outspoken and admired critic was Lester Ward. The argument between them was by no means the only ideological conflict of this contentious period, but the scholars of the time regarded it as by far the most significant. Ward did not challenge Sumner's scientific assumptions. He only added Comte's taxonomies to them, which hardly made his system more flexible. His message was that evolution had made humanity capable of mastering nature and of transforming society through democratic governmental action, which meant not a return to ideas of rights and consent but universal education guided by social science. This would bring about a "sociocracy," in which an informed public and a powerful executive would soon prove that art could triumph over nature. Not that Ward offered any specific examples of how political invention or social technology would work. He was keen on statistics and on the diffusion of knowledge; but beyond that, the big picture was his real terrain. And while Sumner finally recognized that science was unstable, Ward never doubted that it was the rock upon which social engineers would stand. Yet for all their differences, they inhabited the same intellectual universe, in which society was a determined organic whole, subject to laws that social science would eventually fully grasp.

Even Thorstein Veblen shared many of these assumptions, but he does stand out as a conspicuous nay-sayer. His eyes were fixed on the enemies of progress, on the atavistic, nonproductive plutocracy of America that stood in the way of the productivity, the instinct of workmanship, and the egalitarian values that industrial society demanded and could evoke. Quite apart from the lasting interest of his assault on the betrayers of the work ethic, Veblen is a fine example of the diversity of American social theory. He was also an unclassifiable moralist. In this no one resembled him more than Charlotte Perkins Gilman, who argued that the domestication of women away from the productive process was out of step with the demands of a society geared to efficient production. Every line Gilman wrote shows an outraged sense of justice, but she could not resort to the liberal vocabulary that could best have expressed it. The notion of individuals as items in an evolutionary whole seemed no less necessary to her than to Veblen. These were certainly voices of protest, and they illustrate two things at least: that American intellectual life even in that rather dismal age was anything but uniform and that one cannot pin conventional ideological labels on them. And none of them—not Sumner any more than Veblen—felt at home in the muscle-flexing, imperialist, and megapolitical world of Theodore Roosevelt.

It was time for a generational change and for the emergence of reform-minded political movements, of which a new political science was to become a part. It was more modest in its intellectual ambitions and perfectly frank about its civic ideals. I refer specifically to the birth of the study of public administration and of municipal government, inspired by what Charles Merriam called "a saturnalia of political corruption," which mobilized political scientists. They took an empirical turn to the investigation of actual political conduct and institutional functions and considered what could be done to put them on a more honest path. It was the beginning of contemporary political science.

As the memory of the Civil War receded, neither fatalism nor struggle seemed quite so ineluctable. Their and our university culture favored more contained, pragmatic, and specialized social sciences. The surrounding cities offered an open field for reform-minded study, as their condition affected many a conscience. Charles Merriam was the perfect representative of this new, university-based, city-wise social science but also a Janus figure; and that is why I shall end with him. He looked back to Sumner and ahead along with John Dewey. And through his students he became the architect and guide of American political science as it developed after World War II.

The great theoretical question for him was, "What did democracy mean in the days of the union, the railroad, the trust and of modern business organization. . . . What was to be the theoretical and practical program of democracy?" He had no use for the crude Darwinism that equated social success with biological fitness, nor was he a racist in any of its numerous forms. Nevertheless, in retrospect, it does seem clear that he was as overwhelmed by change and uncertainty as his predecessors. And so he looked to statistics and to depth psychology—both poorly understood—and applauded all that was being done in the name of eugenics with little reflection and with baseless expectations of permanence. However, he also followed Dewey in his efforts to construct a meaningful democratic theory that took change for granted.

Merriam and Dewey did not return to the doctrines that had guided American politics before the Civil War. The Constitution was thought to be seriously flawed, especially the separation of powers. In any case, processes, not structures, mattered. Everything Dewey said against abstraction took root among Merriam's students. This was not, however (as it is often said to be), just a revolt against juristic formalism. It was, rather, an effort to realize an ideal of an impossibly perfect science that had reached the ultimate determining causes of change, which would permit accurate predictions, professional expertise, and unchallengeable political reform.

Merriam's own theory restated Dewey's notion of social planning not as a matter of fixed governmental blueprints imposed on the citizens but as a continuous process. If Dewey insisted on the need to create a public, that is, a body of actively engaged citizens, Merriam hoped for political learning by doing and for a new prudence. Both mixed democratic participation and social science, and this corresponded to the emerging practices of both state and national governments. Perhaps regrettably, Merriam was less inclined to see science— as Dewey did—as a state of mind, rather than as an accumulation of facts. In the face of unceasing change, however, both did offer a philosophy of citizenship in which the capacity for perpetual adaptation to novelty was sustained by information and communal activity. The outcome was that the democratic tendencies of the social sciences generally and the overt ideology of mainstream American political scientists were now in harmony. They were to be both good democratic citizens and rigorously objective adherents of the ethos of science.

With that, I have come to the door of the present. But I cannot close without remarking that in the wake of World War II and the Civil Rights movement, we no longer feel compelled to despise the values expressed in the language of rights, justice, liberty, and consent with which American political theory began. I hope that I have shown that its history has been a profound meditation upon our political experiences and our peculiar and often tragically flawed institutions. I expect—indeed hope—that others will give different accounts. However, if one were to cast aspersions on American political theory, it should not be that it is Oedipally attached to liberalism but that like the rest of the political classes of Europe and America, it failed to understand itself and lacked the imagination to project a plausibly better future. If we can learn to do better, it will be because democracy is itself dynamic. The history of American political science is a part of its development, which was neither painless nor uniform; but it has been an intellectual adventure of the first order.

Note

This essay is the presidential address presented on 30 August 1990 at the 86th annual meeting of the American Political Science Association in San Francisco. I offer these remarks for the records of the Association rather than as a scholarly paper.

PART TWO

American Distinctiveness

CHAPTER EIGHT

Positive Liberty, Negative Liberty in the United States

Translated from the French by Stanley Hoffmann

S ince its publication in 1958, the famous conference of Isaiah Berlin, *Two Concepts of Liberty,* has held a preponderant position in all the discussions on political freedom among English-speaking philosophers. It has been much criticized, but it is still the analytic foundation of most of our arguments. The reason for this is that Berlin has given us a very precise definition of negative liberty, and he has defended it against all other possibilities. According to him, negative liberty is the possibility of fulfilling our projects without coercion. In counterpart, Berlin has defined positive liberty as the victory of our higher self over our passions and our interests, and also over our inferior self, which happens to be our true self. In politics, this freedom has often justified paternalistic and oppressive regimes.

Since liberalism has spent half a century trying to define itself against totalitarian ideologies, these distinctions have been found very useful. But this conception of freedom has also been criticized for being too narrow. This does not seem fair to me. Vague definitions are rarely accurate. What I want to explain here is that this contrast between the two freedoms is not relevant to the history of American political thought, which is focused on the idea of rights. The reason for this insistence on rights is to be found less in the legacy of Locke than in slavery, whose memories still haunt us. Rights are not this open door that allows us to reach our goals, which is how Berlin defines negative liberty, but they allow us to realize our goals *against*

This essay is translated from the French, "Les visages de la liberté," *XXXIIe Rencontres Internationales de Genève* (1980), with kind permission from Editions de la Baconnière SA.

others. In the United States, the struggle between master and slave is not a metahistorical Hegelian image, but a daily fact, which has not yet disappeared. Rights are claims addressed to the government, asking it to act positively in order to protect the freedom of minorities, of blacks, of the weak, and of all those who are second-class citizens. One wants to prevent the masters from oppressing anyone. Nor are rights what Berlin calls the conditions of freedom without which one cannot enjoy negative liberty. Rights have an independent value. Nor are they acts of liberation; they are freedom itself, because they constitute a perpetual social process without end, a way of political life. They are the result of a history of freedom which must always be understood with slavery as its background.

But slavery is not the whole answer. The legal institutions of the United States have also contributed to increase considerably the importance given to personal rights. And it is the meeting between those two legacies that has created in the twentieth century a liberalism which expresses itself in ever more frequent and ever more demanding claims aimed at obtaining more rights. As Tocqueville had already noticed, all political problems in the United States become legal problems because all of them are resolved sooner or later by courts, and especially by the Supreme Court. Ever since the birth of the Republic the people have consented to the principle of judicial review of legislation, because it has always been believed that a written constitution requires the existence of a court with the authority to decide whether a law adopted by the two houses of Congress and signed by the president is really constitutional. Since all our rights are inscribed in the Constitution, every citizen can and must claim his or her rights before the judiciary. American political culture is radically legalistic and focused on the courts. Above all, the rights of minorities are in the hands of judicial magistrates and not in those of the legislators, who act for the majority of the citizens who have elected them. It was therefore inevitable that one had to go to courts and not to the legislative assemblies in order to demand that racial discrimination and all the other signs of slavery be erased from political life. In short, freedom means that every person has the right to defend himself effectively in a judicial court against all those who would like to deprive him of his full citizenship and of his constitutional rights. This freedom is not a passive enjoyment, but a form of permanent political action.

It is strange that in a country as democratic as the United States, there should have been those two anomalies: slavery and the supremacy of courts. The former violates the most fundamental idea of democratic justice. The Declaration of Independence says that no government can be just if it is not based on the consent of the governed. This declaration may not be a law but it is not a simple pamphlet either. It is a promise of political morality made at the birth of the Republic. But the slaves never had the opportunity to consent to anything. It is only very slowly that democratic principles have begun to impose themselves, and most of the time this has not happened in a democratic way. The Civil War in the nineteenth century, and now the courts, have accomplished much more than the elective representatives of the people. The slaves were not liberated by the majority, but during the war, whose initial cause had not been to put an end to slavery but which ended up by doing it in any case. Even Lincoln, who was opposed to slavery, was not an abolitionist. Like most Americans, he hoped that slavery would disappear gradually and legally.

Democracy is nevertheless defined by the sovereignty of the people or by majority rule. The Constitution begins with these words: "We the people." But even though there is not a single word about a court such as the Supreme Court to be found in the Constitution, it is in fact nine old judges who, unless the Constitution were to be amended—something that is extremely difficult—are the sovereigns. They have the last word. This is an institution which is obviously irreconcilable with democracy, but results from the conjunction of the three following facts: legal traditions inherited from the Colonial and Revolutionary period, distrust of any government, and a democracy which had little confidence in itself. This convergence has given to the United States two sovereigns, the people and the Supreme Court. This means that there is no sovereignty in the United States. There exists a process for resolving conflicts inherent in a federal and pluralistic system and for protecting the rights of citizens. Given this complicated situation, the drama of freedom in the United States is not a simple fight between liberty and equality, between the minority and the majority, or between the individual and the masses' state. It is the quest of a political situation in which justice and freedom would be inseparable because all the rights would be respected. Until such a utopian state comes into being, which nobody believes possible, political liberty remains the pursuit of rights.

What happened to Isaiah Berlin's two liberties in such an ideological and historical milieu? We must remember that he gave his lecture in the middle of an ideological war, which mobilized terrifying fanati-

cisms. As the word "freedom" has a huge prestige, even the most oppressive ideologies pretended to be its defenders. Berlin's first task
therefore was to distinguish so-called negative liberty, the liberals' liberty, from the false liberty of their totalitarian enemies. Negative liberty is "the open door," or the possibility to act without being hindered by anyone. My freedom is as vast as the space in which I can
do everything I want without anybody's intervention, and particularly
without the intervention of officialdom. And he noticed something
which has escaped many of his critics: that the poor also like their
negative liberty; they too refuse to be controlled and manipulated in
their daily life. The absence of freedom is just one more deprivation
they have to bear.

Berlin's second purpose was more philosophical. In separating liberty from all other political values he wanted to demonstrate that it is
impossible to combine them into a single public good. We must
choose among them. There is no platonic harmony and no way of
justifying the supremacy of a single dominant idea. Promoting public
health, education, and justice, improving the standard of living, encouraging the arts and sciences, protecting nature, are all valuable social goals, but they are independent of freedom, and indeed they could
limit my capacity to do whatever I like. Maybe these other public
goods are the conditions that make liberty possible, but they are not
liberty itself. In any case, one has to choose. But the necessity of choice
is not the only consequence of this multiplicity of political values. It
also implies tolerance and political pluralism. And these two ideas,
individualism and pluralism, are obviously very well adapted to the
social conditions and to the present situation of political conflicts in
the United States. They have therefore vastly contributed to the success of Berlin's essay among American readers.

And yet these theories have been severely criticized. There is no reason to suppose that the multiplicity of political values leads to any
definite consequences. It can lead us to anarchy, or to the arbitrary
imposition of one or the other of these values, just as easily as to
tolerance. The notion that the necessary incompatibility of values has
only the liberal implications that Berlin attributed to them has been
questioned. A second criticism is more philosophical. It states that
justice and fairness are the necessary conditions for the pursuit of all
other public values and must therefore have absolute primacy. One
must note that this criticism, which tells us that neither freedom nor
any other public good is possible without justice for all, carries so

much weight in the United States because it is rooted in the history of slavery and in the lasting consequences of slavery which are still visible everywhere. This does not mean that justice and freedom are the same thing, but only that in the historical circumstances of the United States justice could have a supreme political value. This is not my concern here, even though these objections against Berlin have been raised by American authors.

What strikes me is that the contrast between the two liberties is not relevant to the history of the United States and does not correspond to our own experiences. I believe this even though I share the fear of those who believe that if one makes the smallest concession to positive liberty one is already on a slippery slope toward the hell of totalitarianism. Nevertheless, it seems to me that positive liberty cannot be reduced to the experience of being liberated from our lower passions by reason—an experience which encourages the ideology of governments that call themselves scientific and that terrorize and oppress us because we are less enlightened than they are. Berlin himself says that this result is a perversion of positive liberty, and not its true meaning. He begins by defining it as something far less threatening. It is the desire to be one's own master and not to be dependent on anyone. But immediately he finds dangerous illusions here. For instance, one may have the feeling of being master of oneself without being really free. One can reach psychological autonomy by detaching oneself from the world like Epictetus in chains, but this is not political freedom. Furthermore, to subject oneself to a necessity that one understands—to knowledge—is not political liberty either. But these are illusions which are not inherent in positive liberty.

In fact, wanting to be master in one's own domain is obviously the other side of negative liberty. How can one do what one wants if one is not master in one's domain? The problem arises at the political level. Voting, choosing representatives, or being governed by members of one's own ethnic group are not the same thing as negative liberty. Subjecting oneself voluntarily to political masters is not the same thing as being without any master. Berlin is right to condemn the identification between those two ideas effected by nationalism. But the desire to be one's master at home must not lead us immediately to personal fantasies or collectivistic ideologies. It is easy to demonstrate that positive freedom has often been perverted and that when it is, it is not authentic freedom but an incentive for individuals to submit to ethnic groups and to their leaders. However, to say that the right to take part in political life and the fact of being an active citizen are no more than statutes and conditions of freedom, but not freedom itself, amounts to reducing negative liberty to a psychological state that is passive and empty of political content. Finally, what can the expression "being master in one's own domain" mean if not the right to act politically in an effective way?

As is often the case, this analytic philosophy has no sense of history or any sense of the social content of ideas. This makes it useless for political thought. If one wants to find something concrete we must come back to the writers whom Berlin cites with so much admiration, Benjamin Constant and Tocqueville. They are the best champions of what I would call the liberalism of fear, but they are not identical. Both defend an aristocratic liberty because they are afraid that democratic forces might destroy the space necessary for private life. But Constant thought about the Jacobins, whereas Tocqueville was worried by democratic culture. Very few Americans have shared Constant's opinions because he says nothing about the good uses of private life. Who wants to be a free man similar to this neurotic character, Adolphe? Tocqueville, on the other hand, has always meant much to Americans critical of themselves, and especially among conservative intellectuals. One of the reasons for this is his emphasis on how much voluntary associations can accomplish, even though he lamented the absence of great individual geniuses and distrusted the egalitarian spirit which stifled individuality in the United States. Parenthetically, I would like nevertheless to remark that there were many aspects of American culture that he did not see, in particular the importance of the inner life of Protestants. And because of this we have to question again the idea of a democratic culture. To be sure, there are democratic morals, but is there a whole culture in the anthropological meaning of the term? I doubt it. In politics, it is absolutely evident that what Tocqueville was afraid of was a government that would be soft but oppressive and perhaps militaristic. Strangely enough, the most radical among the American democrats contemporary to Tocqueville also feared a government that would be too active and possess excessively extended powers, but not for the same reasons as Tocqueville.

Tocqueville was in the United States at the beginning of the most creative period of our history insofar as ideology and literature are concerned. It was the age of Jackson, a period during which the democratic ideas which are still alive and popular appeared. It is in the fifteen years preceding the Civil War that abolitionism developed, and with it a doctrine of justice which can be summed up in the expression *equal protection of the laws,* that is, in the demand that laws be applied equally to all, an expression that one finds also in the famous Fourteenth Amendment of the Constitution, which finally became, in modern times, the foundation of civil rights, that is, the idea of equal liberty for all citizens. Democrats and abolitionists have contributed to the formation of a liberalism of rights which is neither negative nor positive, but a combination of both. It is this liberalism that I want to examine here, rather than add to the criticisms of Berlin's thesis. On the contrary, I will use his own distinctions in order to illuminate the perpetual struggle for freedom in the United States. To say that these distinctions have another meaning in a historical context very different from the one that Berlin was thinking about amounts not so much to contradicting him as to thinking through his ideas thirty years later. I do not want to deny that these two liberties exist in the United States; I only want to say that they are deeply linked to one another.

Negative liberty was at the heart of the mentality of Jacksonian democrats, a mentality which was born just when Tocqueville was in the United States. They repeated night and day that "the best government is that which governs least" and which costs nothing. They still say so. What were they afraid of? Certainly not absolute monarchy or a military dictatorship in the Napoleonic style. Their greatest fear was that the rich would take away their political rights and use their money to buy the elective representatives and the other civil servants and to establish a protected and unremovable elite. Less government, less corruption, and above all no theft of the rights of citizens, this is what they wanted. It was clearly a natural reaction in a republic with egalitarian political institutions and an inequalitarian civil society. This inequality of wealth was accepted as just and natural by the majority of the people, but at the same time they asked that all citizens be treated in the same way by the government and that they all have the same political rights.

The political worry of democrats was also exacerbated by the distrust which they felt toward Europe in general and toward what they called aristocracy in particular. That fear also had its roots in the political realities of this period. Metternich's Europe was infinitely distant from America. The United States was the only democratic republic, and its citizens felt very isolated. They were also conscious of the contempt that the Europeans had for them, and they repaid them hundredfold. When the young Walt Whitman was still a journalist in

Brooklyn, he boasted that the good days of these rotten old systems of Europe were gone, that the evening of their life had come, and that this heralded a glorious dawn for oppressed people. It is *here,* in the United States, he wrote, that the flag of freedom had been planted, and it is there that the capacity of men to govern themselves would be tested. All the traces of feudalism were going to be destroyed.

How did democrats such as Whitman imagine what feudalism had been like in Europe? Certainly not as we learned about it from Marc Bloch. And why was he so afraid of it? After all, there were no hereditary political privileges, and titles of nobility were banned by the Constitution. He thought that feudalism was a system of monopolies of wealth and of political authority. According to Tom Paine and other democratic writers the barbarian kings who conquered Europe had divided all their lands among their hordes of warriors, with whom they had governed without any law or justice. This nobility had used its monopoly of property in order to seize political power. Moreover, it had been helped in this plot against the people by a Church which was as monopolistic as it was. This danger had not disappeared. The question of knowing "whether the people or property will reign will always remain open," according to a Jacksonian senator.

The best remedy against aristocracy thus conceived was negative liberty: no intervention by government in the economic or religious life of the citizens and no obstacle to their freedom to do what they wanted. Any political power endangers their rights. Taxes, for instance, can always be used in order to increase the armed forces, which could then deprive artisans and farmers of their rights and put government into the hands of the rich and the idle who, like the Europeans whom these people admired in secret, had nothing but disdain for honest labor. They would enslave the poorer people. And the fear of slavery can be found everywhere, including in the language. One always hears the cry "we are going to be reduced to slavery." This was a charge already hurled at the British during the Revolution. Indeed, the word "slavery" has a very precise meaning in the United States. One knows what one is talking about and what one fears so much. It is not an empty metaphor. Without a government one cannot enslave anyone. Slavery is forced labor under the coercion of laws.

Nevertheless, a minimal democratic government had at least one duty: the protection of human rights. And the president, the only person elected by the majority of the whole people, could act as a tribune. His duty was to protect the people against an army of rich, cunning, and aristocratic predators. In that period, there was very little confidence in the courts, which were dominated by undemocratic interests and whose acquired rights were too well protected. Only the president, an old hero of the War of 1812, could defend the rights of the people in reducing as much as possible the powers of government. To be sure, these ideas are not coherent, but they have established a very lasting state of mind. This unreasonable confidence in a negative power which would defend rights has in the twentieth century been put at the service of President Roosevelt, and even of Ronald Reagan. To sum up, democratic negative liberties mean a very limited government which has nevertheless enough strength to protect the people's rights against the people's enemies.

What did the citizen do with this ideology of natural rights? He voted, he went to political meetings where he listened to tireless speakers, and above all he knew that he was not a slave. He hated the blacks and he was afraid to be reduced to a social condition in which he would be not much higher than a slave. He knew very well what slavery was, and even though slavery was limited by law to blacks, he was afraid of it. The slave had no rights, and should he, a white artisan, have fewer rights than the aristocrats, he would in a sense be closer to slavery than to liberty. This was one more reason for negative liberty and for a limited government which would not have the means to reduce him to what would be called, after the Civil War, a second-class citizenship, the political condition of the blacks. The great fear was that of not being superior to "Niggers." "The only support of the working class is the great principle of the equality of rights." Without it, "we are white slaves," said the first American trade union leaders. These sentiments were expressed endlessly. This was the nightmare of the radical democrats.

This democratic ideology was not far removed, in certain of its aspects, from the public convictions of the great slave-owning planters of the South. This may seem strange, because these planters, with their rural state of mind, their penchant for duels, and their taste for the novels of Sir Walter Scott, gave the impression of resembling the old European aristocracy, and they were often accused of being aristocrats. This was an illusion. The cotton plantations were commercial enterprises, their lands were a commodity like any other, and they did not share the ancestral ideology of European nobility. They were in fact the most anti-European Americans. They had a passion for their rights and for the Republican spirit, which was even sharper than among the democrats of the North. From Burke to the abolitionists this has been noted and well understood. For the owners of slaves who could see every day what a total lack of freedom meant, liberty was their most precious possession. To be free was the essence of their identity. As Richard Hildreth, one of the most intelligent abolitionists, put it, the passion for personal freedom is nowhere more violent than in the hearts of aristocrats raised in freedom and who have learned to appreciate its value, since they could see every day the terrible contrast of servitude. Not to be a slave was of incalculable importance for them. The smallest reduction of what they considered to be one of their rights immediately appeared to them as an attempt to enslave. All their debates and all their rhetoric, whether on taxes, on tariffs, or on what mattered above everything else, their constitutional and natural rights to own human beings, were filled with this fear of being enslaved. Nobody liked negative liberty more, and nobody talked more of civil and natural rights than those masters of slaves. Indeed, they were masters of their domains and they felt free. Assuredly, they benefited from negative liberty.

It is true that the masters of the slaves of the South had fewer personal liberties than the citizens in the North. They were obliged to serve in semimilitary groups in the case of slave revolts. They had to control their slaves and they were responsible for the slaves' behavior. And since they were afraid of abolitionist propaganda, their rights to talk and to read freely were severely limited. Their cultural life was also stagnant. European immigrants did not want to settle in the South. Even though slavery was limited to blacks it was an institution which did not inspire much confidence among Irish peasants. They all settled in the big cities of the North. Like the Yankee artisans, they too hated the slaves more than slavery. This was caused by their violent racism much more than by the fear that the emancipation of the slaves could cause a fall of the wages of white workers. For them too, being free meant not being a slave. This is how the ideologies of the masters of the South and the democrats of the North met and converged.

How can one tell someone who enjoys as vast a freedom as that of the slaveholders that he is not truly free? It seems to me that theirs was a perfect negative liberty. They felt free, and they had enough power to be able to act without any hindrance. It is with this situation in mind that liberals turned toward another idea of rights, which was more appropriate to a state of nature such as Hobbes's than to a modern republic in which even the masters talked incessantly about civil rights. One was beginning to think about more political, more legal, and more realistic changes than the deportation of blacks to the West Indies or to Africa. Trusting too much in the spirit of the Constitution, the political abolitionists hoped until the last hour that the courts would, case by case, abolish slavery. For that was the place where one had to claim the rights inscribed in the Constitution. But that plan failed. The Supreme Court declared that blacks could never be citizens in the United States and that they had no right that any white had to respect. Three years later the Civil War began.

The lesson of this story is not fatalistic. A hundred years later the ideology of natural rights and the spirit of independence of the masters served extremely well the cause of the descendants of their former slaves. Also, even though one still believes in natural rights in the United States, one knows perfectly that despite the Declaration of Independence they are not self-evident. They are constitutional rights, and the courts decide what they mean in practice. One is far from the unlimited negative liberty of the slaveholders. Equal protection of the laws, however, should not be understood as a request for an equality which could limit negative liberty, but as the political and legal realization of the idea of natural rights. For, if blacks are human beings, they have rights, and the negative liberty of the masters ceases to be a monopoly.

In order to get there, one had, however, to introduce certain elements of positive liberty into the idea of human rights. The first step toward this goal was made by the abolitionists, who were mainly Protestant radicals. This may be difficult to understand in Europe. We must remember that slavery in the United States was the harshest possible; only ancient Greece had known a comparable system. Emancipation was forbidden by law, and the free states were obliged to send fugitive slaves back to their owners in the South. This meant that all citizens were implicated in slavery, a fact that weighed heavily on the conscience of a minority of abolitionists. Even though Europeans had had slaves in the eighteenth and nineteenth centuries, those slaves did not live among them; they were very far away, overseas, and very well hidden. Only the Americans had an enslaved working force at home. In those circumstances, slavery was not only an anomaly in a constitutional democracy, but also an outrage for modern enlightened opinion anywhere, and Americans knew it. But nothing has been more important than the awakening of religious conscience. The most famous abolitionist, William Lloyd Garrison, had quarreled with all the churches of Boston because of their lack of zeal. He was a church all by himself, the incarnation of the Protestant principle. In his eyes, slavery was a pact with the devil, and a contract with pure and absolute evil. The will of the majority, positive laws, had no value for him. He only knew the will of God, and he knew what his duty was. He was called "the great liberator," and the following words are inscribed on the pedestal of his statue in Boston's central park: "I will not compromise, I will not deceive, and I will be heard!" He thought that it was impossible to believe that one was free when one was obliged by the government to be allied with moral evil. Abolishing slavery would free one from an unbearable sin. Moreover, he did not want to be obliged by the state to help enslave his fellow human beings. How can one say to such a man that he is free when he does not feel free? Obviously, he was seeking both liberties, the negative and the positive one together. To him they were inseparable. But this did not have any threatening implications. On the contrary, he obliged the citizens who talked so much about rights to take them seriously. This is because American slavery was a phenomenon unlike any other.

The idea of a spiritual enslavement to one's lowest inclinations was, according to Hegel, an internalization of the old relation between master and slave, and I think he was right. But what was happening in the United States before the Civil War was the opposite movement. The sense of enslavement to one's lowest drives was externalized and made visible in slavery, which was still a social reality. One finds manifestations of these feelings not only in the passionate rhetoric of Garrison, but also in Lincoln's speeches, even though he was not an ardent abolitionist. He too presented the liberation of slaves as a moral duty. He said that the fight against the injustice of slavery was analogous to the fight to overcome drunkenness. Both were conquests over oneself, and he believed that one could not accomplish either by force but only bit by bit. As we know, he had to learn that he was wrong, and the cost was terrible. Lincoln was profoundly religious, and Thoreau was not. And yet Thoreau's language was very similar to Lincoln's. He talked about the division of labor, for instance, as a kind of slavery we impose on ourselves in the same way. It was terrible to have an overseer from the South, but even worse to have one who came from the North, and worse still to be one's own overseer and to enslave oneself to useless labors. This was the old internalization. But Thoreau immediately came back to actual social slavery. The government which enslaved blacks could never be his own government because he was too good for such a regime. Nobody had the right to oblige him to do evil, and to contribute to the enslavement of others. How could one think that one is free when one knew that the taxes one payed would be used to enslave blacks? To refuse to pay them was an assertion of both liberties at the same time. Moreover, this was liberal positive liberty.

Negative and positive liberties, despite our contemporary fears, are not necessarily in conflict. It seems to me that even though one is right to separate freedom from the conditions which make it possible for it to flourish, negative liberty itself is just a condition for more active and wider freedoms. The fact of acting without hindrance and the existence of open doors can be considered as simple conditions for claiming positive rights and freedom, such as those demanded by Garrison, Thoreau, and the other abolitionists. What is in fact more problematic for the United States is that neither the liberation of the slaves nor their claims to their rights have been accomplished by a democratic process. The emancipation of the slaves has never been popular. It was a consequence of the Civil War, and it was the courts which abolished legal racial discrimination after the end of the Second World War. The will of the majority has always been opposed to it.

After the Civil War, three amendments to the Constitution and a series of federal laws guaranteed all legal rights to the emancipated slaves. This was the work of a minority of republicans from the North and it did not last. Ten years later, the nation only wanted to forget the war and the blacks and their problems. Indeed, blacks had been reduced to a social condition barely superior to slavery in the South, and they were confronted by racial hatred in the North. Courts did not protect their rights. Segregation, that is, a life that was supposed to be "separate but equal," had been approved by the Supreme Court. The laws originally written with the intention of protecting the rights of emancipated slaves were now used by courts exclusively in order to protect economic laissez-faire against the attempts of the government to regulate the conditions of work and trade. There are unique ironical circumstances in the history of the United States.

The era of negative liberty for private enterprise ended with the New Deal, but the resort to courts in order to claim the rights of racial minorities through the application—at last—of the laws and doctrines that had existed ineffectually for a whole century began only ten years after the Second World War. The first right that was revived and which led to all the others was the right to ask the courts to listen to the grievances of black citizens and to concern themselves seriously with the rights of ascriptive minorities. This is the "open door" without which nothing would have been possible. But it indicates already that liberty can mean not that public authorities should do nothing, but that they act so as to protect minorities and to educate the whole people. This is what, in principle, had always been expected of them. Negative liberty does not mean a passive government. It requires a political will which is, indeed, a manifestation of positive freedom.

The rights guaranteed by the Constitution and by the Bill of Rights have two functions. The first, which was of the highest importance for Jefferson and for all his liberal heirs, is the right of citizens to oppose the government, which is always suspected of having tyrannical ambitions. When one forbids the government to make any law that establishes a religion or interferes with freedom of religion, or any law that limits the freedom of the press, one provides individuals with the possibility of defending themselves against official interventions in their private lives. But there exist also declared rights which require that the government do something. Most of the constitutional rights protect people accused of crimes, and these are cases in which the government is obliged to act. It has, for example, to constitute a jury of the neighborhood. When one requests the equal protection of the law for minorities, one claims a right of that kind. The government is asked to act, to ban official segregation and racial discrimination in general.

As I have already stated, tribunals have an extraordinary authority in the United States. Their decisions are enforced by executive power. Sooner or later, they are obeyed, often without much enthusiasm. However, the effects of judicial decisions may not be felt for ten years or so. Twenty years after racial segregation in the schools was proclaimed illegal, most schools are not yet integrated.

Nevertheless, many things have changed. Like the Bill of Rights, the constitutional decisions of the Supreme Court have always been accepted, not only as authoritative decisions, but also as lessons of civil education, as political education that puts discussions and debates at a higher level than that of the daily political speeches. They function, somehow, like the preambles to the laws in Plato's *Laws*. Even those who never agree with the decisions of the Supreme Court learn something during the discussions in which they participate. Thus it is through a mix of coercion and education that the rights and dignity of the citizens, including those of blacks, have been gradually asserted.

For a foreign observer, it may seem that the conflict between the former masters and their previous slaves was a conflict between two negative liberties. One wants to be free to do whatever he wants with an inferior whom he despises, and whom he regards as a piece of property that has been stolen from him. The other wants to be free to do what all other citizens can do without any distinction among persons. But is it really a matter of two negative liberties, that is, of possibilities to act without obstacle, of doing what one likes as in the state of nature? It seems to me that social conflicts cannot be understood in this way. Domination, property, slavery, segregation, discrimination, racial classifications, and citizenship are all legal conditions defined by law and protected by public power. All entail positive rights—or the absence of such rights.

The real conflict, then, is among those rights; and the choice one has is of deciding which rights the bureaucracy should strengthen and which it should reject. One has to choose, but not between two negative liberties or between negative liberty and positive liberty. Courts must make a choice between two rights, each of which entails specific political constraints. As soon as one recognizes that blacks are citizens, exactly like all the others, this choice is made. Especially as both parties still faithfully believe in natural rights, despite whatever skeptical intellectuals may say.

But the changes in behavior which these decisions require afterward, and which they will require for a long time still, mean that the right to claim one's rights will remain the first of all rights. When all liberties are positive liberties, the right to fight for one's own rights and for other specific rights is the most important of all freedoms. It is an endless process.

Were the old masters "forced" to be free? Certainly not in the sinister sense that Rousseau had in mind. Any reform imposes new constraints on someone. But no one has ever said to the racists and to the segregationists that they were liberated when they became obliged to respect the liberty and the rights of other citizens. To the extent to which it has been possible to awaken their conscience and to make them more conscious of the rights of others, their positive liberty has perhaps been broadened. But what matters is that the old masters themselves have accepted the process through which constitutional rights have been worked out. When their effective rights were diminished the only defense they could present in order to safeguard them was local custom, an excuse which the Constitution has not recognized since the amendments added after the Civil War.

In the United States, legal freedom offers to citizens the possibility of claiming their rights in court, and indeed it requires that they do so. For it is the characteristic of a good liberal citizen that he fight for his rights, which can never be sufficiently extended and sufficiently respected. In such an ideology and in such a political practice negative liberty and positive liberty are not in conflict, they are mutually supportive.

References

Ashford, John. *Agrarians and "Aristocrats."* Cambridge: Cambridge University Press, 1983.

Berlin, Isaiah. *Four Essays on Liberty.* Oxford: Oxford University Press, 1969.

Blau, Joseph, ed. *Social Theories of Jacksonian Democracy.* New York: Bobbs-Merrill, 1954.

Burke, Edmund. "Speech on the Conciliation with America." *Works* 3 (1881).

Dumond, D. L. *Anti-slavery: The Crusade for Freedom in America.* New York: Norton, 1961.

Fogel, Robert. *Without Consent or Contract: The Rise and Fall of American Slavery.* New York: Norton, 1989.

Foner, Eric. *Reconstruction.* New York: Harper and Row, 1988.

Fredrickson, George M. *The Inner Civil War.* New York: Harper and Row, 1968.

Hildreth, Richard. *Despotism in America* (1854). New York: Kelley, 1971.

Lincoln, Abraham. *Speeches and Writings.* New York: Library of America, 1989.

McCloskey, Robert G. *The American Supreme Court.* Chicago: University of Chicago Press, 1960.

McKittrick, Eric L., ed. *Slavery Defended.* Englewood Cliffs, NJ: Prentice-Hall, 1965.

McPherson, James M. *Battle Cry of Freedom.* New York: Oxford University Press, 1988.

Myrdal, Gunnar. *An American Dilemma.* New York: Harper and Row, 1944.

Paul, Arnold M., ed. *Black Americans and the Supreme Court since Emancipation.* New York: Holt, Rinehart and Winston, 1972.

Smith, Timothy. *Revivalism and Social Reform.* New York: Abingdon Press, 1957.

Thoreau, Henry. *Walden and Other Writings.* New York: Bantam Books, 1971.

CHAPTER NINE

The Boundaries of Democracy

I f "we the people" are the sole source of public authority, who are the people? If democracy is government by and for the people, who does and who does not constitute the people? No question has been more vexing for modern democratic thought, because it arises not only when self-government is defined, but also whenever democratic governments have to consider their relations to aliens and to other states and peoples. What boundaries mark a democratic people off from others? Few if any territorial boundaries have ever been chosen by a people. Most have been set by war and accident. Are there justifiable boundaries? Or are there no defensible borders, so that the people are, as has been plausibly argued, all mankind? If that is not the case, or at least not yet, how are aliens to be separated from citizens and the territory of a democracy marked off from the land of others? How, above all, are generations to be sorted out? How are the dead and the living, the old and the young, and the past and the present to be divided or joined? Consent, after all, occurs only here and now. These questions have troubled American democrats from the first, but especially during the intellectual flowering of the eighteenth century.

Tocqueville by then had already noted that when one spoke of democracy in America, there was much that was uniquely and entirely local. Most significantly Americans were an emigrant population, there was endless land, most people belonged to one of the numerous Protestant sects, three different races lived on the continent, and,

This undated essay was previously unpublished.

above all, there was slavery. These characteristics impinged deeply upon the structure of practice and thinking in America, especially in deciding upon its own membership.

The origins and end of the formative era of American democratic thought are not easily set. They surely go back as far as New England Puritanism, especially as it altered under the pressure of conflict with England. And it obviously must take us through the works of Tom Paine and Thomas Jefferson. Its end might be seen in that revival of intense democratic sentiment which is rather loosely called the age of Jackson. The tensions that had prevailed in democratic thinking then became overt. As is often the case, the end or the denouement makes manifest the deepest conflicts of a preceding era, and so reveals the implications of much that has now come to a close. On one side there were the radical Jacksonian democrats like O'Sullivan, the editor of *The United States and Democratic Review,* who argued passionately that the nation of futurity must expand to fulfill its destiny to bring democracy to the entire continent, perhaps even to the whole hemisphere.[1] There could be no geographic boundaries to a providential design. Against this vision Albert Gallatin, who had been secretary of the treasury under both Jefferson and Madison, thundered with no less a sense of providential endorsement, "Your mission is to improve the state of the world, to be the Model Republic, to show that men are capable of governing themselves . . . by your example to exert a moral influence most beneficial to mankind at large." As for the fashionable idea of the "hereditary superiority" of the Anglo-Saxon race over the Mexicans, Gallatin was sure that democracy must reject such a claim, as it rejects all hereditary claims.[2] What is most curious of all is that both O'Sullivan and Gallatin were perfectly convinced that their respective views were those of the Sage of Monticello, whom both revered. Which of the two was the true heir of the original promise of American democracy? Quite possibly both were equally entitled to wear the mantle of Jefferson, in whom all the built-in contradictions of democracy found their meeting place.

At the opening of the road to Jefferson stand the New England Puritans, whose "atrabilious philosophy" he detested and whose descendants loathed him as a second Jeroboam who had turned Israel from the law.[3] They were, nevertheless, democrats—if not in theory, at least in their electoral practices. Not all members of the community could be members of the Congregational Church, but those who were did elect their ministers. And more relevant, magistrates were elected annually by all the freemen. Puritans thought that government was both very important, because it was of God, and very negative, because it was there to punish and restrain us in our fallen and sinful condition. To be a magistrate required a calling, a special fitness for the office, and while election did not prove that a man really had a vocation to govern, it was at least a sign to that effect. A people's refusal to reelect a man was similarly a clear indication of his failure to have been truly summoned to the office. While the freemen who were entitled to participate in these annual elections were not the entire male population, the practice is by any standard very democratic. To insist that magistrates be qualified to exercise their functions is, moreover, a denial of hereditary authority. Merit as it is perceived in the personal qualities of a potential magistrate, rather than in his birth, is the sign of a true calling. The origin of this way of choosing one's governors was not political, but part of the normal rules governing companies, which became part of a polity with the settlement of a territory. Inadvertently the result was democratic. In theory, the clergy took no direct part in governing. In actuality, it was they who decided what the tasks of government were to be, and who could be a member of the community at all. Eventually it was not possible to require voters to be members of the Congregational Church, but for a long time one had to show that one believed what the rest of the community was supposed to believe. It was in short a democracy that was both exclusive and authoritarian.[4]

To guide the magistrates and the people as a whole the clergy delivered particularly political sermons on the yearly election day. These annual sermons were unique to New England and their immediate purpose was to be a "watchman upon Jerusalem's walls, whose proper business is to descry dangers, and give seasonable notice thereof, to observe the sins of the times and the awful symptoms of God's departure."[5] The content of these sermons was a review of the events of the past in terms of biblical hermeneutics. It was not a new interpretive system, but the occasions to which it was applied were highly original. It was assumed that the Bible, especially the Old Testament, contained the "types," which we would now call archetypes, of all possible political events and experiences. The way to understand one's own world was to relate it to the appropriate biblical type of which it was the antitype. That is how one could understand who one was, what had already happened, and what was likely to occur. The clergy was meant to show the community to what biblical events they were to look in order to discern the meaning of their most recent political conduct. The question "who are the people" was answered in no uncertain terms. The Puritans were the people of Israel. As such they were apart from every other people. They were, of course, not the natural heirs of the ancient Hebrews, but their replica. The Old Testament was their story as a prophecy to be reenacted. First and foremost, they must attend to the Exodus from Egypt, then to the Babylonian captivity and its end, always a dreadful warning. David's story was naturally significant, but most of all Noah seemed to apply to the early comers, who had also started out anew after crossing a flood of water more awful than the original deluge. Getting across the Atlantic was a terrifying experience and it made the founding of a new settlement in a wild and empty country seem very much like Noah's re-creation of mankind after all the other people had died. It was not difficult to fit themselves into these prophetic molds. It is not a historical way of relating past and present, because it does not involve thinking in terms of sequences or of continuities at all. Events are not connected in a chain. The new people of Israel relived the original biblical experiences exactly as they occurred then. The only obstacle was intellectual, to fully know which were the right reference points. That was the work of the learned clergy, especially in the election sermons. As many historians have noted, the "errand into the wilderness" which the Puritans undertook was both a real experience of life in a wild country, and a recollection of Isaiah and John the Baptist in its spiritual significance. They had come to the natural wilderness to save the garden of the Church from the wilderness of the world which had not yet fully responded to the Protestant Reformation. The society they would set up in New England would be a beacon that would lead the rest of mankind to a full Reformation, and by setting an example of holy living would bring Protestantism to its realization. They were on an errand for all mankind. This was not just a self-imposed task; they had been chosen. They had covenanted with the Lord, repeating the covenant of Abraham. If they fulfilled it He would reward them, though this was not wholly certain. If they failed in their duty He would punish them. So every public misfortune was a divine penalty inflicted for some wrongdoing. Moreover, because they were the best, the only people of Israel, they failed absolutely when they erred at all. The election sermons therefore had only one subject, declension. There was always a falling away from the covenant, and as the years went by, from the standards of virtue that had prevailed among the first settlers. Only they were truly Noah-like. Since then there had been drubbing, adultery, idleness, and unthriftiness. As their just reward God had sent epidemics and King Philip's War. When the people were obedient God would send them magistrates like Moses or Nehemiah and all would be well. Mostly the election sermons were terrifying warnings, and at the end the people said "Amen" in a horrifying repetition of the Deuteronomic precedent. Since everything had already happened once before and was constantly being repeated, it was not difficult to know what the boundaries of political life were. Even profane history had its lessons.[6] Classical history also contained types. The corruptions of the Romans had brought their own version of the Babylonian captivity. The clergy had read their Tacitus and Sallust and the relevant pages in St. Augustine and they could see that pagan decline had its own awful lesson to teach. The psychological and political decline of the Romans indulging in easy and luxurious living was a natural addition to the sacred history of the people of Israel. It thus made perfectly good sense to speak of Sir Edmund Andros as a second Nero and to see the fall of Rome as a replication of the punishment of Israel. In fact the two are very often juxtaposed. That these awful imprecations and warnings should be addressed on a political occasion to the entire people carries a more than politically democratic meaning. There is implicit in this entire way of defining the people a complete collective responsibility for the fate of the community. Everyone's actions mattered to them all. And if they seem self-absorbed in their recollections and prophecies, they did believe that they were acting for all mankind.

How could this political theology have been integrated with the philosophy of John Locke? Unlikely as it may seem, it did happen, gradually, but surely. First of all there was the great common experience of felt oppression under James II. The idea of a basic social contract was not so alien either. The Puritans had not only taken up the covenant of Abraham with God, but had also contracted with each other to fulfill together the terms of that first covenant. Their society was built on a mutual promise to bear the communal responsibility to fulfill the mission of Israel. To resist tyranny and in any case to watch the magistrates carefully, even as one obeyed them dutifully, was part of the belief system that was no less familiar to Locke than to them. They were therefore quite prepared to accept a secular explanation of their difficulties with England as well as a purely political justification for resistance, as long as these did not interfere with or replace their biblical understanding of their situation. Locke was simply added on to a religious doctrine of government. And New Englanders were ready to hear his message by the eighteenth century. John Wise, a perfectly orthodox preacher, gives us a very good idea of how Locke was taken in as a spiritual lodger in Puritan thinking. Not only did Wise dwell on the social contract as the way Israel had come together for the greater service of God, but self-preservation was also a duty to Him. The instinct for self-preservation was divinely given and a sign from God that He wanted us to preserve His creation. Had not Noah saved himself thus? The Puritans had come to America like Noah to preserve themselves, as he had, for God's sake. Natural rights, the most important point for American democracy, after all, were also not beyond the Puritan embrace. Wise reminded them of their duty, and thus right, to resist tyrannical and specifically papist rulers. Every Protestant Englishman had a right to resist with all his powers an evil as great as a papist king. And as the English government seemed to favor the Catholics of Quebec more than its Protestant subjects in New England, the latter had every right and duty to resist. Here was a danger against which they had an obvious right to preserve themselves. The great Mr. Locke had simply explained to them in immediate terms what they already understood from contemplating the story of Noah. His prescriptions were perfectly compatible with their own sense of their situation.[7]

By 1776 the New England clergy stood on the brink of a chasm. The most famous election sermon of that fateful year had as its title "The Church's Flight into the Wilderness," and others had themes that were just as tense. Obviously there was much to dread, especially when the local Assembly was disbanded and martial law imposed. And no sermon of 1776 reflects the Puritan reaction to these events better than Harvard president Samuel Langdon's Cambridge Annual Election Sermon. It was entitled "Government Corrupted by Vice and Recovered by Righteousness," and was based on Isaiah 1:26, "They have deprived us of our Judges."[8] According to Langdon, British Liberty was about to expire as the military government had deprived the citizens of Massachusetts of their legitimate magistrates and had condemned them to the equivalent of the Babylonian Captivity. These afflictions must be regarded as a divine punishment because the people had sinned. The chief sinners were the American Tories who now supported the king, probably a great part of the population of Massachusetts then. What had these people done to arouse the divine wrath?

They had lived idly and luxuriously, they had supported the corrupt ways of London, and they had set papists and savages upon us. It was they who were the real rebels.

It is very important to understand this part of Langdon's claim. He and his like were not modern revolutionaries. The future played no part in his thinking at all. To defy authority was, moreover, utterly wrong. It could not, therefore, be admitted that the New Englanders were in revolt. On the contrary, it was the king and his American friends who were in fact rebelling against the law of man and God. The local Tories no longer accepted biblical morality, but a mere Platonism, while the English violated the rights of loyal American subjects. It was not an easy thought to accept. Like most Americans, Langdon spoke of England as a parent, and filial piety was not a trivial duty for a child of Israel. Only by convincing himself that the king had become a cruel parent could he justify his disobedient conduct, and it is in this frame of mind that invoking the Lockean rights of man became an obvious resort. There is, moreover, hope; for the people of Israel had not fallen into anarchy, after all. It had found new and virtuous judges in its towns and villages, and above all the Continental Congress meeting in Philadelphia was composed of good men. Not everyone had been tainted by a decadent Platonism. The king was indeed a tyrant and a just war against him was called for, but all this would act as a scourge and Israel would emerge cleansed from the ordeal. It would come out of a corruption and decline like Rome's and the Babylonian captivity and would be restored to continue its mission.

The purely political pamphlet literature of the years preceding 1776 was very different from Langdon's sermon. It tended, like the second part of the Declaration of Independence, to consist of lists of complaints and lacked the sense of hovering evil and cosmic horror that marked Langdon's sense of the situation. It was not enough for him to itemize grievances; he had to find the right biblical model, and he saw palpable failure and danger, and in the end, the promise that the people of Israel would come through. Was it still the same people of Israel, though? The citizenry of Massachusetts was, thanks to English policy and the pressure of endemic labor shortages, increasingly heterogeneous, and in referring to the virtuous magistrates at Philadelphia Langdon was acknowledging their membership in a larger and spiritually highly diverse polity. The question of who the people were was thus suddenly open. That mutual agreement was the only satisfactory entry into citizenship had always been accepted, and birthright had followed as new generations grew up. Who however qualified for full acceptance by those already in place? Who could be naturalized, once the citizens were no longer just the people of Israel and the "principal nation of the Reformation"? It was not clear now. And later democratic thinkers did not find it easy to answer.[9] That did not abate the New England faith in a universal mission to act for the rest of unreformed mankind. The universalism remained. It should not, however, be exaggerated as an element in American democratic thought. The Puritans were not its only fountain and origin, and to be a "redeemer nation" has been only one, and by no means the most significant, aspect of America's self-definition.[10] Even as Langdon was delivering his traditional jeremiad, Virginians and Pennsylvanians were making quite different appeals for resistance, and preparing a far stronger case for the rights of man, as not just one, but the sole ground for political action. A secular public was waiting for a new message. Two years into a war, they were not yet quite ready to make a complete break with their "parent" country. It was Tom Paine's genius to be able not only to mobilize them, but also to speak very meaningfully to traditional New Englanders. *Common Sense* is a brilliant pamphlet, and as Edmund Randolph said, "It put the torch to combustibles."[11]

It is a great mistake to think of Tom Paine as a marginal figure in American political thinking. He did not take a direct part in building its enduring institutions, but the rhetoric of radical journalism owes him much even now, and he was much read by the Yankee pioneers moving westward. More significantly he certainly impressed Jefferson genuinely and through him became a lasting voice in American democratic discourse. The first effect of his pamphlet was spectacular not only as a unifying force, but also as a revelation of what democratic feeling in America was then, and in some measure would remain. Baptists in Virginia, tired of the Anglican Filmer-like sermons of Jonathan Boucher; Pennsylvanians fed up with Quaker passivity; deistic Virginia gentlemen, even John Adams, who came to hate Paine; all were moved by *Common Sense*. The title itself is a stroke of genius. "Common sense" means shared and universal understanding. It is everybody's birthright. And it is also the untutored intelligence of everyman. Finally it implies an active, "can do" attitude, a ready, practical approach to one's problems, efficiency in short. The first thing that Paine did with the notion of common sense was to turn a local squabble into a struggle for the salvation of the world.

> The cause of America is in a great measure the cause of all mankind. Many circumstances hath and will arise, which are not local but universal, and through which the principles of all Lovers of Mankind are affected and in the event of which their affections are interested.[12]

A struggle for freedom is inherently important for everyone who hopes for it anywhere. That was not a new idea for his audience. Even more familiar was his recalling of biblical examples and a pervasive use of sexual imagery in his condemnations. "Society is a blessing," but government is "like dress a sign of our lost innocence," combines the two. For we do not need much government, and certainly Americans did not need the sort of government the English were inflicting upon them. Paine's state of nature was not quite Locke's. It was more familiar, a natural wilderness to which colonists came and in which they cooperated in order to survive. That certainly corresponded more than the Hobbesian version to the experiences of Americans. It followed that if settlers needed some government, it was merely to supply "the deficit of virtue," but it did not seem to be a great debit and would soon be made up. Neither the Puritan sense of sin nor the restraints it called for remained, but even as they listened to old notions, Americans were absorbing a transforming doctrine. All men, not just the children of Israel, were now fit for good government. Frequent elections and limited authority would make the magistrates indistinguishable from their electors. Why had this not always been the case? In Paine's view, it was human pride that urged rulers on to overstep their bounds. And that pride was the supreme sin was no news to Paine's Christian readers. The antecedent biblical type for this political pride was the dreadful story of Jewish royalty. When the people of Israel wanted "to be like all the other nations," they acquired kings, like the heathen. Samuel and Gideon warned them against it, and the consequences were known to all of Paine's readers. "Monarchy is in every instance the Popery of government." Joined to this religious language was a decidedly secular vocabulary also designed to desacralize and demystify monarchy. Consider the origin of the English kings, "a French bastard landing with armed banditi." Unruly descendants of a bastard, acting against the consent of nature, they were surely not chosen by God to govern anyone. To Paine, the kings of England were, in fact, the offspring of the lowest of the low, the criminal classes. And they showed no improvement. They waged war and distributed patronage only to their favorites. They were "crowned ruffians" and no one should be impressed by them. The parental bond, if it ever existed, was broken by them. Indeed "even brutes do not devour their young" as the king of England was then attacking Americans. Americans were not, however, children, but adults ready to rule themselves. Above all, and this really was a new thought, they were superior because they were young, not old and senile like the English. Paine was urging Americans and all mankind to stop looking to the past as a guide.

> The sun never shined on a cause of greater worth. 'Tis not the affair of a city, a country, a province or a kingdom, but of a continent, of at least one eighth of the habitable globe. 'Tis not the concern of a day, a year, or an age, posterity are virtually involved in the contest, and will be more or less affected, even to the end of time, by the proceedings. Now is the seed-time of continental union, faith and honor. . . . By referring the matter from argument to arms, a new era for politics is struck: a new method for thinking has arisen.[13]

Everything was to be new, and new was better. Newest of all was the expectation of a permanent, continental, democratic government. The very size of the new nation made all the old metaphors of politics obsolete. To Paine, the notion of a continental family was absurd. It would be a marketplace where all the nations would meet to exchange goods and ideas, a universe in its very character. The New World had been an asylum for the persecuted lovers of freedom all along; now its vastness would make all who came countrymen. Ancestor worship could mean nothing to such a population and its youth would last. "Youth is the seed-time of good habits." Europe may have still believed that old age was the time of wisdom and good counsel, but America knew better. The world must be renewed all the time. That, Paine cleverly noted, was the real meaning of Noah's survival. So the most traditional of memories was brought to bear on the news that "the birthday of a new day is at hand."[14] And the revolutionary call went out to all, not just to Americans. They may have been acting as messengers for mankind, but all were asked to come and join the struggle against the past.

> Oh ye that love mankind! Ye that dare oppose, not only the tyranny, but the tyrant, stand forth! Every spot of the old world is over-run with oppression. Freedom hath been hunted round the globe. Asia, and Africa, have long expelled her. Europe regards her like a stranger, and England hath given her warning to depart. Oh! receive the fugitive, and prepare in time an asylum for mankind.[15]

There can be no doubt that for Paine the boundaries of democracy were meant to embrace all those who loved freedom.

America would also be open in another way. It would trade with anybody, without any barriers. Like many other eighteenth-century writers, Paine was convinced that commerce was a source of peace. Every exchange was to be welcome. Wealth and population would mean geographic expansion, of course. The continent would soon contain more people than Europe. There was, after all, room for all. It was really to be the business of the world, or rather of its youth. For America would have no part of the old international order, with its treaties, and balances, and wars. It would be huge, and self-contained. These views were not ignored in Europe, as readers of Felix Gilbert's *To the Farewell Address* know. Well might the English and the Spanish in America tremble.[16] There seemed to be no limits to the power that Paine foresaw for America. He talked as if ships and a whole navy could simply jump out of the trunks of trees. It was all meant to be defensive power, but very threatening, by any standards.

What boundaries, if any, did Paine envision for this huge new democracy? There were to be none between ruler and ruled, citizen and emigrant, old and young. The only wall was ideological. Those who did not reject the past were not real friends of freedom. They had no place here. The American Tory, Paine wrote, was just a traitor. A captured English soldier would be set free or sent home, but the Tory was to be executed. He may not have been a traitor in the old common law, but he was disloyal, and not just to a cause, but to the future. The providential tone as Paine spoke of the "chain of extraordinary events" must have stirred his readers deeply.[17] And they may also have responded to the hope of a political future free from the corruptions of the old order. There was something here for every republican free from both the religious and social restrictions of Europe, but it was all presented in the language of the oldest of memories. The promise was absolutely dazzling. There was to be power without aggression and a mingling of all the nations without conflict. All this would be possible for young, democratic citizens who needed little government, and who were determined to assert their rights. Those who believed all that were welcome, and those who did not were excluded and not immune from attack. The standard for democratic citizenship was ideological. Anyone who wanted to be a democratic citizen belonged to the people, and those who rejected the ideology of the New World ought to remain in the old and decrepit order of the European past.

North America had enough room for them all and it would be strong enough to defend itself against foreign incursions, if it had to do so. But it would do its best to enter into no political relations with other states, all the more so since it wanted no part of their old and disreputable conventions. This came as close as possible to defining the democratic people as mankind in general. It set ideological rather than territorial boundaries, but it did so in the confident belief that the Western Hemisphere could accommodate all democratic people whatever their national origins might be.

For American democratic thought Paine's greatest single achievement was the profound impression that his writings made upon Thomas Jefferson. Jefferson helped with the publication of Paine's later books, and came to his aid when the old radical fell upon hard times. *The Rights of Man*, especially, was very close to Jefferson's deepest beliefs about one set of boundaries, those between generations. Paine argued there that no generation owes anything to another. The world belongs entirely to the living. And from as early as 1784 to as late as 1824, two years before his death, Jefferson repeated over and over again his conviction that there was an absolutely impassable barrier between generations. The newness of Noah's second world, after all, did imply a gulf between past and present, and to perpetually repeat his voyage implied a recurrent rebirth. "The earth belongs in usufruct to the living. The dead have no rights, the earth belongs to the living." Each generation must be as self-ruling as every other. "One generation," he wrote, "is to another as one independent nation to another." There were no natural bonds joining them, and the social distance was as complete as the physical one. Every generation, according to his calculations, lasted for about nineteen years. It followed that all the existing laws should be revoked at the end of twenty years and every generation be as free as its predecessors to create its own society. It was not just a matter of newness—majority government did demand the consent of those who were alive in the present. It was inherent in democracy that the present alone should matter. One could not vote if one was dead or not yet born. And the "consent of the governed" was not an idle phrase for Jefferson.[18]

The immediate and often repeated occasion for expressing these sentiments was America's foreign debt. In Jefferson's view, America ought not to borrow from foreign bankers and saddle future generations with debts. Moreover no generation should feel obliged to repay debts incurred by their predecessors. They should simply repudiate these impositions to which they had never given their consent. We simply had no right to transmit debts to our progeny. They, however, had every right to refuse to honor them. When James Madison objected that America would lose all its credit, once it was known that it might renege on its debt after nineteen-odd years, Jefferson replied that that was exactly what he hoped for. If no Dutch banker would lend us anything we would avoid indebtedness. The temptation would never arise at all.[19]

It was not only the prospect of international indebtedness that provoked Jefferson to emphasize the independence of generations from each other. In fact he thought that constitutions and all subordinate legislation should be completely revoked every twenty years. A constitution was an agreed precommitment to the structure and limits of governmental authority. Who, however, could be democratically precommitted? Only the generation that tied its own hands for the sake of its own purposes. It could not bind future generations. That was not consent. Laws simply must be renewed. When James Madison objected to these arguments, he raised only prudential, not philosophical, arguments. Constant change, he pointed out not unreasonably, would be inefficient in the extreme; it would make each generation utterly irresponsible with no regard for their successors, and in any case, people built their lives on expectations of the future. It would be too frustrating and it could not be done.[20]

If Jefferson had been interested, say, in making the trains run on time, he might have agreed, but that was not his aim. He wanted to recognize all the implications of a genuine democracy, not to arrange an easy one. The barriers between generations, between those majorities that could consent and dissent, and those that could not, must be absolute. There could be no abridgment of the rights of the living.

There was a great deal of hopefulness in this separation of the old from the young. The young were expected to be superior to their immediate elders, just as every generation is to be better than its remote ancestors. The vehicle of this perpetual improvement was education. And indeed, in this view, education becomes the the most important business of society, all but replacing politics. It was certainly Jefferson's hope that Virginia would invest all that it possessed in a system of education that would ensure that every generation of citizens at every level of society would be better informed and more deeply learned than its predecessors. One might, of course, wonder whether education might not actually encumber the young with the traditions and beliefs of their teachers, but that depends on the kind of education that they receive. If mathematics and the natural sciences are stressed, and history is presented as a source of edifying illustrations, then one might hope for flexible and future-directed people. In any case, nothing could be worse than to keep teaching the "Gothic" ideas of our ancestors.[21] By 1816 Jefferson thought that American political wisdom had come a long way since 1776, and he urged far-reaching institutional changes upon his native state.

The way to avoid the errors of the past was to recognize that history need not be repeated in America. With the years, moreover, as he saw America expanding, Jefferson came to stress the importance of geography rather than history in the curriculum. Especially after the Napoleonic debacle he came to look upon European history as a cycle that moved from tyranny to rebellion to reformation to oppression and to renewed tyranny and so on forever.[22] The study of history ought to have only one purpose, to get America off that treadmill. The young who absorb this warning fully would by that fact alone be superior to all earlier generations. Moreover, the longer Americans lived in freedom, the better they would know how to preserve and enhance it. This also was a view of history not as continuity, but as radical discontinuity. Americans had no ties to the European past. They could pick and choose useful information from it, but they had no enduring memories of it. And they certainly were not hostages to earlier generations. They could not benefit from them except as warnings. The gap Jefferson wanted to create would be not only moral, but proprietal as well. He hoped to weaken hereditary positions of every kind, beginning with primogeniture in Virginia. No generation had a right to determine the fate or to enfeeble the force of consent of succeeding generations. No one ever was more seriously Noah's spiritual heir than Jefferson, even though he never mentioned him. He was not given to quoting the Bible.

The prospect of rational men who would constantly recreate their society had immediate implications for America's relations to the rest of the world. What sort of treaties and agreements with other nations would be suitable? Given the unregenerate condition of other states, the government of the United States would enter into commercial treaties to facilitate trade carried on entirely by its individual citizens. For only individuals could engage in commerce, as in everything else, and they should be entirely free to do so at their own choosing. Apart from

helping them to achieve that end, and to promote free trade generally,
America was to avoid all binding agreements with other states.[23] They
were another bond that could not be imposed upon later generations.
Even the kinds of treaties he could bear reveal the intensity of Jefferson's individualism. Unlike Madison, he had no interest in groups or
minorities. Only individuals can act as students, traders, and citizens,
and the democratic majorities they might form consist of discrete individuals. "Nothing then is unchangeable but the inherent and unalien-
able rights of man," he wrote to his old friend Major Cartwright in
1824.[24] They and they alone were unnegotiable. Every other principle
and institution must be subject to change.

The most important international consequence of these assumptions was that America was to close its doors to the political infections
that would come to it from Europe. Not only were England and
France a thousand years behind America morally and politically, but
they exercised a malignant influence.[25] Insulated from the parental
danger and kept from the contamination of the Old World, Americans
would flourish. They would develop a new common man and a new
ethos. The whole language of paternalism would go, as newness was
all. "The great extent of our Republic is new. The sparse habitation is
new. The mighty wave of public opinion which has rolled over it is
new." [26] And new was better. Jefferson never doubted that. Newness
was, moreover, what Europe found so difficult to absorb. That was
why the French Revolution had failed. But "irresistibly" the message
of the rights of man would spread to Europe. It would cost millions
of lives to establish them there. It must come; awakened by our Revolution "they can never retrograde." [27] Simply by pursuing its own goals
America would in time bring down the Old World which still endan-
gered it and oppressed its own people. The cost in lives and blood
did not trouble Jefferson particularly. Presumably he thought the price
worth paying. Freedom had, after all, not been achieved painlessly in
America either. His view of history, moreover, encouraged such an
attitude. Consider that he wrote that "a two-penny duty on tea unjustly imposed in a sequestered part of the world" had transformed
the condition of all its people and even of mankind.[28] History was not
just mindless, it was impenetrably crazy, in fact. To forget the past was
not just morally good for us, it put an intellectual nightmare behind
us as well.

Although we were to avoid the contagion of the Old World, Jefferson did not expect America to close its doors to persecuted Europeans. Immigrants were to be made welcome. In his first inaugural address he repudiated the Alien and Sedition Acts with "shall oppressed humanity find no asylum on the Globe?"[29] Free and virtuous patriots were to come to America. Those who were neither patriotic nor liberal might presumably be wiser to remain in Europe. Jefferson also worried about crowding. If America became too populous it too would have its Paris, with its *canaille* instead of a population of virtuous farmers. But for all his misgivings, he resigned himself to manufacturing and commerce, the twin engines of these unwelcome changes. First of all, national defense required wealth, and without commerce there could be no riches. Secondly, the majority of Americans wanted commerce, and the needs of defense and the voice of the people were imperatives Jefferson never ignored.[30] "The first object of my heart is my own country" was not a vain utterance from Jefferson. Patriotism dictated a policy of "free commerce with all nations . . . political connections with none."[31]

The hope was that strength would mean peace. What of the Western Hemisphere? As early as 1786 Jefferson already believed that "our confederacy must be viewed as the nest from which all America, North and South is to be peopled."[32] To get off the wheel of history, America's geographic boundaries were to be expanded to the limits of natural possibility. The Spanish and English would just have to leave, and the French were bought out when as president, Jefferson purchased Louisiana. The local residents were never asked whether they consented to this arrangement, and the Creole population was far from eager, in fact, to fall under the rule of the United States.[33] Evidently, the consent of the governed had its limits as a principle, especially when applied to people who for traditional and religious reasons were, in Jefferson's view, not yet ready for freedom. To control its future, to stay out of European "broils," the hemisphere must remain open only to the United States. The entire rationale for the Monroe Doctrine is in a letter that Jefferson wrote to the then president.[34] Not only must the hemisphere have no boundaries excluding Americans, it must keep Europeans out. For as long as the latter were excluded, even the most degenerate of populations might be restored. It might take acres of blood and centuries of time before Catholic Spanish Americans would be ready for self-government. But he hoped that the Mexicans might manage it because they at least were not Europeans. If we protected them from that blight, they might be reborn under our auspices.[35]

There was, of course, one large group of Americans who had no reason to look forward to Jefferson's program with anything but terror. Indians were not ready to forget their ancestors, did not think of themselves as unattached individuals, and showed no disposition to be virtuous citizens of the United States. They were, nevertheless, incontestably a part of America. Were they to be a barrier and a limit to the Jeffersonian vision of democracy? It was Jefferson's hope that one could bribe them and bribe them again to peacefully settle down to agricultural pursuits, and then convince them to trust their new government, which had nothing but their welfare at heart. They were to become good and obedient children, but quite obviously not citizens.[36] The cultural boundaries of democracy were evidently as rigid as the generational ones. The geographic expansion of democracy met a temporary obstacle in the Catholic Spaniards, but an absolute one in the Indian. He could never be remade into a New World citizen. I do not mention slavery, because it cannot be made part of any modern democratic vision at all, and Jefferson knew that perfectly well. He simply refused to think about it, and when that was not possible, did so with a mixture of fear, shame, and racism. The Indian could not yet be so readily ignored. He had to be considered, and so he was, in a way that had nothing to do with consent. He was left to his historic fate of dependence, which meant, in effect, removal and destruction. He was an obstacle to the errand into the wilderness, whether it was Puritan or democratic or both.

Who then were the people? What were the boundaries of democracy at the end of the first era of American history? Were the people the consenting members of a model society that had no other relations with the past or the external world except to be an example of democratic virtue to all mankind? Did American democracy exist only to show that "our experiment will still prove that men can be governed by reason"?[37] Or was it an expansive empire that would create a vast new society at any human cost and sweep away all that did not fit into its renovated continent? The boundaries of democracy would be drawn very differently in the two cases. Membership always depends on the purposes of the polity, whether it be the people of Israel intent upon fulfilling the Reformation, or a new people inviting members of every nationality to its land to be free, or a new, efficient democratic culture rushing over a continent. At the end of the era the Jacksonians and their critics had not come to an answer. Perhaps we can never reach one, because we cannot know what we should aspire to become.

Notes

1. Norman A. Graebner, ed., *Manifest Destiny* (Indianapolis: Bobbs-Merrill, 1968), pp. 15–29, 135–43.

2. Ibid., 192–93.

3. Henry Adams, *The History of the United States of America during the Administration of Jefferson and Madison,* ed. Ernest Samuels (Chicago: University of Chicago Press, 1967), pp. 61–62, 107–8.

4. Edmund S. Morgan, ed., *Puritan Political Ideas* (Indianapolis: Bobbs-Merrill, 1965), pp. xiii–xlvii.

5. A. W. Plumstead, *The Wall and the Garden: Selected Massachusetts Election Sermons, 1670–1775* (Minneapolis: University of Minnesota Press, 1968), p. 16.

6. Perry Miller, *Errand into the Wilderness* (Cambridge, MA: Belknap Press of Harvard University Press, 1956), pp. 1–47, 141–52. Sacvan Bercovitch, *The Puritan Origins of the American Self* (New Haven: Yale University Press, 1975); and *The American Jeremiad* (Madison: University of Wisconsin Press, 1978), passim.

7. John Wise, "A Vindication of the Government of New England," in Morgan, op. cit., pp. 252–67.

8. Morgan, op. cit., pp. 352–72.

9. James H. Kettner, *The Development of American Citizenship, 1608–1870* (Chapel Hill: University of North Carolina Press, 1978), pp. 65–128.

10. Ernest Lee Tuveson, *Redeemer Nation* (Chicago: University of Chicago Press, 1968), gives a very full account of this element in the Protestant evangelical tradition, but it should not be read as giving it an exaggerated importance.

11. David Freeman Hawke, *Paine* (New York: Harper and Row, 1974), p. 47. James T. Boulton, *The Language of Politics in the Age of Wilkes and Burke* (London: Routledge and Kegan Paul, 1963), pp. 134–50.

12. *Common Sense,* ed. Isaac Kramnick (London: Penguin, 1976), p. 63.

13. Ibid., p. 82.

14. Ibid., pp. 107, 120.

15. Ibid., p. 100.

16. (Princeton: Princeton University Press, 1970), pp. 36–75, 107–11.

17. *Common Sense,* pp. 117–18. *The American Crisis: The Writings of Tom Paine,* ed. Moncure Daniel Conway (New York: G. P. Putnam, 1902), 1: 170–79, 204–7, 215–17, 250.

18. All references are to Thomas Jefferson, *Writings* (New York: Library of America, 1984). To James Madison, September 6, 1789, pp. 959–64; To John Wayles Eppes, June 24, 1813, pp. 1280–86; To Samuel Kercheval, July 12, 1816, pp. 1395–1401; To Major John Cartwright, June 25, 1824, pp. 1490–96.

19. To Archibald Stuart, January 25, 1786, pp. 843–45.

20. Marvin Myers, *The Mind of the Founder: Sources of the Political Thought of James Madison* (Indianapolis: Bobbs-Merrill, 1973); To Thomas Jefferson, February 4, 1790, pp. 229–34.

21. To William Green Munford, June 18, 1799, pp. 1063–66; To John Adams, October 28, 1813, pp. 1304–10; To Dr. Joseph Priestly, January 10, 1800, pp. 1069–74.

22. To Samuel Kercheval, July 12, 1816, pp. 1395–1406.

23. *Report on the Privileges and Restrictions on the Commerce of the United States in Foreign Countries* (London: J. Debrett, 1794), pp. 435–48. To James Monroe, June 17, 1785, pp. 802–9; To G. K. von Hagendop, October 13, 1785, pp. 834–37.

24. To Major John Cartwright, June 5, 1824, p. 1494.

25. To James Monroe, June 17, 1785, pp. 802–9. To George Wythe, August 13, 1786, pp. 857–60.

26. To Dr. Joseph Priestly, March 21, 1801, p. 1086.

27. *Autobiography*, p. 97. To Richard Price, January 8, 1789, pp. 935–39; To John Adams, January 11, 1816, pp. 1374–77.

28. *Autobiography*, p. 97.

29. *First Annual Message*, p. 508. To Jean Nicolas Demeurier, April 29, 1795, pp. 1027–29.

30. To John Jay, August 23, 1785, pp. 818–20; To George Washington, December 4, 1788, pp. 930–35; To Benjamin Austin, January 9, 1810, pp. 1369–72.

31. To Elbridge Gerry, January 26, 1799, p. 1057.

32. To Archibald Stuart, January 25, 1786, p. 844.

33. Dumas Malone, *Jefferson the President: The First Term, 1801–1805* (Boston: Little Brown, 1970), pp. 348–63. Alexander De Conde, *This Affair of Louisiana* (New York: Scribner, 1976), passim. The purchase of Louisiana was the incident that made Theodore Roosevelt call Jefferson "the first imperialist of the Republic." Merrill D. Peterson, *The Jeffersonian Image in the American Mind* (London: Oxford University Press, 1960), p. 270.

34. To James Monroe, October 24, 1823, pp. 1481–83.

35. To Alexander von Humboldt, December 6, 1813, pp. 1311–14; To Lafayette, May 14, 1817, pp. 1407–9.

36. To Charles Carroll, April 15, 1791, pp. 976–77; To Benjamin Hawkins, February 18, 1803, pp. 1113–16; To William Harrison, February 27, 1803, pp. 1117–20; To Alexander von Humboldt, December 6, 1813, pp. 1311–14; *Third Annual Message*, pp. 512–13; *Second Inaugural Address*, pp. 520–21; *Sixth Annual Message*, p. 527; To the Chiefs of the Cherokee Nation, pp. 561–63.

37. To George Mason, February 4, 1791, pp. 971–72.

CHAPTER TEN

The American Idea of Aristocracy

merican political theory has traditionally been thought of as something only Americans could find interesting. What there was of it was generally thought to be too local or too derivative, too much a mere repetition of European themes to concern anyone but the natives. The latter, in turn, in this, as in other matters, resorted to isolationism. American intellectual history, or American "studies" more generally, were important but only as illustrating something uniquely and incomparably American, meaning, to be exact, "not European." What mattered about America was all that most sharply separated its institutions and its literature from European practices. It would be unfair to say that this always implied self-glorification at the expense of the older culture. Quite the contrary, the comparisons were often profoundly unflattering to American culture. Nevertheless, what made the study of American ideas significant, for better or for worse, was that they were significantly unlike those of England and France. It is, of course, perfectly obvious that America's most distinctive institutions, representative democracy, federalism, and slavery, set it radically apart during much of the nineteenth century. The endurance of the first and the aftermath of the last still make the United States quite different from other political societies, in fact. It is by now obvious, however, that representative democracy, at least, is far from peculiarly American, and one might therefore suppose that the typical ideologies that cluster around it have now become generally significant. Perhaps the most notable of these is the centrality of

This undated essay was previously unpublished.

majorities and minorities as basic units of political life around which so much reflection turns. That is not really surprising, for these are the primary realities of electoral politics and constitutional government. Minorities immediately claimed the attention of the most celebrated of the Founders of the American constitutional system, James Madison. They remain the focus of the attention of all those who see civil liberties as the very heart of American political values. Majorities, however, have not been seen only as the potential menace of the few. They also have their rights. It is their consent that is the heart of the democratic creed. And at all times, majorities have, in a world far from safe for democracy, felt threatened by "aristocrats." The meaning that the word "aristocracy" held in America in its first fifty years as an independent country is very close to what is now called elitism. And it is embedded now in the mental world of all democratically governed people. It is my argument that this notion, in all its resonances, owes more to John Adams, the second president of the United States, than to Pareto, and that it does so because it is inseparable from the context of the electoral politics of a vigorous representative democracy.

As a rule, "aristocracy" has been a word of praise, and it still is when it simply means some group that is "best." By the end of the eighteenth century when it was applied only to the hereditary nobility, it came to be despised in America and later among French revolutionaries. After the Revolution in the newly established independent United States, however, the term acquired a wholly new meaning as it was attached to people who had no relation whatever and bore no resemblance to the old European nobility. Although still a highly pejorative term, it was no longer a remnant of antifeudal feeling, but an expression of the uneasiness that attended representative democracy. For then as now it was a highly egalitarian political system within a society that was both in principle and in fact entirely inegalitarian both economically and culturally, and is so even if we do not take slavery and race into account. "Aristocracy" was from the first a word that expressed a not unreasonable fear: that social inequality would destroy free electoral politics and damage that equality of rights which the Declaration of Independence proclaimed. Indeed, what would "created equal" mean in an unequal society? At the very least it could and *did* mean that there would be no hereditary offices or titles and that entail would have to go. That was all that the word "aristocracy" had meant for centuries. And even during the course of the Revolutionary War it still carried its old meaning. There is no pamphlet that damns the entire monarchical, aristocratic, and traditional order of Europe more passionately than Tom Paine's *Common Sense* and *The Crisis*. The American Tories were always excoriated as "aristocrats," adherents of an irrational, primitive, brutal, and tyrannical hereditary order. But abusive as it was, this was traditional usage. It is only after the Revolution, when the new political order was being forged, that the word "aristocracy" began to acquire its later, peculiarly local meanings. During the debate over the adoption of the federal Constitution in 1787 many Anti-Federalists already argued against a more centralized government, because it would become "aristocratic" in a new way. That is, it would be both socially and geographically *remote* from the electorate. Large electoral districts, moreover, would be open only to rich and clever candidates, leaving, as one speaker at the New York Convention put it, "us illiterates 'without rights.' " This illiterate then went on to quote Thucydides and Hobbes, but his point is clear enough. Aristocrats were those who could and would scheme and plot to monopolize political offices. The deepest source of this apprehension, moreover, as all these speeches make clear, was not just in the new proposals for a federal government, but in an older American Whig fear, which by the late eighteenth century was fueled by a very diffuse sense of "corruption." That is why the suspicion of aristocracy is not set against any great trust in the people, as one might expect. That is one of the odd things about it.

No figure in the early history of the Republic mirrored and thought through these attitudes more urgently or intensely than did John Adams, a most distinguished heir of Massachusetts' cultural puritanism. "Corruption" still had all the old resonance for him—heightened psychologically because of his own, and his contemporaries', conviction that the old bonds of religion had been wrong and that individuals ought indeed to strive against all the old authorities. At the same time he never doubted that "emulation," ambition, and self-assertion would be corrupting, and were merely nice words for greed and aggression. He was nothing if not utterly self-divided. Thus he had worked for years to get a declaration of independence, and when it was finally accepted he was clearly triumphant. But still, he wrote to his redoubtable wife, Abigail, "I was not transported by enthusiasm. The people will have unbounded power and the people are extremely addicted to corruption and venality, *as well as the great.*" In his eighties Adams could still fight against the removal of the last property qualifications for voting in Massachusetts, at the same time that he worried about the excessive influence of the wealthy and orthodox in Massachusetts.

The prevalence of distrust, indeed of a political misanthropy, in American political thinking cannot be overestimated and it has long survived its Puritan and Whig origins—from which Adams was already quite remote. But alarm at corruption in a free and competitive society was never far from his mind, and it flared up especially when he was challenged, as he was twice particularly. The first time, some years before the French Revolution, Turgot and Condorcet and some of their friends criticized the new constitutions of the various American states for their caution and for having two legislative houses, even though both were elected. They thought that the "upper" one, with its higher property qualifications for both voters and representatives, amounted to a denial of equal rights. Adams was stung in his deepest sensibilities—his political fears were being not only ignored but distorted. He replied in a work of three volumes and of utter unreadability, but his points are clear enough. In the absence of any hereditary political privileges, he replied, the two chambers were designed to protect the people against the designs of the great and not to deprive them of their rights. For though there were no garters, crosses, ribbons, or titles in these states, differences in wealth, education, and family names made a lot of difference in any society; so that members of the same family were often elected over and over again in perfectly free elections. If there were only one house, these people would quickly dominate it by manipulating and overawing the other members, and in the end they would demoralize and fleece the people through their excessive influence. If they were tempted into the upper house, they would be isolated and conspicuous—always under public scrutiny. They would also act as a check upon the people, by being able to veto undesirable legislation, for the people would be as "unjust, tyrannical, brutal and barberous" as the great—or anyone else who had uncontrolled power. The reasoning is not wholly plausible or sound, but it reflects clearly what Adams thought an "aristocrat" in the worst sense was: anyone who through undue influence "controlled any vote other than his own." If they were fenced off properly in their upper house, they would not be able to bend elections to their own ends, and might even act to prevent the majority from abusing its strength.

The second challenge to Adams's mistrust was far more important, both for him and for America: Thomas Jefferson. During the Revolutionary era they had been very close friends, and then after fifteen years of bitter political enmity they were reconciled and for the last thirteen years of their lives they carried on a correspondence that remains one of the real treasures of American intellectual history. Jefferson, Adams noted unhappily, feared only "the one"—a king, whereas Adams himself feared "the few." Consequently Jefferson promoted a plan for what he called a "natural aristocracy" through a system of education, and indeed he was the founder and architect of the University of Virginia. In this he reflected the ideas of his French friends who also dreamed of replacing politics with education. He had as early as 1781 in his *Notes on the State of Virginia* explained his scheme to one of these Frenchmen. Virginia would, Jefferson hoped, be divided into a hundred small units, each one of which would be largely self-governing and would maintain a school which all its children would attend for three years, free of charge. The state would then pay for six more years of secondary education for very able students who could not pay for themselves. "By this means twenty of the best geniuses will be raised from the rubbish annually, and instructed at the public expense." The best ten of these would then be sent on to university to become, in due course, the teachers, legislators, and judges of their state and nation. Only in this way could intelligence and academic ability, which is what Jefferson meant by "natural aristocracy," compete successfully with wealth. Primary education would create a citizenry capable of self-government and of protecting its rights, while higher education would create competent government, run by men of talent. The "rubbish," in short, would benefit from this arrangement. I dwell on that awful word, since Jefferson was to be so revered as a democrat, not entirely unjustly since he hoped to see those small units democratically governed. He was in his way no less ambiguous a democrat than Adams, however. Jefferson balanced participation with his "natural aristocracy," while Adams balanced popular and restricted legislatures.

In any case, full of enthusiasm, Jefferson wrote to Adams that he believed that "innate qualities of talent and virtue" would be made to rule in Virginia. To be sure "innate" and "hereditary" qualities were of greater interest to Jefferson than to Adams for other reasons. Jefferson thought nature was generally very partial in distributing talents, since it denied them to black people altogether. The question of uncovering what was innate was for him important precisely because so much *was* inherited and thus "natural." Mere man-made artificial aristocracies of wealth would "shrink into insignificance" just because education advanced "natural" aristocrats. Science, however, is progressive, and "talents and enterprises are on the alert," so there could be no obstacles to the pre-eminence of these "natural aristocrats" who would be released by education to act as an energetic force, free at last from mere artifice. "The best government is one that most effectually selects the natural aristocrats for its offices," that is, the one that leaves the matter to the universities, in fact.

The word "meritocracy" was to be made famous by Michael Young's splendid British spoof, and it has remained a fixture in the American language. Obviously it hit a native nerve, given the respect which Jefferson personally, education generally, and careers open to talent especially have enjoyed. The first voice to protest was not surprisingly Jefferson's friend John Adams. All aristocracies, Adams wrote back, begin with some sort of display of "virtues and talents," usually "genius, strength and beauty," and go on to being hereditary classes, supporting repressive and corrupt regimes. An aristocracy of "natural talent" would be no different. "Your distinction between the aristoi and pseudo-aristoi will not help the matter. I would trust one as soon as the other with unlimited power." "You will say," he went on, "that our Elections are pure?" In fact, they were not all they should be, because "every national Interest and honour" was already being sacrificed "to private and party objects." America was becoming "disaggregated"—the word was, I believe, his invention. Unlike the younger and far more realistic Madison, Adams saw no safety in a multiplicity of mutually restraining factions. Corruption was not to be so easily checked. Factions would only display jealousies and rivalries and practice "cruel rapacities upon the people," and the more intelligent, the worse. Philosophy and religion in any case would never govern nations, and whatever "esteem" they might earn would never rival the admiration that is aroused by beauty, appearance, riches, and a famous family name. Even a Harvard degree—which Adams clearly thought little of—could win an election in the absence of any other sign of merit. Prestige would come from anywhere, however illusory, "as long as it attracts the notice of mankind." The political consequences were, moreover, always the same. The people would vote uncritically for candidates with empty but conspicuous qualities who would then use their edge entirely for their own advantage. He wished his old friend luck, expressed his own admiration for learning, but refused to place any credit in the scheme.

Now Adams was in fact interested in promoting learning for its own sake. He founded the American Academy of Arts and Sciences and he was a well-educated, indeed a learned, man, but he had well-founded doubts about the political merits of intellectuals. He was perhaps too fond of Jefferson to hurt his feelings by mentioning it, but to another correspondent he explained that he thought that there simply was no connection at all between intellectual talent and political merit. Why, after all, do scholars work at their subjects? For reputation? To be sure, knowledge promoted "virtue and happiness" and should be cultivated. But as a form of personal prestige it is like every other claim for more votes than one: politically dangerous. Moreover, there are just as many educated "knaves and hypocrites" as unlettered ones, and "intelligence has no association with morality." Just take a look, Adams went on, at the internal government of academies; when there are elections for new members, there are just as many intrigues and parties as in the state legislature; all these philosophers, divines, physicians, lawyers, poets, and orators are in strife with each other. Even before the natural aristocracy "became a hereditary caste, in sum, it would *not* give the people good governments." To Adams it was clear that all intrusions of personal eminence into electoral politics were "aristocratic," and were bound to be reprehensible eventually, because sooner or later the less gifted many would be victimized.

The response of later democrats to Adams was curious. Throughout the early nineteenth century and after, Jefferson remained their revered patron saint, "the sage of Monticello." Yet Adams's cast of mind was really the more representative of nineteenth-century democratic attitudes, though this remained unacknowledged. The necessity of an educated citizenry, capable of defending its rights, taking part in politics, enjoying the self-respect that education gives, remained a primary part of the democratic program throughout the nineteenth century, but Jefferson's aristocracy was quietly forgotten. Adams, on the other hand, was said to be too much of a "political fatalist," just another Sir Robert Filmer. He thought that because aristocracy was usual it was inevitable, democrats complained. The new generation of radical democrats who were associated with President Jackson in the 1830s were more confident than Adams had been—or so they thought. If one prevents hereditary offices and political monopolies of any kind, and above all limits government to a bare minimum of activity, one can stop aristocracy from destroying democratic electoral politics. The real conflict was not, as Adams had thought, between virtue and corruption, but between rights and concentrations of power, whether based on religion, military force, or commerce. For America only the latter mattered, and the Jacksonians saw the "money power" at work in one place, the Bank of the United States, the chartered bank of the federal government. And the bank was a danger not because it pursued damaging economic policies, but because it posed a terrible political threat. As Jackson himself put it in his Farewell Address of 1837, if the bank's charter had been renewed, "government would have passed from the hands of the many into the hands of the few." By controlling the currency a group of rich men would be able "to exercise more than *its just portion* of influence in political affairs." The laboring classes of this country "are in constant danger of losing their *fair* influence in the government and cannot *maintain their rights* against the influence of this 'paper aristocracy.'" Redistribution of wealth was not what Jackson had in mind—nothing was more absurd to him and to his supporters than the idea of equality of property or talent among men (not to mention Native Americans and blacks). But in politics, numbers were what had to count, and anything else was "unfair." It was, in fact, his duty as president, the only official elected by the whole people, to protect the many against the schemes of "aristocrats"—that is, anyone who tried to acquire more than his share of influence, more votes than one, especially by using money to work on voters and congressmen.

The only answer to the aristocratic threat, according to the radical Jacksonian press, was less government. Law could not create equality but it could always foster "artificial" inequalities of wealth; so the less law the better. This was hardly a very sanguine view of American politics and indeed no more confident than Adams's had been. Moreover, it was thought that America was becoming more unequal and that "the crafty and indolent were depressing the condition of the labouring and middling classes." There is no evidence to support that contention, but it is very important for the American theory of aristocracy, which is always nostalgic, which always harbors a fantasy vision of a more egalitarian America in some past. There is always "declension," to use the favorite term of seventeenth-century Puritan sermons. Aristocracy is the proof of this increasing decline and fall. Even relatively cheerful democrats thought so. James Fenimore Cooper, the author of the *Leatherstocking Tales,* once so very popular in Europe, was at one stage of his life an ardent supporter of Jackson. He even had a little theory of history to support his hero. Americans during the early frontier days had been an equal, cooperative people struggling against nature. Once settled, a ruthless, greedy, crude struggle for individual wealth began. This had to be controlled by law and government. It should be a democracy, but tempered by democratic "gentlemen" who would bring culture, candor, and balance to politics and protect the people against its predators. This ideal "American Democrat" is a version of Jefferson's "natural aristocracy" but with a very great difference. Cooper and the Jacksonians did not see Americans as a very active people but one that needed protection against incursions and aggressions, especially from this new "paper money" aristocracy out to grasp unfair political advantages. The duty of gentlemen was one of "trusteeship," of care for the politically inept and threatened.

There was also a note of nationalism now in this polemic, wholly unknown to Jefferson and Adams. To a degree, that was simply part of a new intellectual era America shared with Europe, but it was also a reaction *against* Europe after the Napoleonic Wars. America was very isolated in the age of Metternich. It was engaged in a political process of democratization, while Europe seemed to have returned to repressive monarchy. Americans began to identify themselves as a democratic *nation* as against Europe and with a unique mission to preserve the light of freedom in a dark world. Cooper, not surprisingly, hated Sir Walter Scott—as would Mark Twain rather later—and both loathed the "feudal" values he was selling especially successfully in the South. Which brings us to another twist in the Jacksonian picture of the malevolent aristocracy: the content of education. Education was good, but what it taught was not. The editor of the leading Jacksonian journal, the *Democratic Review,* was sure that American colleges were "dens of feudal subversion" which taught the rich to despise farmers and mechanics. For what did they read? English literature, which was indeed "as rich and glorious, as it was a vast collection of intellectual treason." We would be better off not speaking English, since our former enemies influence us so. The answer was to create a democratic, anti-aristocratic American literature, but the editor was no fool, and he knew that his problem was insoluble. Shakespeare was not going to go away. Perhaps one ought to keep the educated out of government altogether. In short, he entertained none of Cooper's hopes for their possible conversion to democracy. These two men had each inherited one of Adams's fears—Cooper saw the danger of excluding, the editor of including, "the few" in the institutions of a democratic government. Only the glimmer of a new democratic culture seemed to offer any hope. And in the poetry of Walt Whitman it was soon to find its voice and celebration.

What is also interesting is that the past inspired such misgivings. America's early primitive democracy was said either to have fled, or at the worst to have never really gotten started at all. Though it is often said, it is only partially true that democrats ignore history and that they are often indifferent to the past. After all, the majority that has to consent to government is alive here and now; no generation had the right to impose itself upon its successors, in Jefferson's view. Yet he was anxious to keep Anglo-Saxon and Native American languages alive. The Jacksonians were also ambivalent. They thought the past saddening or useless, but they were also eager for a new kind of history, not one about great men, about aristocrats, but the history of mechanics, inventors, and of general populations. This rejection, indeed fear, of Europe's aristocratic past gave modern statistical and social history and indeed social science its first impetus. Adams wrote up all the old republics, and his successors, most of whom were not nostalgic, but in search of a suitable history for a democracy, began to write the history of the people. That is the real and primary origin of social history and indeed of social science generally in America. Its most distinct feature, the effort to describe the lives and opinions of the many, has in fact always been obvious. What, after all, could be more democratic than survey research?

Politically then, aristocracy is by 1830 un-American, as well as a monopolistic conspiracy on the part of the rich to deprive the people of their full political rights. Nationalism was added to democratic suspicions. There is no hint that this puts the sacredness of private property or of competitive activity into doubt—as I have said. So Alexis de Tocqueville, who visited Jacksonian America, wrote, "The people do not want the rich to sacrifice their money, but their pride." Tocqueville had interviewed a considerable number of rich and eminent Americans and while he thought a "commercial aristocracy" a very disagreeable prospect, he did not think it a very likely one. Americans were too mobile socially and geographically to settle into a hereditary pattern of any kind. He was too impressed by the stability of democratic society and institutions to be much concerned about aristocrats, especially as he saw the legal profession, open to all, yet always cautious and formalistic in its thinking, as fulfilling all the useful purposes of an aristocracy. What did surprise him was the enormous fear and foreboding so many old-rich Americans felt. They clearly trembled for their property, in spite of the complete absence of any real threats. Tocqueville thought that money simply made men uneasy. A marquis, rich or poor, at home or in exile, is still a marquis; that is what he *is*. But money comes and goes. Anyone can potentially make and lose it. I would add consent as a source of their worries. The consent of the governed is the basis of democracy, and while the many certainly consented to property, they had not, as we saw, consented to all the ambitions of the rich. Of all "aristocratic" aspirations the one that was most completely rejected was an effort at imitating the European aristocratic habits, to be idle, indeed to despise work. And the rich did long for European ways. It was not the rich as such but the "indolent," the idle-rich, who roused the greatest loathing among Jacksonian democrats. Wealth had to be earned; "independent of industry" it was unjustifiable. It was odious because implicitly it meant that labor was regarded as impure, demeaning, degrading, and despised. It was undemocratic. It was not just a cultural challenge, it was a denial of the national ethos. America's most famous book about its aristocracy is therefore, not surprisingly, Veblen's *The Theory of the Leisure Classes,* written in the last years of the nineteenth century. It is one of a long line of jeremiads launched against the idle rich, who refused to participate in America's productive work and instead indulged in atavistic displays and exploits, to emphasize their aloofness from industry and commercial enterprise. Veblen was relatively indifferent to their political activities, but his contemporaries the "populists" were not. Their case against the bankers, the "money-power," had not altered since Jackson's days. Those few among the educated and rich who chose to go in for social good works tended to follow Cooper's political lead. These "progressives" as they were called actually made a college president, Woodrow Wilson, president. However, what is interesting is how little was new in all of this. Veblen with his lament about atavism, and the populists with their outcry against monopolized political power, added nothing to the original idea of aristocracy. Nor did the "progressives'" denunciation of corruption sound particularly novel. That is especially true of John Adams's most recent and self-acknowledged heir—C. Wright Mills, whose *Power Elite* in the 1950s summed up the entire ancestral tradition. His book was very popular in Europe as well. He had little use for Veblen and his like who worried about mere manners and conspicuous consumption—that was just "monkey business." What really mattered was that twentieth-century America had suffered a precipitous decline, a fall from egalitarian grace. It was corrupt. The people were a fragmented, passive, powerless, and gullible mass-society. The various elites of the wealthy and professionally privileged had coalesced to form a "national power elite" which was able to control access to political office and influence. Representative democracy was a mere sham, a shadow of its former self. The controlling elite was made up of just the kind of people Adams had feared, successful, ambitious, and manipulative individuals capable of dazzling and extracting the submission of the misled and deprived majority. This version, the oldest one, of America's political attitudes had emerged again in all its vigor, to abate after two turbulent decades, but not likely to disappear entirely. Indeed even though the word "elitism" is now used very carelessly as an all-purpose condemnation of any inequality or inegalitarian opinion, its original political character ought to be remembered. Without the democratic idea of the rights of the majority it tends to lose all genuine political meaning.

There are several more general propositions that suggest themselves in this story. One is that moral and political beliefs are enormously enduring. The physical and institutional life of America has been transformed since John Adams first uttered his cry "I fear the few," but the ideas born in the first fifty years of its independent political life remain relatively unaltered and are as vigorous as ever. The second, lesser, but not insignificant consideration is that the electoral politics of representative democracy give rise to quite specific social perceptions; and among these, the tension between the rich and the poor will be seen as a conflict between the minorities and the majority. The fears entertained by minorities, not always rich or aristocratic, have of course had a profound effect upon the American theory and practice of civil rights, which is well known. There is another side, however, which I have tried to present today: the fears that the majority felt of "aristocracies," of the successful few who would take more than "their fair share of political influence," who could command more than their own vote. It is the balance of these two fears that I think gives representative democracy its specific character and endows John Adams and his heirs with a more than local or antiquarian interest.

CHAPTER ELEVEN

A New Constitution for a New Nation

The title of this paper may seem paradoxical since it appears at the head of an essay that is supposed to discuss the influence of classical antiquity on the framing of the United States Constitution. It is, however, meant not to deny that the Founders reflected frequently and deeply upon the political history of European antiquity, but to note that it was by considering that remote past that they came to realize fully how very novel their project was, and to give the phrase *Novus ordo seculorum* its full impact.

We ought not to forget that every person who had a secondary education in the eighteenth century had read some of the classical authors. Certainly he would know some Cicero and Plutarch and he might also have read some of Tacitus's lurid historical writings. These, rather than the great Greek philosophers, were the favored authors of the time, and all were readily available in translation, so that no great knowledge of the ancient languages was required to read them.[1] They formed the young minds of all sides of every controversy, of loyalists no less than patriots during the Revolution, and of Anti-Federalists just as much as of those who wrote the Constitution of 1787. The classical authors whom everyone read did not point in any one political direction; they were simply part of the common understanding of an age. Because they provided a familiar pool of illustrations during debates they were an important vehicle for the self-understanding of the opposed parties to any controversy, but they served all sides equally well. Their influence was genuine but diffuse.

This undated essay was previously unpublished.

Nevertheless, modern constitutionalism, of which the United States Constitution is the first complete example, depends upon certain philosophical conceptions which had their origin in ancient Greece. The very idea of the rule of law depends on Aristotelian logic, that is, on syllogistic reasoning. There has to be a general rule, a specific case that falls under it, and a necessary conclusion. And while Aristotle knew perfectly well that forensic argument could rarely be so exact, the syllogism was for him and has remained the standard not only of the fairness of the law, but also of its rationality. Both the civil and criminal law of a city were rational only if they were logically deduced from the most basic rules of justice which distributed the burdens and benefits of society to its citizens and which corresponded to their deepest political beliefs.[2] So one might well say that Aristotelian logic was a necessary, though not a sufficient, condition for constitutional political theory, which must have the rule of law at its very center. For whatever else it may be, it is not arbitrary government.

The second set of politically relevant ideas and examples that were derived from classical antiquity concerned republican government, since with a few minor exceptions most medieval and modern states were monarchies. Here Polybius (200?–118 BC) and Cicero, as well as general histories of Rome, were decidedly significant. From Polybius, the exiled Greek general who had contemplated his Roman conquerors at their height, they learned the theory of the mixed constitution. Aristotle had already explained that a polity in which both the rich and the poor with their different interests and ideologies ruled jointly might be more stable and less prone to injustice than most other regimes. Polybius had a more institutional version of the mixed regime. In the normal course of historical change, he argued, monarchies become tyrannies and are overthrown by virtuous aristocrats, who in time decay into oligarchies which are overturned by law-abiding democrats, who eventually fall into mob rule. Sooner or later a new monarch restores order and the cycle, based on the permanent human passion for power and wealth, resumes. Only Rome had brought this process to a halt by devising a division of powers between the aristocratic senate, the democratic popular assemblies, and the monarchical consuls and other magistrates. In this version of the mixed constitution each political class had a veto to prevent the others from straying from the path of public duty. It allowed republican government to endure and to frame good laws which made virtuous statesmen and citizens.[3] Not only did it force every part of the political society to stay within the limits of its assigned sphere of authority, but the special talents of each one were put to the service of the whole. To be sure, the ideal of the mixed state did not remain a republican notion. Americans were most familiar with it in its English form as a mixture of a monarch, lords, and commons. However, as very few of the Framers thought a return to English government either possible or even desirable, they looked to the history of republics for models. Ultimately, after much discussion, both the classical republics and mixed constitutions ceased to matter in 1787. John Adams had still managed to write the mixed republic into the Constitution of Massachusetts and he certainly was an ardent admirer of Polybius, but he was a relatively isolated intellectual figure, with his truly Puritan sense of corruption and declension as the only constants of public life.[4] In fact, the mixed constitution was laid to rest rather early on in the Constitutional Convention when Charles Pinckney got up and said out loud what everyone knew, that there was nothing to mix in America, that rich and poor were too much alike to require separate institutional embodiments.[5] "We the People" had a very new meaning; it was neither the plebs of Rome, nor the commons of England, but everyone. Moreover, the energetic young men in Philadelphia had absorbed the history of the Revolution in a way that put them at an enormous distance from all of classical antiquity and even from Adams's last colonial generation. They thought that change was good, desirable, and necessary. It was not a sign of decay or corruption, but of improvement and reform. Not cycles but steady progress summoned them to write a new constitution. They were to be sure, as has often been noted, without illusions about human moral capacities, but they had a lot of confidence in new knowledge and the institutions it could help them build. They certainly believed that political science had come a long way in the recent past. And when they talked of advances in the science of government they meant one author above all others, Montesquieu, whose *Spirit of the Laws* was a widely used college text and, apart from the Bible, the most frequently cited book in the year 1787.[6] From its pages they learned, among other things, that the functional separation of governmental powers was the primary way to avoid concentrations of political authority in too few hands, and that this was the way to achieve the real end of modern constitutional government: political stability without the oppression of individuals.

Indeed, even the idea of the rule of law, or the government of laws not of men, as they then said, was a set of notions drawn from English theory and practice as it was expounded by Montesquieu and, after him, by Blackstone, rather than from ancient philosophy. The rule of law was not, as it had been for Aristotle, the rule of reason guiding a city to justice, but the protection of the rights of individual citizens against arbitrary governmental actions. For Aristotle the rule of law covered potentially every human activity, public or private. So also, Cicero's notion of law as the expression of the consensus that ties a people into a city, is remote from the way law figures in modern constitutional thinking. The latter is built on a distinction between public and private life, and it is the task of law to keep every public agent within the limits of his assigned sphere. Such a view of law could have no place in the classical ideal of government, whose highest aim was to educate its members according to a shared ideal of human virtue and political rationality. In contrast every member of the Convention of 1787 agreed that it was the chief aim of good government to protect the liberty and property of individual citizens. The modern rule of law assumes that only a restricted number of activities and relationships may be ruled at all, which puts a vast distance between it and ancient legal ideals. The wide circumference of the private realm, to which guaranteed religious freedom is a testimony, was a response to Christian sectarianism, which is utterly remote from the creedal world of classical paganism. This is in itself enough to recall the limits of the law's reach in eighteenth-century constitutional thought. Limited government has its roots in the divided loyalties created by biblical religiosity and in denominational conflict, not in ancient philosophy. And one might well argue that without the Bill of Rights the spiritual objectives of the Constitution were incompletely stated. Its origins are to be found in England, not in classical antiquity.

The framers of the Constitution were, in fact, well aware that they owed a lot to English legal precedents and that this in itself made them relatively modern. Their favorite author, Montesquieu, had explained that quite clearly, for he had a very strong sense of the differences between modern and ancient politics. The invention of the compass had transformed Europe.[7] The symbolic power of that instrument was not lost on Montesquieu. Not only had it meant new worlds, new wealth, and immense power, it also meant a different sense of direction, and a wholly altered relationship to nature—in short, an unprecedented culture. It pointed into directions which men had never taken before. Politically that meant, among other things, a new idea of the best possible regime. Of the two models of free government, the old

Roman Republic and modern England, only the latter was still practically relevant. Comparisons between the two polities were, however, possible and even instructive. It is as a contrast and as the illumination that comes from the alien and remote that the classical republics could still serve political understanding. And not the least important lesson of their history was the course of their decline. Montesquieu feared despotism above all else. And one of his objects was to show that any form of government, even a republic, can become a despotism, which is an irreversible disaster. Republican Rome had fallen into that state and it was an awful example and warning.[8]

What mattered most to Montesquieu's immediate heirs, such as *The Federalist Papers*'s Publius, was therefore his analysis of the strengths and weaknesses of republican governments. What did Montesquieu think a republic was? It could be democratic or aristocratic, that is, the citizens ruled and were ruled in turn, or they elected permanent magistrates. Religion was manipulative or insignificant. Republics were small cohesive communities in which citizens were carefully selected for political membership and knew each other well and felt an intense emotional commitment to each other and to their city. Republics were ruled by unspoken rules that arose insensibly from their physical and moral development, rather than by consciously made laws such as govern modern states. Indoctrination, early education, constant vigilance by censors and fellow citizens were indispensable to maintain the ancient cities. They could last only as long as they remained deeply traditional societies, wholly geared to public purposes in which every institution served to maintain the disciplined egalitarian and military structure of the community. While they were free states because every citizen was at liberty to rule as well as to be ruled, they were insecure because they were excessively demanding. The citizens became unruly or military expansion destroyed their cohesion.[9]

At no time did Montesquieu suggest that republics of this kind could or should be restored in a wholly transformed modern world. They were scientifically significant only for purposes of comparison. The famous chapter on the English constitution in *The Spirit of the Laws* is in fact a comparison between England and Rome as two examples of free states. Both were systems in which the political classes could take part in governing without being controlled or repressed by the others. In England representation served "the general will" of the people far better than direct democracy could in a large country. The king and the House of Lords served freedom by dividing and balancing the power of the state. Consent was at the very heart of this regime and so was personal freedom. Unlike the ancient republics it was governed by deliberate legislation, not custom. The cornerstone of English freedom was a judiciary that was completely independent from other governing agents. It was impartial, aided in its justice by popular juries, and dedicated to one end, the security and freedom of every individual. It is on this capital point that England proved its superiority to Rome, where each one of the branches had some judicial power so that judges were never wholly independent. To be sure in democratic republics punishments were meant to be fair, because the life of every citizen was precious, but their institutional means were not adequate to that end.[10] Without the separation of powers, Montesquieu's great invention, no republic could be truly free. It was his deepest belief that the criminal law especially, but also civil law, must be withdrawn completely from the political arena if the life, liberty, and property of the individual are to be secure.[11]

The second new feature of a modern state is commerce, about which Rome knew nothing, while it is the benign object of English government. While there had been ancient commercial republics, they did not in Montesquieu's view pursue trade consistently. In the new European world commerce not only would soon eliminate Machiavellian foreign policies and war, it must also reduce prejudice, refine manners, and promote justice, frugality, economy, moderation, labor, prudence, tranquility, and order. These are not the Aristotelian virtues, but the democratic virtues of ordinary people. Moreover, the character-building powers of commerce and the dynamics of the political system relieve the English of any need to cultivate self-restraint or ancient virtue in order to maintain their regime. They must and are ready to pay high taxes and to sacrifice everything for their freedom, but that is all. A modern free state demands only that everyone pursue his interest with determination and speak out and reason, no matter how badly. Religion must play no part in politics, and in England it seems to have no place even in private life. These are unexceptional men and excellent citizens and this is the very model of what the modern state should be like.[12] The only probable alternative is despotism. The absence of unity did not disturb Montesquieu. Even in the classical republics, that was not what virtue meant. Real political harmony was perfectly compatible with dissension and disagreements of every kind. What passes for unity usually is despotic and only amounts to "dead bodies buried next to each other."[13] Nor did Montesquieu bewail the absence of great men. Unlike the ancient historians, he did not believe that these celebrated individuals had ever played a very significant part in social change. His historiography was exceptionally impersonal, a matter of deep causes and incremental change. If Caesar had not destroyed the enfeebled republic, it would have been some other general.[14] Nothing could be more remote from classical political science. And much as they admired George Washington, the Framers also followed the wisdom of the modern age and planned a political system that did not require great statesmen in order to succeed in its aims.

This was the political science that Madison and Hamilton had learned in their youth and that is how Montesquieu came to be written into *The Federalist*.[15] Publius took the remoteness of classical republics for granted, even though the Anti-Federalists did not. They were convinced, quoting Montesquieu, that only a small and cohesive society was fit for republican government and they considered the states quite comparable, culturally and demographically, to the ancient cities. It was an illusion that Publius did not allow them to entertain for long. In fact, it was the misgovernment and irresponsibility of state governments that led to the Convention in the first place, and inspired James Madison to develop a theory of the modern extended republic.[16] The second battle fought with rival examples from antiquity was about the success or failure of the ancient confederacies, which might serve as models for the new federation. Montesquieu, who had pointed to the military advantages of this arrangement for the smaller republics, was again often and inconclusively quoted in the Convention.[17] One can hardly blame Benjamin Franklin, who fully recognized the irrelevance of this line of thought, for protesting during the Convention that these discussions were "a proof of the imperfection of the Human Understanding. . . . We have gone back to ancient history for models of Government, and examined the different forms of those Republics which have been formed with the seeds of their own dissolution and now no longer exist. And we have viewed Modern States all around Europe, but find none of their Constitutions suitable to our circumstances."[18] He suggested that the Convention try prayer instead, which, for Franklin, amounted to an expression of despair. As intelligent as ever, even in old age, he had put his finger on the difficulty that the Framers confronted: that there were no precedents, no models, no examples to guide them in their utterly novel enterprise. It would all have to be their own invention. Apart from the inheritance of English law, they would be obliged to create federalism, representative democracy, and a separation of powers that did not, in fact, exist even in England, in spite of Montesquieu's idealized account of its institutions. According to Publius, their own brief experiences and the modern science of politics would have to direct them. There was nothing else.

In keeping with all these considerations, classical antiquity served Publius mostly as an awful warning of all that could go wrong in republics. In this he was actually following local traditions. The memory of Rome was not a particularly heartening one for those who remembered not only the palmy days of the Republic but especially the history of the Empire. Protestants had little use for anything that the name Rome might suggest, in any case. And had not St. Augustine told them all there was to be said about the morals of the Republic when he reminded his fellow citizens that their revered ancestors had found glory in the rape of the Sabine women?[19] Was there anything to be added to Tacitus's account of the horrors of even the early Empire and his cynical hints that the Romans had never been all that different? More secular readers might have come to agree with David Hume that there was no correlation between the personal virtue and the military success of the Romans; they were pretty degenerate even at the height of the Republic.[20] When at the federal Convention the history of the old republics was mined for warnings, its members were far from being eccentric.

It is therefore not surprising that the very first three words of the Constitution are a declaration of political independence from the entire European past. "We the People" is a declaration of popular sovereignty which makes the consent of the citizens the sole legitimate ground of government. The implications of this momentous novelty are spelled out very clearly in *The Federalist,* which remains our best interpretation of the original Constitution. This was to be a republic based not on virtue, but on the consent of people with diverse interests and a shared concern for life, liberty, and the security of property. It is to be governed not as a direct democracy, but by elected representatives and by a federal government that had only a very tenuous resemblance to the unsuccessful confederacies of ancient Greece. Intellectually that meant a new political theory, based not on the sanctity of tradition, but on a political science that uses the experiences of the past merely as illustrations, or as data for framing general propositions about both good and ineffective political institutions. Even this is less important than calculation based on reasoning from careful observations of current American and English political institutions and conduct. Eventually Madison was to say that even Montesquieu had only opened up the science of politics which America was now fast developing.[21] That was certainly part of his and Hamilton's enduring intellectual self-confidence, but also of their awareness of the novelty of their enterprise. What could possibly be learned from old chronicles in a wholly new political scene? Their main use was negative. The only time Rome is mentioned with full approval in *The Federalist* is to demonstrate that the presence of two concurrent taxing authorities is compatible with achieving greatness. The power of both the states and the federal government to tax the same citizenry does not, therefore, have to lead to any dire consequences at all (34). With that exception, the institutions of antiquity were treated either as suggestions to be discarded or as examples of everything that was to be avoided.

The rejection of the example of antiquity begins very early on. Unlike Montesquieu and most liberal political theorists, Publius did not think that commercial states were particularly peaceful. Commercial republics, he noted, pointing to Athens and to Carthage, were inclined to go to war. And they did so for no good reason. War is always an option. Pericles apparently dragged Athens into war in order to please a prostitute (6). There was no need to dwell on the conduct of military republics, since they were completely irrelevant to the civilian ethos of America (8). The message of antiquity was, however, clear. Unless the states accepted the proposed Constitution and united under it, they would sooner or later go to war against each other. That did not mean that in other respects the states and the proposed federal republic were not superior to other forms of government. They were genuine republics designed to preserve liberty and property (36). The new extended republic, unlike the little republics of antiquity, would moreover be able to protect the public against the local factions that might threaten freedom and property (45 and 85). It would have the strength to do so because it was overtly grounded in the consent of the entire American people, "the only legitimate fountainhead of power" (49). The people would not only ratify the Constitution, but would go on to elect representatives who would hold well-defined office for a limited time. That was the real mark of republican rule in the modern era (22 and 39). Without a union this would be impossible, as the history of the ancient cities proved. Their internal divisions were a perpetual invitation to foreign intrigue and to treachery on the part of the very men to whom the people had entrusted the powers of government (22). "It is impossible to read the history of the petty republics of Greece and Italy without feeling a sensation of horror and disgust at the distractions with which they were continually agitated, and at the rapid successions of revolutions by which they were kept in a state of perpetual vibration between the extremes of tyranny and anarchy" (9). If one remembered that they were far smaller than any of the American states and if one accepted Montesquieu's argument that the ancient republics were possible only as long as they remained tiny, then there were only two choices for the American states. They must either become thirteen monarchies, or unite into a modern extended republic, built on principles of an improved political science that was unknown to the ancients. The latter knew nothing of a self-correcting electoral system that was both energetic and free. Should the Constitution be rejected, the states would also become "little, jealous, clashing, tumultuous commonwealths, the wretched nurseries of unceasing discord and the miserable objects of universal pity and contempt." A genuine confederate republic would avoid all that, for it would have the resources to quell any uprising in any of the states as well as to provide for the common defense (9).

When one considers the scorn that Publius heaped upon the endemic disorders of the republics of antiquity, one might suppose that unity was his highest political aim, which would scarcely be compatible with his ardent championship of liberty. That was not the case, however. It was his view that America could overcome the tension between freedom and unity thanks to the practices of representative government. In this it was again ahead of the ancient republics, for although the Athenians had understood representation, they did not use it fully, and so fell prey to personal tyrants (63). There was far too much direct participation by the entire body of citizens in every branch of the government, and especially in Athens's popular assemblies. "Had every Athenian citizen been a Socrates, every Athenian assembly would still have been a mob." Such a crowd was bound to give way to unreasoning passions and was invariably manipulated by some wholly unprincipled leader (55). In contrast to this lamentable spectacle, "is it not the glory of the people of America" that "they have not suffered a blind veneration for antiquity?" Though they have shown "a decent regard for the opinions of former times," they have now embarked upon "the experiment of an extended republic" and posterity will be grateful for this innovation. "Happily for America, happily we trust for the whole human race," they have rejected the past and "pursued a new and more noble course" (14). Representative government in an extended republic is such a vast improvement because, unlike classical democracy, it has a built-in remedy against the ruinous conflicts of factions. Far from having to crush differences of interest or political and religious opinion, they are encouraged to flourish. The greater the multiplicity of religious sects and of more tangible interests, the more likely these groups are to form changing and flexible electoral coalitions, none of which has a motive for crushing the others (10 and 51). Bargaining replaces the tumult of popular assemblies, as order and freedom are reconciled in society generally. The representatives, moreover, can deliberate calmly and save the people from occasional follies, and still remain close enough to the electorate to maintain their trust. The electoral system creates a disposition in favor of liberty, and the separation of powers prevents the concentration of authority in too few hands. All this was possible only thanks to America's great political invention, the large republic governed by representatives of the people. The small republics of antiquity knew nothing of this and even their leagues were inadequate to defend them. The one confederation that had central institutions sufficiently strong to be at all effective went down in military defeat like all the others. Such were the costs of smallness, an awful warning to the states (17 and 18).

The specific institutions of the ancient city-states also failed to pass muster. Rome had so feeble an executive that it had to resort to dictators in moments of danger, which was a dangerous expedient (69). The consuls who made up its plural executive were often at odds and would have been so more often if, as patricians, they had not been joined in fear of the people (70). And finally, worst of all, ancient politicians did not really know how to put a constitution together. They had to find individual legislators who were driven to resort to violence and superstition to impose a basic law upon their republics. The men who together had written the proposed Constitution of the United States were in every way their intellectual and ethical superiors. They had managed to introduce stability and energy into a limited republican government designed for a free people (37 and 38). And they had done this by "quitting the dim light of historical research" and following reason and good sense (70). Antiquity had very little to teach them, except to remind them of its many errors.

One might argue that Publius did not really understand himself or his debt to antiquity, but why should we accuse him of such obtuseness? He did not deny that there was much to be admired in the classical past, but unlike the French radicals of his day, he did not have to look to it for an alternative to a hated monarchical and clerical regime. That was behind him, and he could look forward to a resolutely modern republic, because he was in fact faced with new circumstances. Intellectually Publius followed Montesquieu to the last. The final papers of *The Federalist* echo his every thought on the necessity of an independent judiciary and the protection of the accused in criminal cases. And the Bill of Rights which completed the Constitution is mainly devoted to rendering the procedures of the criminal law compatible with individual security and freedom. This is the very end of modern republican government and there is nothing in antiquity that resembles it. It created a legal system to protect the property and freedom of individuals, not to teach them civic and martial virtue. To have fully understood that and to have recognized that antiquity was too remote to copy, and not worth regretting, was no mistake on Publius's part. America had discovered the future. And if Publius longed for fame, so have many other men who were far removed from Plutarch's heroes. Nothing suggests that he would have wanted posterity to treat him with reverence or to become the object of ancestor worship. The best tribute we can possibly pay him and his generation is to follow their example and to think not about our imaginary roots, but about our responsibilities.

Notes

1. Richard M. Gummere, *The Colonial Mind and the Classical Tradition* (Cambridge, MA: Harvard University Press, 1963).

2. Aristotle, *Nicomachean Ethics*, bk. 5; *Rhetoric*, bk. 1, ch. 1; bk. 3, chs. 17, 18.

3. Kurt von Fritz, *The Theory of the Mixed Constitution in Antiquity* (New York: Columbia University Press, 1954).

4. Gilbert Chinard, "Polybius and the American Constitution," *Journal of the History of Ideas* 1 (1940): 38–58.

5. Max Ferrand, ed., *The Records of the Federal Convention of 1787* (New Haven, CT: Yale University Press, 1966), 1: 397–404.

6. Donald S. Lutz, "The Relative Influence of European Writers on Late Eighteenth-Century American Political Thought," *American Political Science Review* 78 (1984): 189–98.

7. *The Spirit of the Laws*, trans. Thomas Nugent (New York: Hafner Press, 1949), bk. 21, ch. 21.

8. That was the main burden of Montesquieu's pioneering history of Rome, *Considerations on the Causes of the Greatness of the Romans and Their Decline,* trans. David Lowenthal (Ithaca, NY: Cornell University Press, 1968).

9. *Spirit,* bk. 2, chs. 2, 3; bk. 3, chs. 3, 4; bk. 4, chs. 4–8; bk. 5, chs. 2–7; bk. 7, chs. 2, 3; bk. 8, chs. 2–5.

10. *Spirit,* bk. 11.

11. *Spirit,* bks. 6, 12, 26.

12. *Spirit,* bk. 19, ch. 27.

13. *Romans,* pp. 93–94.

14. *Romans,* p. 102.

15. Since there are so many editions of *The Federalist Papers* in use now, I shall not cite references in endnotes, but simply put the number of the individual paper in parentheses in the text.

16. Charles Hobson, "The Negative on State Laws: James Madison, the Constitution, and the Crisis of Republican Government," *Mary and William Quarterly,* 3d ser., 36 (1979): 215–38.

17. *Spirit,* bk. 9, chs. 1–3.

18. Farrand, *Records,* 1: 450–51.

19. *The City of God,* bk. 2, ch. 17; bk. 3, ch. 13.

20. "That Politics May Be Reduced to a Science," in *Essays Moral, Political, and Literary,* ed. T. H. Green and T. H. Grose (London, 1898), 1: 106.

21. Gordon Wood, *The Creation of the American Republic, 1776–1787* (New York: Norton, 1972), p. 612.

CHAPTER TWELVE

Democracy and the Past:
Jefferson and His Heirs

"Democracy has no forefathers, it looks to no posterity, it is swallowed up in the present and thinks of nothing but itself." So complained John Quincy Adams in 1833, somewhat unfairly. For while it is true that Jefferson and his Jacksonian heirs felt no reverence for their ancestors, they were not entirely indifferent to the future. But Adams was right about the inherent present-mindedness of democracy. Majority rule, equal rights, the consent of the governed apply only to people alive here and now, not the dead or the unborn. Only the living can vote or claim their rights. But it was not, in spite of Adams, just democracy that made Americans live in the present moment. Their circumstances also inclined them to reject first the European past and then history generally.

The first departure from the past was begun quite inadvertently by men who were not particularly democratic in their outlook. But the very idea of a constitutional convention was a novel American invention and so were written constitutions. Cromwell had suggested something of the sort, but nothing came of it. That was not all. Hardly had the Convention of 1787 sat down to its labors when it realized that the venerable mixed constitution, whether Roman or English, had no place in America. Charles Pinckney of South Carolina got up to note that there was no class that needed another English House of Lords or Roman senate. There was nothing to mix. The difference between the richer and poorer members of the society was not so great as to require special institutional embodiment. "We the People" was a com-

This 1988 essay was previously unpublished.

plete departure from the entire European past. It does not refer to the Roman plebs or the English Commons. It is everyone here, and no one in Europe. Other battles fought with rival examples from antiquity had the same effect of eliminating the past. When Benjamin Franklin protested that such discussions were "a proof of the imperfection of the Human Understanding. . . . We have gone back to ancient history for models of Government, and examined the different forms of those Republics which have been formed with the seeds of their own dissolution and now no longer exist," he simply put his finger on the difficulty that the Framers confronted: that there were no precedents, no models, no examples to guide them in their utterly novel enterprise. It would all have to be their own contrivance. Apart from the inheritance of English law, they would be obliged to create federalism, representative democracy, and a separation of powers that did not exist anywhere.

In due time, Publius writing *The Federalist* would admit that his own brief experiences and the modern science of politics would have to direct him. There was nothing else. For European history did not offer him positive examples, only dire warnings. Classical antiquity merely featured flawed republics, while the monarchical past had nothing to say to him at all. Americans would simply have to do something quite different. It would not be a tiny direct democracy, but an extended republic based on the consent of people with diverse interests and a shared concern for property and the blessings of liberty. Intellectually that meant that history could be a source not of traditions, but merely of illustrations for general political propositions. It was less important than calculation based on reasoning from careful observations of current practices. Eventually Madison was to say that even their idol, Montesquieu, had merely opened up the science of politics which America was now fast developing. That was certainly part of his and Hamilton's enduring intellectual self-confidence, but also of their awareness of the novelty of the enterprise they were defending.

For in their view, ancient politicians did not really know how to put a constitution together. They had to find individual legislators who were driven to resort to violence and superstition to impose a basic law upon their republics. In contrast, they thought the men who together had written the proposed Constitution of the United States to be in every way intellectually and ethically superior to the ancients. They had created a constitution openly and well by "quitting the dim light of historical research" and "following reason and good sense." And while "the novelty of the undertaking immediately strikes us," Madison noted, new did not mean worse. Quite the contrary. It was too bad that "skill in the science of government still left much to be desired," but the work of the Convention was superior to all earlier acts of law-giving. In contrast to the lamentable spectacle of Athenian disorders, American representative democracy would be both free and stable. Thus "is it not the glory of the people of America" that "they have not suffered a blind veneration for antiquity?" For though they have shown "a decent regard for the opinions of former times," they have now embarked upon "the experiment of an extended republic" and posterity will be grateful for this innovation. "Happily for America, happily we trust for the whole human race" they have rejected the past and "pursued a new and more noble course."

Publius had learned the lesson of a revolutionary war, that institutions are made and unmade and that change was not to be dreaded but welcomed. Hence the pride of the very first of the *Federalist* papers. "It has been frequently remarked that it has been reserved to the people of this country by their conduct to decide whether societies of men are capable or not of establishing good government from reflection, or whether they are forever destined to depend for their political constitutions on accident and force." The proposals and reasoning with which he defended them were thus to signal a new era in political practice and thinking, in which choice and will replace habit and deference. Freedom in Publius's view clearly meant also freedom from tradition.

It was partly due to the traditionalism of his opponents that Publius was driven to his intellectual radicalism, but it was also inevitable that Americans should recognize that the European past was no longer their own. The political science that replaced a useless historiography was embedded in democratic practices. From the first, American constitutional democracy has required considerable amounts of accurate information. Along with regular elections a national census is published every ten years. Beyond that, freely elected representatives need to know as much as possible about their constituents, the voters. Thus Hamilton, who was no admirer of the electorate, scorning even its apparent failure to exercise the right to vote, recognized that the voters had to be understood. In *Federalist 35* we accordingly find a fine voting study of how a combination of economic interest and deferential voting worked in his native New York. That is how we should see politics, "if," as he put it, "we take facts as our guide." I am now concerned not with the accuracy of Hamilton's observations, but with the mind-set that they display, which also comes out in his correspondence, with its constant laments that "the data are necessarily uncertain." As history ceased to be relevant, the social sciences were welcomed, even in their infancy.

If the practices of representative democracy thrust Hamilton into the present, genuine conviction did so for Jefferson and his Jacksonian heirs. The democratic ideology that Jefferson bequeathed to radical Americans was an unqualified majoritarianism, in the sense that it was up to a majority of citizens to decide for themselves, and as they saw fit, how they wished to be governed. They must decide not only who was to hold public office, but also what institutions and laws they would prefer. That at once makes one see that majority government has considerable implications for one's view of the past. For Jefferson it meant first of all a rejection of the European past, which was not just irrelevant, but a record of unmitigated wickedness, political brutality, and religious superstitions. America's future depended on forgetting all traces of that past—it was to be deliberately non-European. "History," he wrote in a letter, "informs us of what bad government is." That appeared to be its sole function. But even more significantly, a democratic people did not need a past of any kind; it must live entirely in the present. In old age, recalling his and his generation's political achievements, Jefferson said that "we had no occasion to search into musty records and to hunt up royal parchments." Democracy was a revolutionary idea and the creation of a liberated people. For what majority was there if not that of the living citizenry of a democracy? "I set on this ground, which I suppose to be self-evident," he wrote to Madison, "that the earth belongs in usufruct to the living." Every generation was new and unburdened with obligations to the past. Jefferson wanted not merely *new* politics, but a politics of perpetual *newness,* as implicit in democratic principles.

This was not the passing fancy of a young man's imagination. Jefferson repeated these ideas early and late in his life, and he never stopped explaining their radical import. "No society can make a perpetual constitution, or even a perpetual law." Since he figured that a new generation entered the political world every nineteen years and as "the earth belongs to the living generation . . . Every constitution then and every law naturally expires at the end of 19 years. If it be enforced longer, it is an act of force, not of right. The dead have no rights. They are nothing and nothing cannot own something."

To Jefferson past generations were not only without rights, they were also inferior, because he believed ardently in the progress of the human mind. The founders of the republic, like himself, had been fine and intelligent men, but future generations would be far wiser and eminently capable of improving upon their institutions. He detested the "sanctimonious reverence" with which some men looked at the Constitution. Ancestor worship was an irrationality no democracy could afford; on the contrary, we should, he wrote, "avail ourselves of our reason and experience to correct the crude essays of our first and unexperienced councils."

Although most Jacksonian democrats shared the Jeffersonian faith in progress, they did not tend to be so adventurous as to suggest that all the laws should be revoked every nineteen years. No doubt they agreed with Madison, who warned his old friend that there was always the risk of an oppressive order being somehow put in place of the democratic status quo. Even rational institutions needed the support of habit and prejudice. And the upheavals of the interregnum would be awful. The rights of property would be in constant jeopardy. Moreover, even if the idea of tacit consent was often abused, it was necessary at least to bind minorities to majority decisions. Nevertheless, Madison did grant a great part of Jefferson's case: that it was wrong to hamper future generations with unnecessary burdens. Democracy did not neglect the future. It refused to limit the rights of later generations with debts, legal decisions, accretions of laws, and institutional arrangements to which they never had an opportunity to consent. Jefferson's heirs were torn irresolutely between his contempt for the burdens of tradition and Madison's prudent fondness for them.

Reverence was simply not a democratic feeling, and the authority of political tradition might be meaningless without the myth of the superiority of the first men, of the heroic demigods who created cities. That was the story that Madison had already laughed out of court in the *Federalist*. In principle the new government did not need traditions, just social science. Consistency was not, however, normal in political discourse, nor perhaps even necessary. Though few Jacksonians were as bold as their patron saint, they did rejoice at the retirement of the national debt, not least because they had at last lifted a burden from the shoulders of future generations. What they wanted to leave their progeny was the greatest possible freedom and a purified institution infused at every turn by the spirit of the Declaration of Independence. They may have felt a greater reverence for the Founding Fathers than Jefferson had, but it was their "Revolutionary Sires" whom they tended to invoke. Like Jefferson they trusted the majority of the living people. Constitutional interpretation was to be left to the people, not the court; offices were to rotate frequently; and the president was to speak for the people. So unmitigated a majoritarianism implies a certain uneasiness about the past. Some Jacksonians believed in continuous constitutional change, while others looked to "purification," that is, to a return to the creative moment. The original Constitution and the Declaration of Independence, it has been said, were for them outside history, a static moment, a reference point. But these principles and rules were not regarded as unalterable; they were merely given. Their authority was not in ancestor worship, such as Hannah Arendt ascribes to the Romans, who alone had both the sense of hierarchy and the reverence for the act of founding that made their traditions utterly binding on posterity. Americans were not like that then, and the efforts to recreate a Roman ideology of authority with the theory of the original intent, is in fact, far from traditional, but constitutes a radical departure from the spirit and outlook of earlier generations, which is a paradox. If John Marshall wanted a free hand for the court, the democrats wanted an uninhibited majoritarianism which would certainly accept the basic structure of the Constitution, but somehow make democratic ideals speak through it more clearly. Many continued to think, as one writer put it, that "the spirit of a people cannot be perfectly enshrined in a specific form of constitution." Certainly not that of a democratic people.

By the end of the War of 1812 even the staunchest of Federalists, George Cabot, noted that "the spirit of our country is doubtless more democratic than the form of our government." It is not surprising that he should have noticed, because that spirit was being asserted then as never before. The Declaration of Independence was about to begin its second career as a promise not yet fulfilled. First of all, Americans began to demand universal white manhood suffrage, and then an end to what they called "aristocracy." Aristocrats were subverters of the democratic order. They owed their wealth and status to laws that favored the rich unfairly. They were also not fully emancipated from the European past, which was revealed in their contempt for work, no less than in their monopolistic practices.

That the democratic ethos should at that time have been especially hostile to anything European is not surprising when one recalls just how alien the Europe of Napoleon and Metternich was to America. Europeans, for their part, no longer admired America as they had before the French Revolution. Americanization was emerging as a word of opprobrium. And while radical Englishmen, like the Chartists, might still look to America with admiration, most Europeans did not expect democracy to endure and did not wish America well. But being so alone in the world was not, in fact, at all disheartening to many Americans. Walt Whitman was far from being original when he wrote in the *Brooklyn Eagle* in 1846 that "the old and moth-eaten systems of Europe have had their day, and the evening of their existence which is nigh at hand will be the token of a glorious dawn for the downtrodden people . . . *Here* we have planted the standard of freedom and here we will test the capacity of man for self-government . . . All that we enjoy of freedom was in the beginning but an experiment. We have been long enough frightened by the phantom of the *past;* let us dare to know that we are out of her leading strings . . . There must be continual additions to our great experiment of how much liberty society will bear." And he not only goes on to contrast the future of America to the horrors of the European past, but also holds out to Europeans the hope that they too would soon be rid of kings and feudal nobles. And indeed Americans sympathized with the European reformers and even saw themselves as their champions. The material point was, however, that Americans must get away from Europe and its awful legacy as soon and as completely as possible. As one Jacksonian journalist wrote, "we will take from the faded escutcheon of feudal Europe its brightest gems and turn from martial glory to the glory of science." They would turn away from all traditions as well, for to say that antiquity confers merit on anything "gives rise to humiliating and degrading thought." Above all, Americans must quit receiving "laws, customs, manners, fashions, morals, literature, arts and sciences from our defeated enemies."

I do not read these pages as expressions of nationalism, but of democracy. After all there was no xenophobic or nationalist rhetoric in the war of independence from Great Britain either. To the last, Americans felt an affinity grounded in language and familial relations for the people of England. And the second declaration of independence, that of Jacksonian democracy, does not have a nationalist tone either. America might indeed be better, but it was so solely because it was unencumbered by aristocracy. The chasm between America and the European past was an assertion of democratic values, not nationalistic particularism. The xenophobic passions of Americans were directed with deadly force against the Native American population, and expressed itself also in virulent racism, and by the forties in a deplorable Anglo-Saxonism, which came to color the expansive ideology of "Manifest Destiny." Nor need we ignore the nativism that met Irish immigrants.

Forswearing the past was not so much a matter of being an American as a democratic citizen. And the heart of democracy was voting. The struggle for universal white manhood suffrage inspired a new and lasting democratic political ethos which took pride in its very newness. When the disenfranchised came to demand the vote they did not claim a historical entitlement, but a natural right. The plans for amended state constitutions were devised by men who felt that they had been denied the status of citizens, and their discontent with prevailing institutions of government became so acute that many states, most notably Massachusetts, New York, and Virginia, had to resort to America's great political invention, the constitutional convention, to renovate their basic law. At all these conventions equal representation and universal manhood suffrage were the main issues. And the arguments reveal with astonishing clarity what democracy meant to this new generation of politically active Americans, as well as to their conservative opponents. The conservatives who defended property qualifications and representation proportionate to the total taxes paid by districts argued that government existed as much to protect property as to defend personal rights. Universal manhood suffrage, they feared, would open the door to public robbers. It would be unjust, moreover, because it was unfair that those who contributed most to the common stock of an association should have no greater influence and power in it than those who contributed little or nothing. The fear of being deprived of one's property seems irrational, given the evident respect that democratic legislatures always showed for the institutions of property. But the anxiety was not quite groundless. For in a government that was based on consent one might well have wondered whether substantial inequalities of wealth were really based on consent, or, at any rate, would always gain it. In addition to fear, there was a view of political society not as an association of citizens, but as a corporation, a joint stock company, in which power and rights were divided proportionately to input. A corporation was a legal body which had a life that stretched over many generations, and membership in it was a vested interest, a guaranteed privilege, not a natural right. Conservatives thought that citizenship should be like that as well. Indeed, voting could not possibly be a natural right, for if it were, one would have to extend it to women and blacks. Surely women were the more virtuous sex, and so their claim was especially strong; while however inferior, the blacks were men. These arguments did not raise a laugh, because they were extremely threatening.

The democratic response was that there was nothing to fear from the poor. Those states that already had universal manhood suffrage had seen no evidence of popular rapacity. And if the poor were really so dangerous nothing could possibly ever restrain them, certainly not disenfranchisement. Moreover, even if self-restraint and virtue were the qualifications for voting, there was no sign that property was morally improving, as the conservatives claimed. Wealth was no sign of civic virtue at all, quite the contrary. Indeed, William Leggett, the radical journalist, reminded his readers of the speciousness of claims to virtue by moneyed men: "Witness the conduct of these pure patriots in the late war." If virtue meant anything it was fighting in the War of 1812, and indeed, the call for the vote had begun with the demand of veterans who felt that if they were good enough to fight they were good enough to vote. If they did not have that right they were mere mercenaries, hardly a republican army. Republican virtue meant patriotism to the democrat, while to the conservative it referred to the probity of proprietors. But virtue, whether that of the better sex or their own, was not the issue for the democratic voter at all; his deepest case was, as one Virginia delegate put it, that the right to suffrage must not be seen "in its technical and confined sense—the right to vote for public functionaries only, but in an enlarged sense as the right by which a man first signifies his will to become a member of government, of the social compact." As such it was the paramount right; the others followed it, even the right of existence. A man without the vote was one-half a slave. For voting was the supreme emblem of status. And equality of social status was what democracy was all about. We might also recall that when Americans spoke with fear of slavery they knew what they were talking about.

To be a white male meant that one had to be a citizen; that was what the Declaration of Independence meant. Now one might well suppose, one Virginian put it, that the notion that all men are naturally equal is "an abstraction of abstractions," but that was so only if one did not appreciate what was meant by the word "nature." It meant necessity. And women, children, and blacks were of necessity unequal. The first two were weak and required protection, and blacks were unalterably inferior. But for all white males the right to participate as equals was a natural necessity, because they had to preserve their lives, express themselves, and protect their families. For them voting was a response to an impelling natural need. It had nothing to do with their personal virtues or their wealth, only with their being men and therefore, as a natural, integral necessity, citizens. It was not, let us note, a historical or a corporate right, but a wholly personal one. And it has been claimed as such by every other group of disenfranchised Americans when they eventually demanded the vote and the political status that it implies.

The struggle for the vote left deep residues of bitterness among democrats, though they were the ultimate victors. And bitterness can create a political mentality. Jefferson had already held to the Manichean political belief that there were two natural parties, one that cherished the people and one that did not, or as his heir Emerson was to put it more delicately, the party of hope and the party of memory. That of course reflects the fundamental condition of American democracy and democratic beliefs, then as now: that political equality should prevail in a society in which wealth is rightly and justly recognized as enormously unequal. That is an uneasy state of mind, to which the danger of an undemocratic tilt is ever present. Hence as Senator Benton, an Ohio Jacksonian saw it, "there never have been but two parties, founded on the radical question whether the *People* or *Property* shall govern. Democracy implies government by the people. Aristocracy implies government by the rich." That was a bit crude: aristocracy meant more than merely the possession of wealth. The essence of the democratic definition of aristocracy was, in President Jackson's words, any group that by its use of its wealth "exercises more than its just proportion of influence in political affairs." It was not wealth as such that was reprehensibly aristocratic, but wealth either gained through governmental favor or used to buy political power and influence. All monopolists and all holders of licenses and charters were aristocrats because they owed their wealth to a government grant. Legal exclusions and owning privileges created aristocracies, not just money. Even more sinister were those who, like the Bank of the United States, were able through their control over the currency and credit to exercise political power that was not responsible to the people, and to use it to manipulate their elected representatives. All this was illegitimate or an "artificial inequality of wealth and power" which a democratic government was duty-bound to prevent. However, "equality of talents or of wealth cannot be produced by human institutions," said Jackson. The democratic government of a highly unequal society did not attempt or even wish to alter the natural economic order, but it did explicitly reject as artificial the use of governmental power to promote the interests of the rich. That was not merely unjust, it was "aristocratic."

Now it may not be exactly what Marc Bloch has taught us about feudalism, but the Jacksonians believed that it had begun as a system of royal patronage. Aristocrats had been the beneficiaries of grants of land and monopolies. "The royal bastard," as Tom Paine called William the Conqueror, had distributed the land to his ruffian band. This was not just a matter of crude party rhetoric. In Emerson's most Jacksonian essay, "Young America," we hear a similar account. Feudalism arose as a rebellion against the excesses of monarchs, but as soon as they wrested power from the monarchs, the barons turned upon the people who had helped them to gain power. In due course trade asserted itself against a decadent nobility, which had installed its own monarchical rulers. It was the merchant who then ruled. And if the people did not watch out, the power of trade would overwhelm it and constitute a new aristocracy of wealth. Governments were not yet free of feudal residues, and so it was clearly the task of Young America to protect itself against the rise of a new moneyed aristocracy. This version of the cycle of regimes owes much to traditional histories of the rise and fall of the Roman Republic, with a new American twist at the end. The triumph and threats of the commercial class were clearly a Jacksonian version of the classical notion of "corruption," of decayed mores ending in imperial oppression. That is why it was in the realm of culture especially that democratic habits would have to be learned: "We are sent to a feudal school to learn democracy," Emerson lamented; "A gulf yawns for the young American between his education and his work," as he was taught systems of thought that were "the growth of monarchical institutions." What was needed was a government free of these elements, but unless the public mind gained more self-respect, that would not happen, nor would America move into a more excellent social state than any yet recorded by history.

How was any repetition of the European disaster to be avoided? The best way to prevent the rise of a feudal caste was simply to have as little government as possible. The fewer civil service jobs there were, the less taxes would be collected, and the smaller the number of projects undertaken by government, the smaller its powers would be and the less harm it could do. And above all, it would lack the means to favor the rich who constantly pressed upon it. Less government meant less artificial inequality because the government was deprived of the ability to establish an aristocracy. President Jackson himself certainly preached the "least possible government" doctrine, but he also had a new and ambiguous view of the presidency that cast him as the tribune of the people. Unlike all other federal officers, he alone was elected by the people as a whole. All the others represented a state or a special interest. He and only he embodied the American people. And his chief task was to protect them against the ever-threatening attacks of the aristocracy, the money-power. If he was to do little directly, he was meant to prevent much. The first task of a democratic government was to stop the rise of aristocracy. And to that end the people were to be heard at every level of the political system. Why not, since the government would do so little?

Not only the political influence, but the manners and attitudes of aristocrats would also have to go. For they were idle and contemptuous of work. These two European aristocratic traits were not wholly unknown in America. The mere rich were unobjectionable, but the "idle rich" were intolerable. "Ruffle-shirted counter-hoppers," "pampered parasites" who accumulated wealth through partial laws, were not to be endured. The great division among men in society was not between poor and rich, but between the "do-somethings" and the "do-nothings." Failure to work was not merely immoral in and of itself, it also expressed a social ideology, the contempt for labor. And there was no denying that physical labor and trade were looked down upon not only by the European aristocracy, but by its bourgeoisie as well. The taboo on work as impure has been extraordinarily enduring, and American democrats were not absurd in denouncing it as an aristocratic assault upon democratic values. By "we the people," William Leggett wrote, "we mean emphatically the class which labors with its hands." They were the majority and their "sole reliance" was the equality of rights. And he was not mistaken in charging his wealthier fellow citizens with not honoring productive labor as democratic citizens should. However, Jacksonian democrats did not despair. Unlike the rest of the world, American workers did have institutions that were in their own hands and so was their destiny. Should they sink back into the European morass they would have no one to blame but themselves. That the danger of re-Europeanization was always present was, however, not denied. Many Americans had very good and specific reasons for their worries. The first factory workers in New England might well fear that the aristocrats were turning Lowell into another Manchester.

To avoid the calamity of European degradation, and the specter of artificial inequality generally, there must not only be less government altogether, but also far more free education. That was the one public activity that did not worry democrats. Education was looked at entirely as an aspect of citizenship. Its object was to democratize the young and to prevent aristocratic tendencies. The curriculum was to concentrate on that and the public school was to make children into young citizens of a democratic republic. There was no talk of creating a "natural aristocracy" such as Jefferson had envisaged. That was one part of his vision for America that was no longer even mentioned. No aristocracy at all for these democrats.

Important as education was for democrats, it was no replacement for personal effort in the race of life. Nothing was more democratic than the ideal of the self-made man. Not necessarily the man who builds a fortune by hard work, but more expansively the model of a perfect human character, of what was called "Young America." Those critics of liberal democracy who claim today that there cannot be an ideal democratic character or a liberal notion of the good life have not really looked at the literature of their own country. They have scarcely glanced at Nathaniel Hawthorne's *House of the Seven Gables* or at Emerson's *Self-Reliance*. Hawthorne offers us a portrait of a perfect young American democrat, Holgrave. This youth has no fixed place in society, nothing inherited, does not stick to a single role in life, and rejects all efforts to restrict and bind him to a place and status. He is self-created because he is socially unfettered, immensely self-reliant, and the master of many skills. America was not nearly open enough for a genuinely democratic radical like Holgrave. It seemed to him, we read, "that in this age, more than in any before, the moss-grown and rotten Past is to be torn down and lifeless institutions to be thrust out of the way and their dead corpses buried and everything to begin anew." And so he cries out,

> Shall we never get rid of this Past? It lies upon the Present like a giant's dead body. In fact, the case is just as if a young giant were

compelled to waste all his strength in carrying about the corpse of the old giant, his grandfather, who died a long while ago and only needs to be decently buried. A dead man, if he happen to have made a will, disposes of wealth no longer his own . . . A dead man sits on our judgment seats and living judges but search out and repeat his decisions. We read dead men's books. We are sick of dead men's diseases and die of the same remedies with which dead doctors killed their patients . . . But we shall live to see the day when no man will build his house for posterity. Why should he? If every generation were allowed and expected to build its own houses, that single change would imply every reform which society is now suffering for . . . To plant a family! This idea is at the bottom of half the wrong and mischief which men do.

Hawthorne spread a fine film of irony over Holgrave's hopes, but as an ardent Jacksonian, a "loco-foco democrat," as he called himself, he basically agreed with the views of this perfect model of Young America, and he made much of Holgrave's integrity and moral independence. Nor was he alone in this. We meet another Holgrave again in Emerson's *Self-Reliance,* where he appears as a New Hampshire lad, and a lot smarter than the snotty city slickers of his day. Both characters perform a dozen or more social roles and hold any number of jobs; each keeps moving without loss of inner balance. Among other things, they exemplify an ethos of the dignity of work and the autonomy that it yields.

Behind Holgrave and Emerson and all of Young America stands Thomas Jefferson, who wrote that "here where all is new, no innovation is feared which offers good." But that is not the whole story. Hawthorne allowed Holgrave to be reconciled to marriage, family, and place. In this he showed, among other things, a deep understanding for Young America, who were not all of a piece. They did not hate the past consistently. Many democrats wanted to abandon only the *European* past. They also hoped that American historians would write a new, democratic sort of history. They longed for a usable, relevant tradition that would dignify labor, rather than war. Bancroft meant to write the history of masses, not of great men. Even Emerson, who in his most Jacksonian moments seemed to be completely uninterested in any history, either that of America or that of Europe, was not constant in his aversion. He agonized endlessly about history. Its burden was that it must be subjective, reduced to biography, which meant two things. First of all that its only value was in each one of us absorbing whatever stories mattered to us personally. Second, that the only really interesting part of history was the story of great men. Emerson was a great admirer of Plutarch, but by great men he did not mean only those whom Locke had called the "great butchers of mankind." For though he admired Napoleon, his great men were the Shakespeares of the past. And yet it seemed to him that in some sense our reverence for these men was not compatible with democracy. It was probably best for us to say "Damn George Washington" and get on with it. "Great men," he cried out, "the word is impious." Even in the case of his representative men, who spoke for and to us because we chose to elevate them, the idea of great men was unacceptable (and not only in the shape of Emerson's friend Carlyle's dominating heroes). They oppressed us and sapped our self-confidence, even if we integrated them into our own minds. In the end Emerson was utterly baffled by his own awareness of greatness and his unshakable conviction that a wise man in his village was as good as any of the great and brilliant men noted in history. After all they were famous only because posterity chose to elect them to that station. What use were they? The very question was meant to put the greatness of the few before the bar of common judgment. And radical democrats, like Ely Moore, the first union man to sit in Congress, wanted even more: an artisan's history, a new idea of human greatness. It was perhaps, after all, important to have a history written for the working many. The history Emerson wanted democrats to read would begin by recognizing that it was only "the mechanical arts" that had raised man's condition above that of the animals. Not property but "mechanical arts" had civilized us. History was made by the producers, not by the consumers, just as the West was visibly being developed by the industrious many. Certainly there had been progress, especially in the modern world, but it was not due to the famous scientists, but to the mechanics. Printing, which was "the preservation of all the arts," was invented by a mechanic. So was the mariners' compass, without which America would not have been found. After that it was the steam engine, again the work of an artificer, and one that had made his life far easier. History books should also stress how many of the distinguished generals and statesmen of the Revolutionary era began life as blacksmiths, bookbinders, and other kinds of manual workers. The point of such a history was to remind the working youth of America of their real place in their country and in the modern world and to make all they could of it. Opportunity was the one thing, he thought, they did not lack, but they did need a better sense of their own worth, and a people's history would certainly encourage them.

It is important to note that technology was seen as not only the creation of the workingman in America, but his great historical achievement and his best hope. It would make life easier for him and everyone else and also increase the value of his work by improving it. In spite of the prevailing agrarian nostalgia, the technological age seemed full of possibilities. Even Emerson shared that view. The garden itself was a human creation and machinery was just a second human hand. History would do honor to it and to its inventors and to the ploughboy on the farm as well. Still, the impulse to invent a new history, rather than inherit one, to look back to find democratic honor, was not the same thing as abandoning the past altogether. And democratic Americans had in fact lived with both these notions ever since. The problem of how a democratic history of the many would really look had not yet arisen and it had not yet been solved. The democratization of values would mean finding out what nameless groups had done as they labored, moved, reproduced, suffered from diseases, and died. If not cliometrics, social history rested on the assumption that these lives mattered.

Let me sum up. Democrats thought that America was the nation of the future, and its great task was to remove the intellectual and institutional impediments to that aspiration. It began with a demand for universal manhood suffrage, which was a matter of civic status, and then turned to other manifestations of political inequality, to the use of government to create unfair advantages and also to intangible barriers to equality, to education, opportunity, and attitudes, especially toward work. Majority rule turned out to require a transformation of the mental world, a turning away from the past or an effort to create a new history. I have chosen to stress its newness for two reasons. First because once it *was* new, but more significantly I wanted to show that innovation itself is inherently a part of an American democratic ideology which, with all its contradictions, has by no means lost all its popularity.

CHAPTER THIRTEEN

Democratic Customs

"She had got to the bottom of this business of democratic government, and found that it was nothing more than government of any other kind." In the last hundred years many Americans have agreed with the disenchanted heroine of Henry Adams's novel, *Democracy*. Before the Civil War there were some who wished that American government were more like all the others, but few, if any, would have denied that it was, in fact, very different. What was the difference that had once been taken for granted and was now denied? Henry Adams's Mrs. Lee had discovered that elections were often dishonest, that many senators were corrupt, that the nation's capital was full of job-hungry party hacks, and that the president "aped monarchical forms," forgetting that he was meant to be a citizen like all others. A formidable and not untruthful indictment, but did it obliterate the difference? After all, Americans had for decades been unique in the opportunities for political participation and for the voting rights enjoyed by its male white citizens in an open electoral system. Representation was not grossly unfair and elementary schooling was generally available. But for Henry Adams corruption had reduced electoral politics to a bad joke and he had discovered, rather painfully, that schooling did not prepare anyone for the actual exigencies of life. Some of his contemporaries, perhaps more cogently, observed that electoral politics did nothing to prevent poverty. English Chartists had long ago called American democracy "a sham." Now it is true enough that voting does not promote virtue or prosperity and that education

This undated essay was previously unpublished.

is only rarely of much practical use. What Adams forgot is that it is a mark of degradation to deny anyone the right to take a full part in politics or the respectability that only formal education can confer. Voting and education are marks of dignity, not means to other ends. That is why the "difference" is more easily recalled in their absence, and forgotten or disregarded when they are taken for granted.

The monumental stability of American politics was recognized quite early, but its democratic practices were not assumed to be normal. In the 1830s, *Fraser's Magazine* could still note that "against the single example of the United States we quote the whole history of democracy" and went on with the mournful list, Greece, Rome, Cromwell, French Revolution, South America, "from Athens to Bogota in sum." Americans were also often concerned, and for excellent reasons. Their fundamental social condition was (and is) incongruous, because political equality was to be maintained amid considerable—and eventually very great—economic and social inequalities. From the very first this circumstance has been a source of profound uneasiness. Could so abnormal a condition last? Even before the Civil War, and without considering slavery, religion, and sex, the paradoxical character of American public life troubled its most thoughtful citizens. Henry Adams's blanket denial may not have been representative of or valid for most of his contemporaries and predecessors, but the tension from which it sprang was widely shared. Moreover, the ways in which public men of every kind responded to it, and the manner in which they dealt with "the difference" in the first decades of America's independent political existence, have set a permanent pattern for political discourse. They drew an intellectual map whose routes continue to guide public argument significantly.

The apparent fragility of the system seems to have troubled the rich more than others. The retrospective observer is as puzzled as were foreign visitors by the intense fears of the wealthy. They clearly thought that "the people" were going to take it all away at any moment. To be sure, in an agrarian economy in which creditor and debtor mean more than rich and poor, there is always ground for mutual fear. Forgiving democratic legislatures and debtors' jails did nothing to calm them. However, with no sign of any organized movement to equalize fortunes and with only infrequent mob action, the rich lived in a state of extraordinary and growing apprehension. The fact that during the Revolution they had acquired an egalitarian vocabulary and that they too had to participate in electoral politics to defend

their interests probably contributed a great deal to this anxious temper. It is not simply as if Hamilton and the younger Federalists almost
welcomed the French Revolution to justify their fears; for they had
felt them well before that. It is rather that their own rhetoric made
them unsure of the legitimacy of their claims to leadership, deference,
and ultimately to wealth. The more democratic their conduct, the
greater their fear for the security of property. Those in favor of popular government were not very threatening. Most only wanted the suffrage, which was due to men who had fought in the militia (war having radicalized a lot of passive farmers), and they agreed with Franklin
that "the important ends of Civil Society remain the same in every
Member of the society: and the poorest continue to have an equal
claim to them with the most opulent." Franklin might well have frightened the rich, since he was one of the very few members of his generation who believed that property was a social right, not a natural one,
and that what society gave it could take away. But who could really
suspect Franklin of incendiary designs? In fact, the democratic politicians were too frightened of aristocratic plots to be very bold. Nothing
could convince John Taylor of Carolina that John Adams was not
plotting to establish a hereditary nobility. Alexander Hamilton was
really attached to the republican form of government, but "everyone"
knew that he was conspiring to set up a hereditary king and house of
lords. The fears of each side were clearly fed by those of the other—
more so than by anything either did, or was at all likely to do.

In fact John Adams did fear the mob, but he was even more afraid
of "the few," as his letters to Jefferson show quite clearly. It was a
nightmare they shared, but to which they reacted in quite different
ways. To cope with the danger of an oppressive aristocracy in Virginia,
Jefferson thought that the abolition of primogeniture, entail, and established religion, along with an increase in the number of jury trials,
would suffice, but only if a wholly new system of education were set
up to create a "natural aristocracy," instead of all the "artificial" ones.
For in spite of his practical involvement he was intellectually indifferent to politics, "a subject I never loved and now hate," he told Adams.
History was for him often, as in the case of his obsession with the
ancient Anglo-Saxons, a source of mythology. At other times it was
reduced to anthropology. The natural sciences alone claimed his full
attention, especially those that might prove economically or educa-
tionally useful. In fact Jefferson wanted education to replace politics.
Primary education would create citizens capable of protecting them-

selves against usurpation and governing themselves directly at the small, local "ward" level. Here education would render ruling superfluous. Secondary education, more selective, would produce intelligent gentlemen and serve as a selection ground for the university. Higher education open only to the few most able would provide the nation with a "natural aristocracy," an elite distinguished solely by its intellectual talents. True merit, as demonstrated by the capacity to learn and advance intellectual, and especially scientific, disciplines, was to replace all other standards for distinguishing ranks in society. That this career open to natural talent would do nothing for equality did not trouble Jefferson, for that was not his aim. What such a system did ensure was change. It certainly did make sense for every generation to reject the political legacy of its predecessors, if scientific knowledge determined and measured all social values. As the former advanced, the latter would have to be adjusted. In this way politics, the struggle of competing interests, the distribution of moral and tangible values, the relations between allies and enemies, all this becomes problem-solving by education and by the already educated. The expected certainty of knowledge replaces the turmoil of political passions.

Adams was far more worried about the dangers of social inequality because he was far more deeply interested in politics than Jefferson ever had been. History was his source of political information and wisdom, and the very basis of his political science. Far from being a traditionalist, in the sense of revering the past with the piety due to one's ancestors, he looked back with the disenchanted eye of a political scientist. In this respect he was no less fact-minded than his friend who looked to nature. His whole disposition was to amass political examples so as to discover general political truths about recurrent political situations. Among these, mob attacks on the security of property and aristocratic oppression were the most threatening as well as the most common. What obstacles could be put in their path? Natural aristocracy he at once recognized as perfectly useless. Every sort of inequality might originate in natural superiority. Sooner or later it would translate itself into wealth, power, and prestige. If it were merely moral merit it would not prevail against the real objects of ambition, good looks, wealth, and power. These gave men reputation and these were the goals of ambition. All of them might be and were used to corrupt republics. In an electoral system an aristocrat was any man who influenced many and controlled more than a single vote. Nor did education help. In his native Massachusetts, education was diligently pursued, and as a result generations of Harvard men, from father to son, could beguile lesser men and govern them. Since Adams was just as eager to promote learning as Jefferson was, he encouraged the latter in all his projects, but he knew that knowledge in fact did not lessen political ambitions and indeed had no effect on morals at all. Only careful institutional engineering, the adroit balancing and separating of constitutionally established powers, would protect the republic against aristocratic corruption. As we know, that was not the actual course of political history. It was, rather, the theory and practice of Madison's organized political parties based on an extensive electorate that settled the relations between the few and the many. It was not a solution that would have appealed to the scientific or moral inclinations of either Adams or Jefferson, for this was not a cure for the underlying disorder. It did not end the ruinous competition that the inherent inequality of men inspired.

The hated Hamilton, whatever he (and for that matter Jefferson) practiced, was at one with his two former colleagues. In his view, parties were symptoms of trouble, not means to its avoidance. He did not look to a general political science, as Adams did, but he also tried his hand at institutional technology. His real worry was known to other intelligent observers of the emergent liberal state: government based on public opinion had nothing stable in it. What was needed in parliamentary regimes based on opinions was some final "pouvoir neutre," in Benjamin Constant's words. In Restoration France it was to be the function of the king to be the final arbiter halting the otherwise endless ebb and flow of conflicting opinions. Hamilton meant to invest the judiciary with that power. Localism and democratic passion being allied, it was to be the judicial duty to arbitrate conflicts between the states and the federal government as well as between the branches of the latter. For "if everything floats in the variable and vague opinions of the governing party, there can be no such thing as rights, property and liberty." Certainly the rights of property could not be left to the whims of changing opinion. When the younger Federalists realized that they were politically dead, their language became that of majority power and minority rights—which would have been more convincing had any of them ever shown the slightest support for the Bill of Rights. Nevertheless, they also were convinced that only the courts and a restricted suffrage stood between them and "fierce and vindictive majorities," bent upon venting "their vengeance upon the heads and fortunes of minorities." The "indolent and profligate" could not be expected "to respect the rights of contract." Society was a partnership in which the rich had a greater share, and therefore greater rights. As universal suffrage moved closer they became convinced that a majority of poor men would use their political power to make property "a booty to be divided among plunderers," according to Storey. Only the judiciary could, because of its position and peculiar rationality, provide protection for the rich in a democratic government of opinions. In short, some way had to be found outside politics to prevent the degeneration of the republic. Jefferson looked to education and scientific knowledge, Adams to political science and constitutional engineering, and Hamilton and his heirs to court-centered legalism. In fact, the last also took up the cause of education eventually, in order to integrate the new voters into society and teach them the rights of property—lessons they had in truth learned very well out of school. Only Franklin really believed in politics as self-correcting. Madison provided the rationale and the skills of an organizer for parties, but only reluctantly at first. Franklin was all but alone in that "first" generation to enjoy politics of every conceivable kind.

Unlike Jefferson, this genuine "natural aristocrat" did not believe that academic learning provided a political education. What was needed was an understanding of history, but not as a storehouse of examples, illustrations, or analogies. History taught "public religion," which amounted to training in self-control, the most essential of the political virtues. It also was useful in teaching logical reasoning, which was important for political argument; and finally for lessons in rhetoric, which was absolutely essential for persuading people to follow one. Franklin himself possessed all these skills to an extraordinary degree, and he thought that anyone "tolerably" capable could achieve much in politics if he applied himself to mastering them. He had every reason to feel self-confident. Anyone interested in bloodless, hegemonic revolution would do well to read his *Autobiography*. It tells one quite clearly how Benjamin Franklin took over Philadelphia by building a party of people who had been excluded from its political life. The "junto" was a club, eventually subdivided into many cells, for the self-education of young tradesmen. That included a new view of politics. For Franklin the end of government was civic improvement, not mere protection of rights. At first without the help of the Assembly, and once he controlled it, with its help, he and his highly organized following paved the streets, put in new street lights, set up schools, built a hospital, organized a militia which elected its own officers, and much more. How did Franklin do it? By persuasion and organization. He was one of the few public men who understood that politics, apart from its military aspects, was not action, but patience; that persuasion took time and cunning and talk, not "deeds." He never confused the language of civics with that of either commerce, science, or war. And he also fully understood the place of self-discipline. Arrogance was bound to trouble a man of his talents and he did not aspire to humility, but he did learn, as he tells us at least twice, to say "I conceive," "I apprehend," "it appeared," and "it seemed," rather than "certainly," "indubitably," "it is," and "is not." What distinguished Franklin was his view of politics as a process of negotiation and association in the course of which men try to improve their lives, not as a way of "solving problems" permanently. He was worldly enough to have risen above fear and cynicism.

It cannot be said that either one of the parties in the Jacksonian age shared these admirable qualities. Their politics were defensive, not venturesome. The democrats continued to fear the encroachments of political aristocracy. Having won the battle for the suffrage, they now turned to education and other prestige values. In spite of Owen and Skidmore, most did not ask for a redistribution of wealth. One may think their measures inept and economically naive, but they did have a very clear idea of what democratic fairness demanded. It was their standing, the respect due to honest industry, to simple merit, and to decent work, that was being threatened by aristocrats, and they meant to assert their due. Even the early trade unionists talked more about self-respect and the claims of work to public honor than about equality of wealth. Most agreed that everyone had an equal right to acquire wealth, not to possess it. It was "special" privilege and "idle" wealth, not their very existence, that aroused their sense of injustice. It was a struggle for recognition for them, the right to a dignified status as workers and citizens. As Tocqueville put it, "the people were not asking the rich to sacrifice their money, but their pride." Above all, the government was to remain neutral. It must not favor the rich. That whole big battle over the bank was not about economic policy, but about the unfairness of a government that gave special support to the commercial classes. Education was for all democrats a great issue because it was the essential mark of social respectability. Ely Moore, an early trade unionist, was particularly clear about that. It was not just the road to economic advancement, but to self-confidence and general regard. Of course, there was not enough education, and much of it was tainted with "feudal" remnants. It was exclusive, class-oriented, and "English" in its general character. And all democrats felt that they faced a conspiratorial aristocracy that meant to deny them this as well as every other standing in society. They were not altogether mistaken.

The wealthy, for their part, were more insecure than ever. Not only did they fear for their newly acquired riches, but they had developed a hunger for social deference. The self-confidence of their revolutionary fathers, who, as a new elite, had successfully assaulted their old English masters, had deserted them. They were socially very uneasy. In this state of mutual disdain Jackson's "popular" presidency looked like the long-expected despotism to the Whigs. To others, like John Quincy Adams, he was a boor, "a barbarian who could not write a sentence of grammar and [could] hardly spell his name." To the democrat, Jackson's policies were "rotation in office," the career open to talent, and an opportunity for those long excluded from political life to participate at last. The opposition saw only inefficiency, corruption, and a degradation of the civil service that forced the "better men" to withdraw from public life. Both sides were right and each deeply offended the other. Neither side ever won. The rich did not receive the social deference they craved, and mere work and decency never got the admiration that wealth and a university degree could bring. However only a log-cabin candidate could win for the Whigs, and the people were not oppressed by a political aristocracy.

Foreign visitors to Jacksonian America rarely, if ever, mentioned social rumblings from below, but all noted the extraordinary snobbery of the rich. Nothing in caste- and class-ridden Europe had prepared them for Boston. It made some observers worry about the ways of "an overgrown bourgeoisie" and about the harshness that a manufacturing elite might exercise if it were to become a permanent ruling class. Most trusted, as Tocqueville did, that the creative force of popular sovereignty, enriched by Western openness, would prevent it. America's most penetrating political analyst, Grimké, thought it very unlikely that there would be any rebellion from below, since the reaction from the ultras of the opposite end of the social spectrum was predictable. It was sure to be terrible. In any case, if the government did not give special advantages to wealth, there would be no sense of outraged justice among the people. As for the "civil aristocracy," it was a widely dispersed third estate composed of capitalists and professionals. Among the latter, lawyers and clergy contributed most to the general stability of political and social life. To this we might well add, today, the professional bureaucrats. Few people liked lawyers then. They were not nearly as popular as Tocqueville thought. But fear and suspicion in no way diminished their ability to make democracy a stable system of government.

Yet if America was steady and democratic in its political life, it was also deeply troubled. The Jacksonian democrats had made their assertion and won some points, but at the same time there was also a crisis of aristocratization, a deep feeling of social frustration among the rich and educated. They hoped to be like the European landed aristocracy of the eighteenth century. Not only did their countrymen refuse to bow to these pretensions, but there were European visitors always happy to tell them that they bore no resemblance, in form or substance, to the hereditary nobility of another age and place. If they had run out of European scoffers, there was always Leggett to remind them of their lack of dignity, manners, and entailed estates. They might toady to every petty lord, but he could still make them feel cheap, and often did. Their withdrawal from public life left them to cultivate an exclusive private society, and while concentrating on business made them richer, privatization made their public life even more difficult. Despising their fellow countrymen, they felt nevertheless obliged to be agreeable, to win a special ruling, to win an election here and there, and to ward off the feared reprisals against open contempt. Some tried large-scale philanthropy, which endeared them to no one. Others developed a dual language, one for private use, the other in the hearing of "the riffraff." The psychological consequence was to make the rich feel deeply constrained and hemmed in. Hence the laments about the difficulty of being individual, free, self-expressive, and original in America. Wealth seemed not to protect them at all. Moreover, they were, as Grund said, "a study in duplicity" with their mercantile hardness covered by showy philanthropy, their dual language, and their public democracy barely hiding their excruciating private snobbery. No wonder Stephen Simpson, a very sober Jacksonian, cried "insincerity" when the Whigs came out for charity schools and the like.

Simpson was not the only one to complain of insincerity. No "civil aristocracy" is immune to inner disruption. It is always able to produce prophets and poets who will look at their country with love and loathing. If religious perfectionism found its democratic expression in the revival meeting, it had an aristocratic voice also. Tocqueville might complain of literary aridity, but he spoke too soon. Pre–Civil War

America got what it deserved and more from its finest minds. The insincerity that had come to flower in America aroused a disgust of more than equivalent dimensions. The poets also had expected democracy to make a moral difference, and it had disappointed them. They knew better than to look enviously at Europe. They glared directly at their own depraved countrymen and in fiction and lecture, poetry and prose, told them how they had fallen. Even to the semidetached observer it is clear that no democracy can do without their song. Sincerity and the strength of character it implies were meant to be part of democratic politics. To lament its absence as Hawthorne and Emerson did is not self-indulgence, but the awareness that mutual respect and seriousness go when frankness leaves. Like voting and education it is not at all useful, but one feels defrauded when it is not forthcoming.

In politics sincerity is not an obvious virtue. Where is one to draw the line between Franklin's persuasive talk, the good manners of democracy, and Hawthorne's Judge Pyncheon? As the latter made his way down the street he only emphasized his social superiority, smiling and waving at all, "for as is customary with the rich when they aim at the honors of a republic, he apologized, as it were, to the people for his wealth, prosperity and elevated station by a free and hearty manner." To "a faithful democrat" there was also something repulsive in "the hang-dog look of a republican official who feels himself less than the least and the lowest of his masters." Was not the majestic dignity of a Puritan magistrate better than this false humility? Not really. "Neither the front nor the back entrance of the Custom House opens on the road to Paradise." Salem's past also had its horrors, and the most distinguished official in its customs house remembered it well. He might despair of the customs of America—his fellow customs-house workers were certainly mere clowns, "leaning on the arm of the Republic." All vitality had left even the younger ones. They had no character at all. And finally Hawthorne was not one to spare his own kind. Even the gluttonous Old Inspector was a relief to "a man who had known Alcott." A cruel and often unjust past, a present composed of hypocrisy, weakness, and imbecility in equal parts, and all this both because and in spite of democratic mores!

Irony was Hawthorne's purgative; self-reliance was Emerson's. Where else was one to turn? Politicians promoted an education designed to integrate children into society, not to develop their individual spirit. The radicals were aimless and destructive, the conservatives without hope or generosity. Neither side had any purpose at all. If there was to be a "natural aristocracy" it might as well begin by turning its back on the division of labor and practice self-sufficiency in earnest. That indeed would be purity, but it was honesty without any social object. Emerson had no illusions about the political value of sincerity. In the face of political corruption "we pass self-denying ordinances, we drink water, we eat grass, we refuse the laws, we go to jail: it is all in vain." These public exhibitions of inner perfection were without any significance. "Obedience to his genius" is the only liberation for an honest man, and it leads away from others. Only a suffocating sense of public hypocrisy could lead a man to such extremes.

As we know, a whole generation of displaced aristocrats, social and moral, came to share Emerson's need for a national purgation—and there was, in fact, something to be wiped away, to be expiated. The men who returned from the Civil War were often different and harder, like Oliver Wendell Holmes, who wrote that war had made him an aristocrat who didn't "value a common life." Many, like Henry Adams, gave up on the "difference" of democratic government. Yet the pattern of political attitudes had been set—only some variations, often important, but not wholly novel, were added. If one looks at generations in thirty- or even forty-year terms one can see that the "differences" in democracy are not only the ones asserted by its defenders and detractors, but also those in the character of their conflicts. An open and equal political order in an inegalitarian society creates a permanent tension between belief and practice, and this inescapable condition is the creative source of a wholly unique pattern of political controversy, which in itself is a great part of the "difference" of democracy as a political culture no less than as a way of governing.

A Casual Bibliography

Adams, John. *Political Writings*. Edited by George A. Peek (1954).
Blau, J. L., ed. *Social Theories of Jacksonian Democracy* (1954).
Douglass, E. P. *Rebels and Democrats* (1955).
Ekirch, A. A. *The Idea of Progress in America, 1815–1860* (1944).
The Portable Emerson. Edited by M. Van Doren (1964).
Fischer, D. H. *The Revolution of American Conservatism* (1965).
Franklin, Benjamin. *Autobiography*. Edited by L. W. Labaree (1964).
———. *Political Thought*. Edited by Ralph Ketcham (1965).
Frederickson, G. M. *The Inner Civil War* (1965).
Grimké, Frederick. *The Nature and Tendency of Free Institutions*. Edited by J. W. Ward (1968).

Grund, Francis J. *Aristocracy in America.* Edited by G. E. Probst (1959).

Hawthorne, Nathaniel. *The House of the Seven Gables.*

———. *The Scarlet Letter.*

Hofstadter, R. *The Idea of a Party System* (1969).

The Jefferson-Adams Letters. Edited by Lester Cappon (1959).

The Portable Jefferson. Edited by M. D. Peterson (1975).

Koch, A., ed. *The American Enlightenment* (1965).

Meyers, M. *The Jacksonian Persuasion* (1960).

Miller, Douglas T. *Jacksonian Aristocracy* (1967).

Miller, Perry. *The Life of the Mind in America* (1965).

Peterson, M. D. *Democracy, Liberty, and Property: The State Conventions of the 1820s* (1966).

Tocqueville, A. de. *Democracy in America.* Translated by George Lawrence (1966).

White, L. D. *The Jacksonians* (1954).

Williamson, C. *American Suffrage from Property to Democracy, 1760–1860* (1960).

INDEX

Anti-utopians, 28, 29, 30, 31–37
Apology for Raimond Sebond (Montaigne), 59
Arendt, Hannah, 176
Aristocracy, 177, 178; American idea of, xi; American distrust of, 117; civic, 194; "commercial," 155; Cooper's view of, 180, 181; Jackson's ideas on, 153, 154, 155; John Adams on aristocrats and, 148, 149, 151, 152, 157; meaning of, in America, 147, 148; and political influence, 157; Veblen on, 156. *See also* "Natural aristocracy"
Aristocratic liberty, 116
Aristotelian logic: and rule of law, 159
Aristotle, 159, 161
Artisans, 93
Atavism: Veblen's lament about, 156
Athenians, 167
Augustine (Saint), 131, 165
Autobiography (Franklin), 192

Bacon, Francis, 6, 97
Bancroft, George, 184
Bank of the United States, 99, 153, 180
Baptists, 134
Barbary pirates: Adams and Jefferson's policy disagreement over, 19
Berlin, Isaiah, 111, 112, 113, 117
Bible: political archetypes in, 129, 130
Bill of Rights, 124, 161, 191
Black District, Midlands: impact on Henry Adams, 85
Blacks, 125, 153; Jefferson's views on, 150; protecting rights of, 112; question of voting by, 179, 180
Black slaves: contact of Europeans with, 5. *See also* Slavery
Blacksmiths, 185
Blackstone, Sir William, 161
Blithedale Romance, The (Hawthorne), 30, 31, 33, 34, 36, 37, 38
Bloch, Marc, 117, 181
Boer War, 88
Bookbinders, 185
Boston: foreign observations of, 194
Boston Common, 84, 85
Boucher, Jonathan, 134
Brand, Ethan, 32
Bright, John, 88
Brook Farm community: Hawthorne's involvement in, 28, 29, 30, 38, 77; members of, xii. See also *Blithedale Romance, The*

Brooklyn Eagle: Walt Whitman quoted from, 177
Buckle, Henry Thomas, 89
Buffon, George Louis LeClerc, Comte de, 94
Burgess, Dyer, 104
Burke, Edmund, xiv, 120
Burns, Anthony, 39
Business organizations, modern, 107

Cabot, George, 176
Calhoun, John, 104
Calvinism: roots of moral pessimism in, 103–104
Cambridge Annual Election Sermon (Langdon), 132
Cannibals All (Fitzhugh), 103
Capitalism, 86; post–Civil War, 85
Carlyle, Thomas, 53, 58, 102, 185
Cartwright, Major, 141
Castes: absence of, x
Catholics: American, 69; of Quebec, 132; Spanish American, 142, 143
Cavell, Stanley, 63
Census, national: mandated by United States Constitution, 4, 98
Chartists, 177, 187
Chaucer, Geoffrey, 39
Checks and balances, 104
Chicago Exhibition of 1893, 89
Chicago School: of political sociology, 92
Choate, Rufus, 44, 45, 100
Christmas Banquet, The, 37
Church of Santa Maria di Ara Coeli, Rome, 84
"Church's Flight into the Wilderness, The," 132
Cicero, 158, 159, 161
Citizenship, 125; deficiencies in American idea of, xvi; and education, 65, 70, 74, 75, 183; Merriam and Dewey's philosophy of, 108
Civic aristocracy, 194
Civic improvement, 192
Civic virtue, xv, 179
Civil law, 163
Civil liberties, 147
Civil rights: and Fourteenth Amendment, 117; movement for, 108
Civil War, 12, 29, 92, 102, 107, 113, 121; and abolitionism preceding, 116; constitutional amendments added after, 126; diplomacy of, 84; drifts toward, 99; and emancipation

United States presidency: Adams's and Jefferson's run for, 19–20
United States Senate, 88
United States Supreme Court, 98, 112, 113, 121, 124
Universal white manhood suffrage: struggle for, 178–180, 186
Universities: and government, 151; Jefferson's beliefs about, 24, 25; rituals and continuity of values in, 3
University of Virginia, 24, 25, 150
Urbanization, 105
"Uses of Great Men" (Emerson), 54
Utopian communities: Emerson's opinion of, 77; Hawthorne's criticism of, xii, 28–38, 47; in Jacksonian New England, 61

Values: democratization of, 93
Veblen, Thorstein, 106, 156
Vetoes: Calhoun's system of, 104
Violent dissent, 66
Virginia: Jefferson's plan for education in, 150; public education in, 24–25; and universal manhood suffrage, 178
Virtue, theory of: and American liberalism, xii
Voters, 92; and Hamilton's view of power of, xi, 6, 7, 8, 9, 97, 98, 173; Jefferson and Adams on, 26; scientific study of, 11, 12
Voting: right to, 3, 173, 179, 188; and political equality, viii; removing property qualifications in Massachusetts for, 149; struggle for universal white manhood suffrage, 178–180

War of 1812, 72, 73, 119, 176, 179
Ward, Lester, 105, 106
Warrantees, 103
Warrantors, 103
Washington, George, 55, 57, 81, 102, 164, 185
Wealth, 193; law and fostering inequalities of, 153. See also Aristocracy
Weed, Thurloe, 86
Welfare: and voting, 9
Westward movement: and providential design, 68
Whigs, 29, 44, 47, 71, 100, 149, 194
Whiskey Rebellion, 26
White male suffrage, 4, 92, 97, 99
Whitman, Walt, 117–118, 155, 177
William the Conqueror, 181
Williams, Roger, 44, 45
Wilson, Woodrow, 156
Wise, John, 132
Women, 93; Gilman on domestication of, 106; in Hawthorne's work, 31, 32, 35, 45, 46; question of voting by, 179, 180
Wood, Gordon, 10
Work: dignity of, 99
World War II: American political science developed after, 107; wake of, 108

Yankee farmers: and self-reliance, 51
Young, Michael, 151
"Young America" (Emerson), 101, 183
Young Goodman Brown (Hawthorne), 35

Zeal: Hawthorne's opinion of, 35, 37